Philosophical foundations of the three sociologies

International Library of Sociology

Founded by Karl Mannheim

Editor: John Rex, University of Warwick

Arbor Scientiae
Arbor Vitae

A catalogue of the books available in the **International Library of Sociology** and other series of Social Science books published by Routledge & Kegan Paul will be found at the end of this volume.

Philosophical foundations of the three sociologies

Ted Benton

Department of Sociology
University of Essex

Routledge & Kegan Paul

London, Henley and Boston

First published in 1977
by Routledge & Kegan Paul Ltd
39 Store Street,
London WC1E 7DD,
Broadway House,
Newtown Road,
Henley-on-Thames,
Oxon RG9 1EN and
9 Park Street,
Boston, Mass. 02108, USA
First published as a paperback
in 1978, reprinted in 1981
Set in Monotype Times by
Kelly & Wright, Bradford-on-Avon, Wiltshire
and printed in Great Britain by
Unwin Bros. Ltd

British Library Cataloguing in Publication Data

Benton, Ted

Philosophical foundations of the three sociologies —(International library of sociology).

1. Sociology—History 2. Philosophy, Modern—History
I. Title II. Series
301'.01 HM26

ISBN 0 7100 8593 1 (c)
ISBN 0 7100 0045 6 (p)

To W.B., H.L.B., and S.L.P.

Contents

Preface

This book is to a large extent the outcome of several years' experience of teaching philosophy of social science at the University of Essex. The attempt has been made to take up philosophical issues in a way that makes evident their relevance to substantive issues in sociology and other social sciences, and in a way that makes philosophical ideas and arguments available to non-philosophers. I don't know whether the attempt has been successful, either in the course, or in the book which arises from it. What I can say with certainty is that any success the book has in these respects will owe a very great deal to the painstaking and persistent criticism and imagination of successive generations of students. The help and encouragement of colleagues, past and present, both sociologists and others, has also been indispensable. This book, like any other, is a social product. If it fails to solve the many intractable problems which it presents, I don't seen why I should be held exclusively to blame.

1 Introduction

There are (at least) two questions which readily arise in the minds of sociology students when they begin courses in the philosophy of social science: why should sociologists have to study philosophy? and what is philosophy, anyway? These are good questions, and like most good questions they are difficult to answer. Partly the difficulty arises from the controversial nature of the questions and the sheer diversity of ways in which they have been answered, but the diversity of answers is itself a mark of the difficulty of the questions. I shall not attempt to give definitive answers, but at least I had better make out as good a preliminary case as I can for the relevance of philosophy before I lose my sceptical readers (the ones I particularly want to keep).

What is philosophy?

It is a (rightly) much respected intellectual practice to begin by defining one's terms, and so it would seem that my first task should be to define 'philosophy'. However, in the specific case of philosophy there are strong reasons for refusing even to attempt a definition at this stage. I shall explain what these reasons are by comparing philosophy with some other intellectual disciplines.

First, the 'natural' sciences. The revolutionary significance of the physical theories of Copernicus, Newton and Einstein, or of the biological theory of Darwin is sometimes expressed by saying that they imposed a new definition on their respective disciplines. On one modern conception of the history of these sciences (to be discussed in more detail later)[1] each science progresses by long periods of relatively unproblematic and uncontroversial 'normal science' punctuated by episodes of sharp intellectual crisis during which the very definition of the science – its very conception of its subject-matter – becomes a centre of controversy. In the 'social' or 'human sciences', by comparison, there is a state of what might be called 'continuous revolution'. These disciplines are split into contending 'schools' or 'traditions' of thought, the research practice of which seems to presuppose a number of radically different conceptions of what it is to study societies. This lack of consensus over fundamentals seems to have characterised the social studies since their inception, so that there never has been a time when a definition of, say, sociology could be expected to gain the assent of any more than one faction of the practitioners of the discipline. In this respect, philosophy resembles the social studies more nearly than the natural sciences. In philosophy, too, there does not exist, and there probably never has existed, consensus about what philosophy is. This, then, is one good reason for not giving a definition of philosophy at the outset.

By why not just give my definition of philosophy and carry on regardless? To do this would be to neglect another important aspect of philosophy – an aspect in which it appears to differ from the social studies. Though I just characterised the social studies as being in a state of 'continuous revolution', and as lacking in consensus over fundamentals, a survey of the sociological literature, for example, does not reveal it to be overwhelmingly devoted to debate over fundamental questions of method and explanation, to controversy over the nature of a science of society. Most sociologists are primarily concerned with the more down-to-earth problems of 'studying society' – or, rather, particular regions or aspects of it: 'Role-distance in jazz musicians', 'Class attitudes to dental treatment', 'The sociology of the betting shop' (followed by) 'Observations on debt collection'. This (not, admittedly, quite random) sample of article-titles from the more respected sociological journals does not bespeak a discipline racked with internal dissent. Nevertheless, anyone who reflects on the explanatory models, the techniques of enquiry, the sets of concepts used in these empirical studies will readily understand that each one presupposes a certain conception of what it is to investigate social reality. This is so even if the researcher does not make his or her more fundamental commitments explicit. By contrast with this, in philosophy there is a considerable amount of explicit controversy over basic questions as to the nature of philosophy and what it is to practise it (I am not, of course, denying that many of the respected philosophical publications are also largely devoted to trivia). Not only does the philosophical practice of the competing schools and traditions of philosophy presuppose conflicting notions about what philosophy is, but a large part of that philosophical practice is itself an enquiry into the nature of philosophy. So we can characterise this difference between philosophy and, say, sociology by saying that whereas in neither of these disciplines is there consensus about the nature of the discipline, sociology does not, unlike philosophy, take controversy about its own nature as part of its recognised subject-matter. A conception of philosophy, then, such as might be embodied in a definition, can only be the result of a philosophical enquiry; it cannot be a starting-point.

Philosophy and the sciences

So far my argument has been negative in intent. But having tried to establish what cannot be done at this stage, I shall attempt a more positive characterisation of the central concern of this book: the relationship of philosophy and sociology. But I shall approach this relationship via a discussion of the more general relationship between philosophy and the sciences. I shall distinguish four conceptions of this relationship (not an exhaustive classification, but one which, I think, captures the most important historical alternatives) and proceed from a critical discussion of each to presenting the outlines of the approach which informs the present work.

First, to adopt the terminology revived by Peter Winch in his important book *The Idea of a Social Science*, are the 'under-labourer' and 'master-scientist' conceptions of the relationship of philosophy to scientific knowledge. Although these conceptions are classical opponents, they have, as will later emerge, underlying assumptions in common.

The under-labourer conception

The under-labourer conception affects to give the philosopher a very modest role – but this humility is, I shall argue, misleading. The seventeenth-century English philosopher, John Locke, was one of the earliest and most eloquent of the 'under-labourers', and his 'Epistle to the Reader' from the *Essay Concerning Human Understanding* is an oft-quoted source:

> in an age that produces such masters as the great Huygenius and the incomparable Mr. Newton, with some other of that strain, it is ambition enough to be employed as an under-labourer in clearing the ground a little, and removing some of the rubbish that lies in the way to knowledge.[2]

It is the task of men like Newton, Boyle and Sydenham to advance the sciences, but their success is limited, and the progress of science impeded by certain obstacles that lie 'in the way to knowledge'. The humble task of the philosopher is to clear away these obstacles to make way for science to progress once more. But what are these obstacles, and what – if any – are the necessary skills of the philosopher/under-labourer? Primarily, the rubbish which must be removed consists of 'learned but frivolous use of uncouth, affected, or unintelligible terms, introduced into the sciences . . .'. Such terms hinder the advance of science because they pass for genuine knowledge, whilst in reality covering up ignorance:

> Vague and insignificant forms of speech, and abuse of language, have so long passed for mysteries of science; and hard and misapplied words, with little or no meaning, have, by prescription, such a right to be mistaken for deep learning and height of speculation, that it will not be easy to persuade either those who speak or those who hear them that they are but the covers of ignorance, and hindrance of true knowledge.[3]

If this is the rubbish that must be cleared away, then the skills required to clear it away will be logical and analytical. The philosopher must be able to recognise nonsense when he sees it, and be able to dispense with it in his own discourse. But now the under-labourer begins to look a little less humble. Why can a man as great as Newton or Boyle not recognise nonsense when he sees it? Why should natural scientists be at a loss when they confront a conceptual or analytical problem, and helplessly call on the philosopher? At work in the under-labourer conception is a narrow and inadequate view of the practice of science itself: scientists concern themselves with factual questions – often of a very general or recondite kind, but factual none the less – whilst concepts are the province of philosophy.[4] I shall return more than once to this distinction between factual and conceptual questions, and the conception of science which goes together with it, for they form part of the most pervasive and influential of all the traditions of thought on the nature of scientific knowledge. For now, suffice it to say that the 'division of labour' between science and philosophy outlined by Locke still has many adherents,[5] and is often expressed in terms of yet another distinction, closely allied to the factual/conceptual distinction. The factual questions tackled by scientists are, it is said, questions 'in' science, and they are to be distinguished from the conceptual questions 'about' science which philosophers ask. The factual questions of the scientist are 'first order' questions; the conceptual ones that the philosopher poses about science are 'second-order' questions.[6] Of course, it is usually recognised that scientists are sometimes forced to confront conceptual questions, for example, about the status of their explanations, but in doing so they are said to be engaging in philosophy.[7]

I shall be developing arguments against the narrow and defective conception of scientific practice involved in these distinctions later, but already it should be clear that they cannot adequately characterise the relations between philosophy and science. There are, for instance, many sorts of questions 'about' the sciences which are not conceptual (though any answer to them may involve conceptual clarification and revision) – questions about the institutionalisation of the sciences in different periods and in different countries, questions about the structural relations between industry, government and scientific research, about the career patterns of professional scientists and so on. Are these political, sociological and historical questions, then, second order? And of what 'order' are the many sorts of questions that can be asked 'about' these disciplines themselves? Similarly, many of the problems which arise in, and constitute the sciences themselves are conceptual problems. Concept-formation and revision, the defence and criticism of concepts and systems of concepts are activities without which the experimentation and observation conducted in most of the sciences would have no sense at all. To take an example that would have been close to Locke's heart: the criticism of vitalist concepts in French physiology in the latter part of the nineteenth century. The opponents of vitalism frequently echoed Locke's 'Epistle' in their claims that the so-called 'vital principle' was no more than a meaningless term designed as a cover for ignorance. But effective criticism (i.e. criticism which had the effect of eradicating vitalism from at least this area of biology) did not come from a philosophical source at all. It came from the physiologist Claude Bernard, who was able to demonstrate by his construction of a new scheme of physiological concepts that the very problems which vitalist concepts purported to solve were false problems.[8]

So, if we take the under-labourer at his word, and concede that the job of philosophy in relation to science is merely clearing up conceptual confusion in the latter, then it follows not that philosophy is 'parasitic' on the sciences (as some critics of the under-labourer conception have claimed)[9] but that the sciences appear as predators upon philosophy. Philosophy is in danger of altogether losing its raison d'être. But there is another way of characterising the task of philosophy which is only implicit in Locke's 'Epistle', but which becomes much more explicit in the body of his *Essay*, and remains very popular with those who today share Locke's philosophical tendency. If it is the job of philosophy to expose and eliminate the use of insignificant terms in science, then it might be thought (incorrectly) that in order to do so philosophy requires a general theory of the distinction between significant and insignificant uses of language. This is, in fact, what Locke attempts to give. Generally, a word is a sign for some idea or combination of ideas. If there is no idea corresponding to a word, then the word lacks significance. This is combined in Locke with the doctrines that the source and foundation (Locke did not adequately distinguish these) of ideas or concepts is in experience (of external objects, through sensation, and of the workings of our own minds, through 'reflection') and that it is these ideas which form the raw materials for the whole of our knowledge. The 'humble' task, then, of clearing away the rubbish which lies in the way to knowledge becomes transformed into the much less humble one of setting criteria for significance and insignificance in the use of language, and thence of erecting standards by which all claims to knowledge are to be judged. Philosophy becomes the last arbiter on questions as to the difference between knowledge and belief, and between these, faith and error. In particular, of course, it was Locke's preoccupation to establish the credentials of physical science as a source of knowledge, and to establish criteria for distinguishing genuine from spurious claims to scientific knowledge. In recent times this has taken the form of a search for a 'criteria of demarcation' between science (implicitly, the only genuine knowledge) and non-science (in Locke's day the principal targets for exclusion were theology and speculative metaphysics, today they have become psychoanalysis and historical materialism). The difficulties for this characterisation of the function of philosophy begin to multiply as soon as philosophy is asked to present its credentials for its claim to authority in examining the credentials of others. More on this later.

The master-scientist, or metaphysical conception

This conception of the relationship between philosophy and science proposes the awe-inspiring enterprise of constructing – or, rather, reconstructing – the whole of (acceptable) human knowledge into one massive logically connected and internally consistent system of propositions. As with the under-labourer conception, this notion of the task of philosophy has its source in sceptical doubt concerning the adequacy of claims to knowledge. Doubt is pushed as far as it can logically go – until, that is, an unshakable bedrock is found upon which the whole edifice of human knowledge can be reconstructed, discarding all the previously unfounded rubble. As with the under-labourer conception, there is an attempt to give general criteria by which genuine knowledge can be distinguished from spurious claims to it. But here genuine knowledge is whatever can be deduced from a small number of self-evident and indubitable axioms or premises. For the French philosopher Descartes (to whose thought much of Locke's philosophy was a critical response), his own existence as a thinking being served as an indubitable premise from which, given certain (also self-evident) rules of inference, he could deduce the existence of God. From the existence of a perfectly good, omniscient and omnipotent God, Descartes was able to deduce the general characteristics of that God's creation, and so logically found the principal laws of the physical sciences.[10] Leibniz and Spinoza were two other classical master-scientists, and by now it should be clear in what respects their conception of the relationship between philosophy and science resembled that of Locke and others of his tendency. Their conceptions differed centrally in that whilst for Locke experience was the source of all knowledge, for the master-scientists deductive reasoning and self-evidence were the hallmarks of true knowledge. Indeed it was precisely the pretensions of system-builders such as these which Locke's conception was designed to deflate – particularly when they insisted on founding science on theology, and mistook self-evidence for innate knowledge.

The master-scientist conception is no longer widely held among philosophers and seems unlikely to be revived (although it is by no means absent from much of the spontaneous philosophising of scientists themselves, and in philosophy, too, a rather more modest variant of the enterprise has been revived under the title of 'descriptive metaphysics').[11] I shall not delay long in criticising it, save to suggest, following Kant, that something must be wrong with a discipline in which answers to its central questions may be just as easily proved as their contradictories.[12]

Two historical conceptions

One presupposition common to under-labourer and master-scientist alike is that the question 'what is the relation between philosophy and science?' has a single answer – the same for all sciences and for all historical epochs. I shall now consider two modern conceptions which challenge this assumption and attempt to characterise the relationships between philosophy and science as subject to historical change.

The first of these conceptions is present in the enormously influential work of Thomas Kuhn. Kuhn's book, *The Structure of Scientific Revolutions*, appeared in 1962 and presented a set of concepts for understanding scientific activity which challenged the hitherto dominant traditions of thought in the history, philosophy and sociology of science. Its impact on these disciplines has been enormous, but ripples have spread as far afield as economics and political science. I shall have occasion to discuss Kuhn's work in later chapters, and so for the moment I shall confine myself to those aspects of his work which are of the most immediate relevance. Against the dominant tradition in the history of science, according to which science is thought of as progressing gradually by the accumulation of empirical knowledge, steadily giving rise to increasingly elaborate theoretical construction, Kuhn poses a conception of the history of science as, like the history of society itself, discontinuous – as punctuated by conceptual leaps and transmutations which Kuhn calls 'scientific revolutions'. What Kuhn gives, in effect, is an elementary periodisation for the history of any science. After its foundation a science will be characterised by a series of periods of unspecified length in which some major scientific achievement provides the methods, conceptual apparatus, standards of validity and so on which govern the research practice of the whole 'scientific community' engaged in this particular scientific specialism. The adequacy of the rules derived from such a 'paradigm' is rarely, if ever, questioned; scientific education amounts to indoctrination into the established paradigm, and the failure to solve a 'puzzle' specified in terms of the paradigm is regarded as a failure on the part of the researcher, not his paradigm. Such periods of what Kuhn calls 'normal science' are punctuated by crises in which at least some of the failures of previous normal-scientific research come to acquire, for a variety of structural reasons never fully explored by Kuhn, a new significance. They acquire the status of 'anomalies' and provoke increasingly divergent revisions of the original paradigm until there can no longer be said to be any single paradigm to govern research practice. Such periods of crisis are resolved only with the general acceptance by the appropriate 'scientific community' of a new set of standards of validity, theoretical concepts, methods of investigation, etc. – in short, of a new paradigm. Two very large-scale examples of periods of revolutionary crisis in science are the shift from a broadly Aristotelian conception of the physical universe to the alternative Newtonian conception which took place between the second half of the sixteenth century and the end of the seventeenth, and the comparable shift from the Newtonian paradigm to a new practice of physics based on the relativity and quantum theories which has taken place in our own century.

Now what Kuhn has to say about the relation of philosophy to science is based on this elementary periodisation of the history of each science. During periods of normal science, scientists – quite rightly in Kuhn's view – hold philosophy at arm's length. Their current paradigm serves them well, and there is no reason why they should concern themselves with fundamental doubts about the whole enterprise. But in periods of revolutionary crisis the situation is absolutely different – scientists are faced not just with fundamentally irreconcilable ways of conceptualising and explaining the physical world, or their chosen aspect of it, but with alternative and irreconcilable conceptions of what counts as an explanation, what counts as a proof, etc. Scientists are confronted with philosophical problems in the midst of their own research practice – and must solve them as a condition of continuing to have a research practice. During these episodes, then, no clear demarcation between science and philosophy, as distinct disciplines, can be drawn.

But it is now apparent that Kuhn's conception of the relationship between philosophy and science leads to the same unfortunate consequences for philosophy as did one version of the under-labourer conception: philosophy seems to lose all point. When science is progressing smoothly, philosophy is at best irrelevant, at worst dangerous, and when science is in crisis scientists solve their own crisis by becoming philosophers. Of course, to show that Kuhn's theory has this consequence for the status of philosophy as an autonomous discipline is not to refute Kuhn. However, there are (fortunately for my theme in this book) independent reasons for rejecting both Kuhn's schema for the history of science and the philosophical position with which it is connected. Some of these reasons will be dealt with more fully later. Suffice it to say that a central difficulty in Kuhn's work is the philosophical and historical weight which is placed on his concept of the 'scientific community'. The limits of this community are not clearly defined, or they are defined in terms of the field specified by a paradigm. But since what counts as a paradigm is itself defined in terms of the scientific community this is no help. One consequence of this is that the application of the concepts of 'paradigm' and 'scientific community' and their cognates to historical cases is subject to no clear restrictions. The 'scientific community' may be anything from the whole corpus of researchers in all the major branches of science (as in the case of the Newtonian revolution) or some tiny group engaged in research in a narrow specialism within molecular biology. Now, if the latter community can have its paradigm and its revolution and paradigm-shift, too, then what is there to distinguish Kuhn's 'discontinuist' conception from the one it was meant to replace – the view of the progress of science as occurring through the gradual accumulation of small-scale advances?

Philosophically, too, the concept of 'scientific community' has a great deal of work to do. Since the replacement of one paradigm by another is the work of the scientific community, and since there are no external 'paradigm-neutral' standards by which to assess the respective merits of rival paradigm-candidates, the very conception of 'progress' in science – of the cognitive superiority of one paradigm over another – comes to rest on the characteristics of the scientific community. This resort to amateur sociology as a means of solving a philosophical problem indicates further serious weaknesses in Kuhn's work, to which I shall return.

The second of my two historically informed conceptions of the relationship between philosophy and science is to be found in some of the work of Karl Marx. I say 'some' because Marx's theoretical positions changed enormously throughout his life, and nowhere did he give a fully elaborated account of his position on this topic. Added to this is the difficulty that almost any interpretation of any text by Marx will be contestable by other, rival schools of interpretation. This is true of all major thinkers, of course, but it is particularly acute in the case of Marx, partly because of the continuing political importance of his work.

The passage which most cogently puts the conception I wish to deal with is from the *German Ideology:*

> Where speculation ends – in real life – there real, positive science begins: the representation of the practical activity, of the practical process of development of men. Empty talk about consciousness ceases, and real knowledge has to take its place. When reality is depicted, philosophy as an independent branch of knowledge loses its medium of existence. At the best its place can only be taken by a summing-up of the most general results, abstractions which arise from the observation of the historical development of men. Viewed apart from real history, these abstractions have in themselves no value whatsoever. They can only serve to facilitate the arrangement of historical material, to indicate the sequence of its separate strata. But they by no means afford a recipe or schema, as does philosophy, for neatly trimming the epochs of history.[13]

Marx and Engels are here speaking of the relationship between philosophy and one particular science – the science of history – but some of what they say applies to the relationship between philosophy and the sciences generally. Philosophy is the predecessor of scientific knowledge; it has its place prior to the emergence of a science, but once the scientific investigation of the relevant field begins, then philosophy loses its point. But this is odd, since both Marx and Engels, though they considered themselves the founders of the science of history, continued to engage in philosophical work. Indeed, it is arguable that much of the *German Ideology* itself – including the passage I quoted – is philosophical in character. How is this to be explained? One possibility is that Marx and Engels were simply inconsistent. Alternatively, the above passage may be read as a characterisation not of all philosophy in its relation to science, but of one branch or tendency of philosophy. Marx later spoke of the *German Ideology* as the text in which he and Engels attempted to settle their accounts concerning their 'former philosophic conscience', and as 'a criticism of the post-Hegelian philosophy'.[14] When Marx and Engels speak of 'philosophy losing its medium of existence' and 'neatly trimming the epochs of history' they are speaking of the speculative, system-building philosophy of Hegel, and of the 'left-wing' followers and critics of Hegel with whom Marx and Engels had earlier associated. This tendency in philosophy had much in common with the metaphysical conception which I have already described, and it seems that it was this sort of intellectual enterprise which Marx and Engels considered to lose its point with the emergence of genuinely scientific knowledge. In the main, the philosophical questions with which Marx and Engels continued to deal were of the sort: How are we to defend our claim to have founded a scientific theory of history? What are the grounds for designating a theory 'ideological', as failing to adequately grasp its object? What are the differences between religious, aesthetic, cognitive and other ways of 'grasping' or 'appropriating' the world? These questions are not quite identifiable as the classical questions of the philosophical theory of knowledge (sometimes called 'epistemology') but they have clear logical and historical connections with them. The central difficulty for this conception of the relationship between philosophy and the sciences is to give a characterisation of philosophy (and found a practice of philosophy) which avoids the error of setting up philosophy as the 'final arbiter' on all questions of cognitive status (the basic error of classical theories of knowledge) without risking the disappearance of philosophy altogether (its disappearance into science, or into the history of science). I shall try to deal with this difficulty more fully in my chapters on Marx and Engels, but since the approach I shall adopt throughout the book lies broadly within this tradition I shall have something more to say about it at the end of this chapter.

What is the relationship between philosophy and the social sciences?

We are now in a position to move directly from the question of the relationship between philosophy and the sciences in general to the more specific one of the relationships between philosophy and the social sciences. I shall briefly discuss two radically opposed accounts of this relationship and proceed to a preliminary specification of the conception to which I shall attempt to conform in the rest of this book.

Positivism

Positivism is a variant of the philosophical theory of knowledge – empiricism – which I attributed to John Locke. For sociologists, positivism is generally associated with the name of Auguste Comte and his philosophical descendants in sociology. For positivists and, indeed, for most empiricists, there is no special problem about the relation of philosophy to the social sciences. In relation to the natural sciences the job of philosophy is to clear up conceptual confusion and to lay down standards of intelligibility, scientific status and validity. Since these standards are universal they apply equally to the social sciences. Positivists often concede that the social sciences have their special problems – there are practical and logical obstacles to the use of the experimental method, social phenomena are far more 'complex', our knowledge of social phenomena must presuppose a prior development of the more fundamental sciences, and so on – but these are, for the positivist, matters of detail or matters of history. Ultimately, social scientific explanations, if they are to count as 'scientific' at all, must conform to the standards already established in the natural sciences. Such pronouncements are usually made in the name of some conception of the 'Unity of Science' – though this may vary from the rather loose notion of uniformity of methods and forms of explanation throughout science to the much more demanding ideal of the 'reduction' of all sciences to the fundamental science of physics. Ironically, such a notion of the unity of science as a logically watertight system of statements, all deducible from a small number of premises, comes close to the very ideal of metaphysics which the positivists are so devoted to debunking. My next four chapters will be given over to a critical discussion of positivism, both as a philosophical theory and in its effects on sociological theory.

Humanism

The most fundamental denials of the positivist characterisation of the relation between philosophy and the social sciences have had their roots in an insistence that the objects of study of the natural sciences and social 'studies' are so utterly different that they require fundamentally different methods and forms of explanation and understanding. I call these conceptions 'humanist' not to identify a particular moral or political commitment at work in them (though such commitments there undoubtedly are) but because they rest on the attribution of distinctive characteristics to human beings and their social relationships. Human beings are conceived as distinctively 'free subjects', as the agents of 'meaningful' acts, as the 'creators' of their social world. It is these distinctively human characteristics which demand a fundamentally different approach on the part of the investigator. They imply that there can (logically) be no such thing as a science of society or that, if there should be, it would be an enterprise different in kind from the sciences of non-human nature.

The controversial anti-positivist (and anti-under-labourer) conception of the relationship between philosophy and the social studies outlined and defended by Peter Winch in his *The Idea of a Social Science* belongs to this broad stream of thought. Winch's view is that philosophy and the social studies have a relationship, in their most basic concerns, which is so close as to amount to identity:

> to be clear about the nature of philosophy and to be clear about the nature of the social studies amount to the same thing. For any worthwhile study of society must be philosophical in character and any worthwhile philosophy must be concerned with the nature of human society.[15]

How does Winch reach this conclusion? Winch's argument is a subtle one and no brief summary can do it justice, but broadly this is the drift of it. Epistemology (the philosophical theory of knowledge) is central to the whole enterprise of philosophy. Such disciplines as the philosophy of art and the philosophy of science are important, not so much because they are helpful to the disciplines which they are philosophies of (as the under-labourers would have us believe), but in virtue of the light they shed on the central questions of epistemology. Art, science and religion are attempts of different kinds to give understanding (also of different sorts) of reality. The 'philosophies of' these disciplines are attempts to give an account of the nature of the peculiar sorts of understanding of reality which they give. As such they are tributary to the central epistemological tasks of accounting for the nature and conditions of possibility of any human understanding of reality at all. And this question of the nature of 'man's' understanding of reality cannot be separated from the question of the nature of the language in which understanding is expressed. 'Man's' understanding of reality, and the language which expresses it are both intimately bound up with social relationships, and not simply as 'a matter of fact' but conceptually. A condition of the use of language to say anything at all is the existence of the social institution of correcting mistaken uses of language, and not only does the understanding of reality which 'men' have affect their social relationships but 'social relations are expressions of ideas about reality'.[16]

On these conceptions of 'understanding' and 'language', conceptions which have their immediate source in the later work of the philosopher Ludwig Wittgenstein,[17] then, the central epistemological questions as to the nature of men's understanding of reality resolve themselves into questions as to the nature and conditions of social relations and the forms of social life as such.

From the side of sociology, Winch argues that 'one can in the end hardly avoid including in sociology a discussion of the nature of social phenomena in general'.[18] A little later this is put in the much stronger form that 'the central problem of sociology, [is] that of giving an account of the nature of social phenomena in general'.[19] The identification is complete; though their starting-points are different epistemology and sociology share the same central problems. But note that this is not the collapse of philosophy into science that we saw could result from one way of taking the under-labourer conception. It is more like the converse. The central part of sociology 'is really misbegotten epistemology', and its problems have been 'largely misconstrued . . . as a species of scientific problem'.

But it is not immediately clear why Winch should claim that the central problem in sociology has to do with the nature of social phenomena in general. Certainly this has been taken by some sociologists to be a problem. In particular sociologists have (mistakenly, as I shall argue later) regarded an answer to this question as a condition of establishing a 'field of operation' for the distinct and autonomous science of sociology.[20] But even for these sociologists it was not exactly a problem of sociology and certainly not the central one. Why should it, indeed, be the central problem of sociology, if the nature of physical phenomena as such, or the nature of biological phenomena as such are not the central problems of physics and biology respectively? The central problem of any science is not something that can be specified *a priori* and once and for all; on the contrary, it is displaced and redefined as a function of the development of the discipline. But this is to beg the question against Winch, since his argument is that sociology – or what he has isolated as central in it – is not a science, but is philosophical in character.

This leads us directly to a central difficulty in Winch's position. Since social relations are thought of as expressions of ideas about reality, the sociological understanding of social relations must be couched in concepts available to the social actors involved in the social relationships to be elucidated. Now, this is a plausible (though not, I think, ultimately acceptable) construction for some social relationships and for some aspects of them. For example, if one person is indebted to another because of a loan, then they stand in a social relation which is in a clear sense an expression of their ideas about reality (i.e. that one has the use of the property of the other on the understanding that it will be returned) and the relation could not even be characterised without the use of concepts ('property', 'use', 'owe', 'return', etc.) available to those who stand in the relation. If we take, on the other hand, the example of the relationship between an employer and an employee, we may find that though they certainly do stand in a relationship to one another, the ideas which the one 'expresses' in his relationship will not be the same as the ideas which the other expresses. The employer and employee will almost certainly differ in their conceptions of the pattern of rights and obligations which constitute their relationship. Even more seriously for Winch, one of the 'partners' to the relationship may not even conceive of it in terms of rights and obligations at all, but in terms of 'power' or 'necessity', of what he or she is 'forced to do' in order to live, or can 'get away with'. Further, there may be ways of characterising this relationship employed by third parties – by economists, sociologists, work-study men and the like which will deploy yet more 'ideas about reality'. But only in the case of some of these conceptualisations is it plausible to speak of the ideas being 'expressed' in the relationship they characterise, and even where it does make some sense to speak in this way, how is the relationship to be characterised when it is 'the expression of' conflicting and incompatible ideas about reality? When we think of new ways of conceptualising our social relationships do we thereby multiply them, and when we change our ideas about our social relationships do we, by that fact, change our relationships? In some limited respects, and for some relationships, of course, the answer to these questions is yes, but to think of this as the whole story is to follow the unfortunate fellow (about whom Marx and Engels speak in the preface to the *German Ideology*) who had 'the idea that men were drowned in water only because they were possessed with the idea of gravity' and that 'if they were to knock this idea out of their heads . . . they would be sublimely proof against any danger from water'.[21] I shall return later[22] to the question of Winch's conception of the social studies and his assimilation of them to philosophy.

Towards an alternative

As I argued at the beginning of this chapter, a conception of philosophy must be the result of philosophical practice – not its starting-point – but my discussion so far has been sufficient for me to at least outline the parameters of the approach I shall adopt, and to distinguish it from the approaches I have described and criticised. What I shall say here is not so much intended as a definitive account of my approach, but rather as a statement of the aspirations of the book and, by implication, the standards of criticism by which I intend it to be judged.

First, as to my conception of the relationship between the 'natural' and the 'social' or 'human' sciences, I shall reject (for reasons I shall expound at length) the 'humanist' contention that there is a fundamental dividing line between these two groups of disciplines, based on their different subject matters. But equally I shall not countenance the Procrustean positivist conception of the 'Unity of Science'. Rather the sciences will be conceived of as a set of cognitive practices with many intersecting and cross-cutting resemblances and differences. The uneven development of the different sciences will be thought of as determining different relations of dependence and autonomy between the different sciences at different times. This is not to deny that the sciences have a unity, but rather to substitute a conception of complex and uneven unity for the positivists' notion of doctrinal and methodological homogeneity.

As to the conception of philosophy which I shall adopt, almost all of what I have to say will belong to epistemology, though not to epistemology conceived in the 'classical' (i.e. sixteenth- and seventeenth-century European) way as the universal legislator for human knowledge. At the centre of the approach I shall adopt is a recognition of the closeness of the relationship between philosophical conceptions of knowledge and the history of the sciences. For this reason my discussions of philosophical theories about the nature of sociological or social-scientific knowledge and the methods by which it is to be acquired will always make reference to the situation in the history of the social studies in which they were produced. Associated with this, also, is my use of philosophical texts written by thinkers most often remembered for their achievements not in philosophy but in sociology wherever this is possible. I do this despite their frequent technical failings, which a professional philosopher will readily recognise, because it is through an analysis of such texts, in their intellectual and general historical context, that the relevance and importance of philosophical investigation to scientific work can best be grasped. Scientists do not, in general, resort to philosophical work for amusement, nor yet for financial gain. They do so, generally, because the scientific problems they face demand it.

The texts which I shall discuss are ones which raise recognisable epistemological questions – questions about what is to count as an adequate explanation, about how much of what is commonly taken for granted really is reliable, about what are and what are not acceptable methods for producing knowledge, and so on. But the importance of the texts I shall be discussing is that these questions are always posed with a definite object – that of making explicit the basic assumptions about the nature of sociological knowledge and explanation which are implicit in the research practice of the writers concerned or of those with whom they engage intellectually.

But it would be a serious mistake to see in these texts simply spontaneous attempts to make explicit what is already presupposed in research practice. It would be a mistake in two respects. First, in so far as the resort to philosophy arises out of problems in research practice, the text will be at least in part an attempt to engage in criticism of the assumptions which are made explicit. Second, and more important, these attempts to render explicit fundamental conceptions of the nature and methods of social enquiry are retreats into properly philosophical territory, and as such make use of the raw materials and implements to be found in that territory: the philosophical methods, concepts and distinctions available in the intellectual culture of the author's time and place. Any attempt, then, to come to grips with these texts and their problems must not only take into account the level of development and current problems of the science whose practice they attempt to conceptualise, but also the philosophical tradition which provides the concepts with which this is done.

From what I have said so far it might seem that what I intend to write is simply a history of the relations between philosophy and sociology, albeit a philosophically informed one. But this is not so – my aim is to engage critically with the philosophical conceptions which I shall be describing but not from the standpoint of the classical philosophical legislator. Rather, an attempt will be made to develop an approach which embodies a recognition of the historical space which separates the texts from one another, and from the present, and also a recognition of the distinctive characteristics and requirements of each branch of knowledge.

2 Auguste Comte and positivist sociology

Central to this chapter will be a consideration of that conception of the nature of scientific sociology which has had the greatest influence both on the practice of social scientists and on their conceptions of what they do. This is the positivist philosophy – or 'positivism' – usually associated with the name of Auguste Comte. I have already said a little about the positivist conception of the relationship between philosophy and the social sciences, and in this chapter I propose to discuss the leading doctrines of the positivist philosophy, as expounded by Comte himself. But Comte's positivism was not a closed and finally elaborated system of ideas. On the contrary, it and its relatives have been subjected to a continuous process of revision, development and sophistication up to the present day, and so I shall devote part of my third and fourth chapters to giving some account of these latter-day developments before advancing the more fundamental criticisms of positivist doctrine.

Although Comte coined the term 'positivisme', he was by no means a profoundly original thinker, either in philosophy or sociology, and it will be necessary to approach his work through a prior discussion of the philosophical tradition to which he belonged, and the traditions of social thought which informed his work. It is also necessary, if Comte's particular combination of philosophical and social thought is to be understood, to speak a little of the economic and political situation in the France of the early nineteenth century.

Epistemology

The aspect of Comte's philosophy with which I shall be centrally concerned is his contribution to 'epistemology', or the philosophical theory of knowledge. The principal questions of epistemology, as I mentioned in chapter 1, are questions as to the nature and scope of human knowledge: what can be known with certainty, and what must be left to faith, or opinion? What is the proper source or foundation of knowledge? A central pre-occupation in epistemology, I argued (though it is by no means always explicit), is the search for criteria by which to distinguish scientific knowledge from the non-scientific.

Although there is a popular tendency in the history of ideas to search for the precursors of modern ideas earlier and yet earlier in the Middle Ages, I shall not follow it. The posing of these questions, as part of a systematic onslaught on traditional forms of knowledge and their credentials, was neither widespread nor did it have a major impact on the development of knowledge itself until the sixteenth and seventeenth centuries. The target of the onslaught was the enormous intellectual achievement of the late Middle Ages: a synthesis of Catholic theology and Aristotelian/Ptolemaic cosmology, which was achieved, in its main outlines, during the thirteenth century by St Thomas Aquinas among other leading Catholic theologians. The doctrines of the Church, the teachings of the scholastics in the universities (themselves predominantly subordinated to the task of educating the future priesthood), and the established medical beliefs and practices of the time all fell within the framework of this colossal intellectual monument. The new movement in philosophy was intimately connected with innovations in scientific knowledge and constituted a challenge to the intellectual authority of tradition, divine revelation and faith, at least in those spheres being opened up to scientific knowledge. And this challenge was not, of course, a purely 'intellectual' one. It had social and political implications of the most profound kind. Descartes, for instance, who was one of the leaders in this persistent scepticism, demonstrated his clear awareness of its political implications by hastily denying them.

> I could in no way approve those cloudy and unquiet spirits who, being called neither by birth nor fortune to the handling of public affairs, are forever reforming the state in imagination; and, if I thought that there was the least thing in what I have written to bring me under suspicion of such folly, I should deeply regret its publication.[1]

This was written in 1637, and it is likely that Descartes had the Inquisition, which had so recently arrested Galileo and forced him to recant his heliocentric astronomical views, very much in mind. To question the intellectual authority of the Church and the scholastics was to question the authority of an institution which was an enormous political power in itself; but more than this it was to challenge the main ideological support of the monarchical form of government. Of course, not all of the philosophical radicals of this period were also political radicals – some found ways of combining political conservatism with intellectual radicalism, whilst many more, like Descartes, disguised their radicalism in their published writings. My point is, rather, that irrespective of the openly avowed political views of individual philosophers, the overall significance of the new tendencies in philosophical thought could not be anything but subversive of the established political and intellectual order.

Of course, to challenge the – by now rather ramshackle – edifice of medieval ideas, the philosophers of the sixteenth and seventeenth centuries needed to be able to point to new, firmer foundations upon which to begin the work of reconstruction or they must run the risk of being discounted as nihilists. There were, speaking very loosely, two main alternatives to faith and revelation as sources and foundations of knowledge: reason and experience. The first alternative – reason – might seem to be not so radical after all, since Thomist philosophy had been quite explicitly an attempt to give Christian belief a rational foundation and defence. But what was distinctive about the rationalism of Descartes was the democratic and individualistic form which the demand for rational defence took. At the very start of his *Discourse on Method* he suggests that 'the power of judging rightly, and of separating what is true from what is false (which is generally called good sense or reason), is equal by nature in all men'.[2] All men, it follows, have the power to submit established doctrine to the test of critical reason (though Descartes denies the propriety of just this, a little later in the text).[3] And the author of the *Meditations* is an isolated individual, seated by his fire, subjecting everything he has hitherto taken for granted to systematic doubt. This is no mere accident of style, but symptomatic of the form taken by the problem of knowledge in the thought of both rationalist and empiricist philosophers. The central question is: what certainty can the individual human subject have concerning the world about him? Not only can the existence of God and the external world be the objects of doubt, but even the existence of other persons. Descartes's answer to the central question, that 'whatever I perceive very clearly and distinctly is true', implies that the 'natural light of reason' is capable of shining in the mind of each secluded individual.

Similarly, for the empiricists, knowledge is founded on the experience of a typified individual subject, and the scope and limits of human knowledge are defined in terms of a psychological theory of the scope and limits of the human mind. Although modern empiricists tend to abandon adherence to such a psychological theory, knowledge for them remains logically tied to the experience of the human subject.

Both the rationalists and the empiricists more or less self-consciously produced their new conceptions of knowledge and its foundation as a defence of the claims of science as a (or sometimes 'the') source of genuine knowledge. For the rationalists the criteria of certain knowledge, the standards by which all knowledge-claims must be judged were plainly drawn from logic and mathematics, whilst for the empiricists it was the experiment and observation which they took to be responsible for the contemporary advances in physical science, that they placed at the centre of their account of knowledge. But though both major tendencies or traditions in the theory of knowledge had, at least in their earlier phases, a close relationship to the sciences, they tended to conceive of this relationship differently. By now the affinity between empiricism and the under-labourer conception on the one hand, and rationalism and the master-scientist conception on the other, should be apparent.

Empiricism

The major philosophical tendency to which positivism belongs is empiricism. Positivism is a variant form of empiricism, along with phenomenalism, pragmatism, operationalism, empirio-criticism, logical empiricism and others. I shall mention some of these more modern variants again in chapters 3 and 4, but for the moment it should be sufficient to give a broad – and necessarily oversimple – characterisation of the leading doctrines of empiricism as a philosophical tendency and to give some indication of its historical significance up to the time of Comte.

'Seeing is believing'; 'the proof of the pudding is in the eating'; 'I saw it with my own eyes . . .'. These are the common-sense attitudes which empiricism articulates into a philosophical theory. Central to empiricism, then, is the conception of a human subject whose beliefs about the external world are worthy of the description 'knowledge' only if they can be put to the test of experience. In classical seventeenth- and eighteenth-century empiricism this doctrine is not clearly distinguished from the proposition that all genuine knowledge has its source or origin in experience. Locke, for instance, devoted the first book of his *Essay* to refuting the doctrine that 'there are in the understanding certain innate principles . . . which the soul receives in its very first being . . .', on the assumption, presumably, that to admit such principles would be to admit the possibility of true propositions not subject to the court of experience (an odd assumption for Locke, since Francis Bacon had already identified the innate contents of the mind as a fundamental source of error).

But most empiricists have been prepared to countenance at least one class of statements whose truth or falsity is independent of experience: these are analytic truths, or 'relations of ideas' as Hume called them. They are true or false 'by definition' or by virtue of the meanings of the terms which make them up. Sometimes such statements are referred to as 'conceptual' statements, and contrasted with 'factual' statements whose truth or falsity is establishable by experience. There is much debate within empiricism about which statements to include in the conceptual or analytical category, some arguing that the propositions of mathematics, for instance, are all of them analytic (and therefore tell us nothing about the world), others arguing, as did Mill, that mathematical propositions are factual. The modern empiricist W. V. Quine has even gone so far as to suggest that there are no analytic propositions at all, arguing that statements simply differ in the degree to which they are protected from rejection on the basis of experience.[4] But despite this disagreement there is a central doctrine which I shall take as the touchstone of empiricism: that there is no knowledge *a priori* ('prior to' or independent of experience) which is at the same time informative about the world, as distinct from our ideas, or the meanings of the terms we use.

Empiricists also differ in the kind and strength of the links they assert between knowledge and the experience upon which it is based. For the classical empiricists an elementary associationist psychology provided the framework for conceiving of this link. The mind was thought of as the initially empty and passive receptor of impressions or 'ideas' through the organs of sense. Ideas so received (or received by the mind's reflection upon its own operations) were the basic units upon which the mind could perform such operations as abstraction, combination, generalisation, etc. to yield systematic propositional knowledge of the world. Later empiricists who dispensed with this psychological theory tended to search for logical links between the meanings of terms, sentences, or whole systems of sentences, on the one hand, and possible confirming or disconfirming observations on the other.

A final source of variation in empiricist theories of knowledge has to do with the content they give to concepts like 'experience', 'perception', or 'observations'. For Francis Bacon (not in the fullest sense an empiricist, but certainly one of its most important forerunners) 'experience' involved practical attempts to change nature, setting ideas to work. The concept of experience in empiricist thought subsequently became progressively attenuated through the metaphor of impressions on a plain sheet to that of an inner display of mental images which serve rather to cut off the subject from knowledge of his environment than to inform him of its constitution.

The history of empiricism[5]

Because of this variability of empiricist doctrine, it is extremely difficult to generalise about its historical significance. In Britain from the mid-sixteenth century an empirical tendency of thought seems to have become dominant among the mathematicians, scientists, craftsmen and merchants who were receptive to new scientific ideas which were rapidly being introduced from the continent. Men such as Robert Recorde, Thomas Digges, John Dee, Nicholas Culpeper, William Gilbert and a host of others were active, not only in translating important scientific works into the vernacular, but in making important contributions of their own to mathematics, astronomy, magnetism, medicine and so on. Perhaps, in part, because of the scholastic resistance to the new knowledge in the universities, and the 'college of physicians', and also because of the resistance on the part of these vested interests to the popular spread of knowledge ('Vile men would, prelate-like, have knowledge hid'),[6] science developed in England outside the universities under the patronage of the merchants, and in close relationship with the crafts, manufactures and methods of transport of the day. Scientists learned from these practices and also, with an eye to the practical application of their knowledge, co-operated to provide free scientific education to the popular classes. It is also beyond question that the newly prevailing current of Protestantism was connected with this combined flowering of science, commerce and manufacture (though the precise form of this connection is very much a matter of debate).[7]

The philosopher (and corrupt politician), Francis Bacon (1561–1627) was able to articulate and combine these existing practical knowledges and scientific traditions with Protestant theology into an intellectual system which, once the power of the monarchy and the bishops was challenged by the Civil War, was a powerful influence on the development of science and industry and of social reform. In particular, his achievement was to appropriate the rigorous separation between God and nature which was central to Protestant theology to serve as a justification for the free exploration by experimental methods of the latter domain, unhampered by theological restrictions. This separation of the two domains enabled Bacon and his empiricist successors to defend the autonomy of the sciences whilst at the same time giving 'to faith that which is faith's'.[8] Science was given further ethical justification in terms of its contribution to the glorification of God through knowledge of his creation and, more importantly, in terms of a conception of human progress through the application of science in trade and manufacture. It is not surprising, therefore, that many of the most politically radical of the parliamentarians – including the Digger, Winstanley and the

Leveller, Overton – together with a group supported by Pym who proposed state patronage for scientific research and massive educational reform, were the bearers of Bacon's ideas. Another of Bacon's intellectual legatees, the political philosopher Hobbes, was by no means a radical, though it is not without significance that his combination of the empiricist theory of knowledge with a mechanical-materialist causal theory of perception and of mental functions such as memory led him to be attacked as an atheist.

The work of the post-revolutionary philosopher, John Locke, can be understood as a compromise between conflicting tendencies, granting (with doubtful consistency) certainty to our knowledge of the existence of God, yet at the same time advancing the claims of the natural sciences. Only in the work of the Irish philosopher, Bishop George Berkeley (1683–1753) do we find empiricism turned back upon itself, historically speaking, to provide a defence for theology and a critique of science. For Berkeley, since all the mind is directly aware of are its own ideas, there can be no justification in experience for the claim that these ideas are 'representations' or 'copies' of a material world outside us. We must, rather, suppose that our ideas are produced in our minds by a beneficent creator.

Enlightenment and revolution in France[9]

In the eighteenth century the centre of the stage, philosophically speaking, is taken by Enlightenment France. Here the rationalist epistemology and the cosmology of Descartes rapidly came under challenge from the physical theory and empiricist epistemology connected with the names of Newton and Locke. The sensationalist philosopher Condillac played the leading role in popularising these intellectual currents in France, and the enormously influential philosophers grouped around the *Encyclopédie* were all to a greater or lesser degree followers of Locke. The empiricist epistemology was, for many of them, combined with atheism and materialism. D'Holbach even turns Locke's own argument against obscurantism in science against theology. 'Theology is nothing but ignorance of natural causes reduced to a system', and the name of God only 'a vague word that men have continually on their lips without being able to attach to it any ideas . . .'. Locke never dared, or was never disposed to draw such conclusions from his epistemology.

The Encyclopedists were also followers of Locke in their political philosophy, which resembled their epistemology in taking the individual subject as its central concept. Social and political institutions were to be judged by the liberty they allowed the individual to dispose himself and his property as he pleased, within the law. The authority of the state was conditional upon the consent of the subjects, sovereign and subjects alike being bound by a social contract whose existence was the sole source of political authority and of civil society itself. But this classical liberal-democratic political philosophy was by no means without its internal problems. A central source of intellectual difficulty and (later, when the philosophy became transformed into a programme for action) of political schism, was that the rights to liberty and property (these rights were hardly distinguished from one another) were seen to conflict with the ideals of democracy and equality once these ideals were conceived in anything more than purely formal or juridical terms. A constitutional monarchy, with a limited property-franchise, on the English pattern, was the political form which most nearly realised the aspirations of these liberal theorists. Others, most notably Rousseau, who came close to producing a critique of the Enlightenment in its own terms, insisted upon the need to restrict the liberty to accumulate wealth in the interests of equality. Though generally regarded as a radical Rousseau was quite ambiguous in his political thought. His conception of economic equality (inequalities should never be so great as to permit of the citizen's selling himself, or being bought by another) implied hostility to the capitalist development of industry, aided by scientific advance, upon which the Enlightenment, following both Locke and Bacon, had based its firm conviction of the inevitability of human progress. Further, in some places Rousseau makes it clear that he favours economic equality less as a desirable end in itself than as a condition whose absence is a threat to the more important end of social order. Rousseau also made a profound break with the individualism of the Enlightenment in his notion of the 'general will' which was to serve as an important source both of French conservative thought and of later socialist and communist political thought.

In England, a century before, the empiricist theory of knowledge, together with the science it defended, had played a part in preparing the intellectual conditions for the English revolution. In France, science and empiricism, together with the political philosophy of liberalism which had also been established by the British empiricists, played their part in preparing the way for the yet more profound revolution of 1789–94. In both revolutions empiricism, science and religious unorthodoxy were partisan forces. They favoured (and, in general, were favoured by) the newly forming bourgeoisie, the merchants, the manufacturers, the artisans and craftsmen, not to mention the professionals, the shopkeepers and the urban and rural labouring poor: in short, they favoured those classes whose political alliance broke the power of the old feudal order, and established the conditions for the development of the capitalist mode of production and distribution, and the social order based upon it.[10]

But in the English case the revolutionary cutting-edge of empiricism became blunted with the achievement of this task – even prior to it. The English compromise between aristocracy and bourgeoisie is mirrored in Locke's compromise in epistemology. In France, the initial phases of revolution seemed set to replace absolute monarchy with a compromise on the English model. But the contradictions in the French social structure, and the exigencies of its international situation, would not allow of this. In the defence of their newly won liberties against international counter-revolution the French bourgeoisie had to call upon and mobilise ever broader and deeper layers of the French masses. But the very extent of this mobilisation, and the far greater differentiation of the 'Third Estate' in France meant that the liberal bourgeois leadership of the French revolution met with a more rapid and far more powerful challenge from below than had been experienced by their counterparts in the English revolution. Those who risked their lives to defend the property-rights of the bourgeoisie felt entitled to their share. Never again, after the experience of the radical-petit bourgeois Jacobin dictatorship of 1793/4 did French bourgeois thought return to the confident liberal individualism of the Enlightenment. The ruling currents in French social thought during the nineteenth century, in contrast to both the Enlightenment and English social philosophy, were preoccupied with the problem of subordination of the individual to the social whole, with the problem of maintaining social order. Only the British ruling class retained the self-confidence to dispense – in theory, at least – with the aid of the state to defend it against the claims of the lower orders.

The positive philosophy

This, then, was the intellectual and social setting which provided both the problems and the raw materials for the 'positive philosophy' and the science of society which was supposed to be its offspring. I have argued that the central preoccupation of the dominant current in nineteenth-century French social thought was the restoration of social order (albeit, for some, a new *form* of social order) and the subordination of the individual to a higher social totality. This is true of the positivist tradition stemming from St Simon and Comte, and persisting to influence Durkheim at the end of the century. But though this positivist tradition presented itself as a break with the Enlightenment and, as a totality, was organised around a quite different set of problems (those problems themselves having an indirect, but none the less real relationship to the changed situation and political problems of the leading class of the Enlightenment), several of the concepts and theoretical projects which were synthesised and fused into the positivist system were drawn from the Enlightenment.

Comte was, for a time, the pupil and assistant of the socialist thinker, St Simon. Their later estrangement, and Comte's subsequent denials of his intellectual debt to St Simon, have led to some controversy as to who was the true originator of the leading ideas of the positivist philosophy. I shall not enter into this debate, since my concern is with the thought, rather than the thinkers. Suffice it to say that in all essentials the thought of Comte is determined, whether mediately or immediately, by the same influences as that of St Simon. For both, forms of society were thought of as embodiments or applications of the systems of ideas which characterised their epoch. The central function of philosophy was to unify and systematise these ideas, a task which was to be repeated with each new epoch. The new form of social order ushered in by the French revolution, then, required a new encyclopedia – a new and up-to-date systematisation of scientific knowledge. But of itself this was insufficient for its task. The existing sciences required more than systematisation – they required extension to a new field, that of man and society itself. The idea of a science of man was not new, of course, but in the eighteenth century the science of man almost always tended to be conceived as psychology, individual men being thought of as the ultimate units of analysis in any such science. Rousseau was one eighteenth-century thinker, as we have already seen, who thought of the social totality as an existence in its own right over and above the individual. There were other thinkers, the conservative opponents of the liberal thought of the Enlightenment such as De Maistre, who also rejected theoretical individualism, but the predecessor in this who seems to have been most important for the formation of the social thought of both Comte and St Simon was Montesquieu. For the latter, 'types' of social order could be distinguished according to their different political systems, there being a regular relationship between the political and other elements in each type of social order. This concept of society as an organic whole, not simply an aggregate of individuals, was taken up and developed by St Simon and Comte. In the work of the former, society was thought of on an analogy with the living organism, requiring not so much a distinct science, but rather a new branch of an existing science, physiology ('general' or 'social' physiology) for its scientific comprehension. Comte and Durkheim, respectively, retained the organic metaphor but were inclined to give successively more autonomy to the science of the social organism than did St Simon. The positivists acquired yet another element in their conception of a social science from Montesquieu: this was the notion that social phenomena, like natural phenomena (or, even 'as' natural phenomena), are subject to general laws, whose operation is independent of the individual will, and often unknown to consciousness. More immediately, though, such a conception of social phenomena as subject to general laws had been put to work for one category of social phenomena by the economist Adam Smith. Classical political economy was, in the first decade of the nineteenth century, becoming widely known in France largely through the work of Smith's populariser, J. B. Say. St Simon's 'utopian' socialism, though critical of classical economics, adopted the same method of searching for general laws governing social life. The search for such general laws was at the heart of the positivist conception of both natural and social life.

Finally, St Simon and Comte thought of the different types of social order not simply as so many alternative forms of human existence, but instead as a historical series, in which the earlier forms are or contain the causal conditions of the later. The series, moreover, has a direction, the later forms in the series being predictable on the basis of the earlier, and representing progress with respect to them. Progress is conceived in the now familiar way as dependent upon science-led industrial development, both Comte and St Simon citing Condorcet as their precursor. There were, then, two sorts of laws governing social phenomena: 'laws of succession' between stages in the series, and 'laws of coexistence' between elements in the different forms of social order. Comte's most significant development beyond St Simon seems to have been his elaboration of the latter field.

Positivism, then, in its classical nineteenth-century form is an empiricist interpretation and systematisation of the sciences combined with a general theory of history and society which can be understood as theoretical articulation of a definite set of political problems.

Comte's history and philosophy of the sciences

The text which best demonstrates Comte's intellectual scope is the *Cours de philosophie positive*, which was published in six volumes between 1830 (the year of the overthrow of the Bourbon monarchy) and 1842. Comte devotes much space to his analysis of the crisis of European and particularly French society, returning again and again to the political necessity of a positive science of society. The following passage from volume 1 of the *Cours* is representative:

> The positive philosophy offers the only solid basis for that social reorganisation which must succeed the critical condition in which the most civilised nations are now living.

> It cannot be necessary to prove to anybody who reads this work that ideas govern the world, or throw it into chaos; in other words, that all social mechanism rests upon opinions. The great political and moral crisis that societies are now undergoing is shown by a rigid analysis to arise out of intellectual anarchy. Till a certain number of general ideas can be acknowledged as a rallying point of social doctrine, the nations will remain in a revolutionary state, whatever palliatives may be devised, and their institutions can be only provisional. But whenever the necessary agreement on first principles can be obtained, appropriate institutions will issue from them, without shock or resistance; for the causes of disorder will have been arrested by the mere fact of the agreement. It is in this direction that those must look who desire a natural and regular, a normal state of society.[11]

The present critical state of society is a manifestation of its transition from a 'military-theological' past (in its Catholic-feudal form) towards an inevitable 'scientific-industrial' future. Each of these social types consists of a typical correlation of institutions, and each is 'governed' or dominated by a characteristic intellectual system or 'mode of philosophising'.

So far the scientific mode of thought has not completely triumphed over its main rivals – hence the 'intellectual anarchy'. Since 'ideas govern the world', intellectual anarchy produces social anarchy, and intellectual order is a condition of social order. The implication is clear: an extension of scientific thought to social phenomena will generate systematic knowledge of society to which all must assent. The general agreement required for social order awaits the foundation of scientific 'sociology'. There are two further, subordinate ways in which the foundation of a science of society will fulfil the political project Comte has set. Hitherto, political thought has been either apologetic or wholly negative and critical with respect to the existing social order. Sociology, by demonstrating the law-governed character of all social phenomena, will set limits to rational political action.[12] Social actors will be disposed to reform what, in each form of social order, can be reformed, and adopt an attitude of resignation towards what cannot. Sociology, then, will contribute to the establishment of a 'moral order' in society. Finally, the detailed scientific knowledge produced by sociologists can be applied in efforts at social reform on an analogy with the application of physical knowledge in the improvement of techniques of production and transportation. Control over nature may be extended to control over man and society by means of 'social engineering'. Later, Comte came to advocate a 'religion of humanity' with a priesthood of social scientists to ensure that the new science of society had the desired political effects.

All Comte's analyses, then, point to the same imperative. The foundation of scientific sociology is an urgent political, as well as intellectual necessity. But by what method is such a science to be achieved and by what criteria is success to be measured? What are the conditions for the foundation of such a science, and why has its advent been so long delayed? To answer these questions Comte propounds a general theory of the nature and development of scientific knowledge. In one important respect this theory breaks with classical empiricism. For Comte the 'knowing subject' is not the solitary individual but the 'human spirit'. This substitution is connected with Comte's rejection of the psychology of the earlier empiricists on the grounds that 'internal observation engenders almost as many divergent opinions as there are individuals to pursue it'. The proper scientific method, Comte argued, was best understood not through introspection but through study of its actual application in the history of the sciences. It is through this study that the cognitive 'progress of the human spirit' can be grasped and so advanced. So, although Comte's epistemology takes as its starting-point an objective idealist metaphysic (as distinct from the 'subjective idealism' of Berkeley) it does represent an important advance in linking philosophical thought about the nature of scientific knowledge and method with historical study of the sciences.

The *Cours* begins with Comte's announcement of his discovery of a 'fundamental law' to which the development of the human mind is subject (primarily Comte's law refers to the human species, but he also believed that his fundamental law was recapitulated in individual intellectual development).

> This law is that each of our principal conceptions, each branch of our knowledge, passes successively through three different theoretical states: the theological or fictitious, the metaphysical or abstract, and the scientific or positive.[13]

There are three incompatible methods of philosophising – ways of rendering comprehensible, of ordering the world. The first is a necessary starting-point for the development of human understanding, and consists in a search for first and final causes, for 'absolute' knowledge. Phenomena are explained by reference to the acts of supernatural agencies. The highest point of development of the theological state is reached when all phenomena are conceived as the effect of a single deity. The second, metaphysical state is merely a means of transition to the positive. In it, supernatural agencies are replaced by abstract forces and underlying entities to which all phenomena are referred. The highest development of metaphysical thought involves the reference of all phenomena to the single entity 'Nature'. But only when it has reached the third, positive state has a branch of knowledge attained genuine scientific status. Comte's characterisation of the positive state, therefore, is his answer to the classical epistemological question as to the criterion of genuine scientific knowledge, but under a historical guise.

Since this is Comte's answer to the question, What characteristics must sociology have to be counted as properly scientific?, I shall return to a fuller consideration of the 'positive state'. For the moment, however, it is necessary to understand that, though all branches of knowledge must pass through Comte's three stages, they do not all do so at the same time. This, of course, was one of Comte's central problems: why has social knowledge not yet reached its scientific maturity, whereas the other sciences have done, or are doing so? The solution to this is provided by Comte's classification of the sciences, and his attempt to give them an encyclopedic ordering. Apart from mathematics, to which Comte gives first place in his ordering of the sciences, Comte is concerned with astronomy, physiology, sociology, chemistry and terrestrial physics. The principal criteria he uses in the ordering are the relations of dependency between the classes of phenomena that each science deals with, the consequent dependency-relations persisting between the sciences themselves, and the further considerations of degree of generality/particularity and simplicity/complexity. The application of each of these criteria yields, surprisingly enough, the same systematic ordering of the sciences. Though there is some confusion in Comte's account of these criteria, this is the general idea: astronomy is more 'general' than say physiology since laws such as Newton's law of gravitation apply to all bodies which have mass, whilst the laws of physiology apply to only a relatively limited sub-class of such bodies – i.e. living bodies. Also, astronomy is more 'simple' than physiology since the former is concerned with bodies only so far as its own (i.e. astronomical) laws apply to them, whereas physiology must take into account that not only its own laws, but also the laws of physics and chemistry combine to produce the phenomena of living organisms. Finally, the phenomena of physiology are 'dependent' on those of astronomy in that the survival and characteristics of organisms are very much affected by planetary motions, whereas planetary motions are unaffected by living organisms.

The ordering of the sciences which these criteria produce is: mathematics, astronomy, physics, chemistry, physiology, sociology. The crucial point about this classification is that it represents not only the rational arrangement of the sciences in any systematic presentation of human knowledge as a whole, but also the historical order of development of the sciences. It is a schematic history of the sciences (schematic, that is, even in Comte, not just in my considerable over-simplification). If, in order to fully understand physiological phenomena, it is necessary to know the principal laws of physics and chemistry, then it would clearly be impossible for the science of physiology to get very far until these principal laws of physics and chemistry were known. 'Social physics', whose phenomena are the most particular, complex and dependent of all, is consequently the last to enter the positive state. Comte's explanation of the under-development of sociology is completed by yet another ordering of the sciences – on the basis of their relative distance from the immediate concerns of men. By virtue of its 'intimate connection with human passions' the development of sociology could be expected to be still further retarded. In 140 years of bemoaning the absence of a Newton or a Galileo in the social sciences, positivists and empiricists have produced no explanation of this deplorable state of affairs which compares with Comte's for elegance or plausibility.

But according to Comte's analysis the intellectual conditions for the foundation of scientific sociology had already matured, whilst political conditions rendered it an urgent necessity. The questions remained, what is the method by which positive sociology is to be established, and what form will it take? The answers to these questions are to be found in Comte's characterisation of the 'positive stage' of human knowledge in general. In the present chapter I shall confine myself to giving an account of Comte's conception of scientific method, together with a restricted set of criticisms. More fundamental criticisms of the positivist conception of science must await further discussion of the development of positivism since Comte's death.

In the positive state, Comte says,

> The human mind, recognising the impossibility of attaining to absolute concepts, gives up the search for the origin and destiny of the universe and the inner causes of phenomena, and confines itself to the discovery, through reason and observation combined, of the actual laws that govern the succession and similarity of phenomena. The explanation of the facts, now reduced to its real terms, consists in the establishment of a link between various particular phenomena and a few general facts, which diminish in number with the progress of science.[14]

A little later in the *Cours* we get:

> It is the nature of positive philosophy to regard all phenomena as subject to invariable natural *laws*, the discovery of which,

> and their reduction to the least possible number, is the aim and end of all our efforts, while causes, either first or final, are considered to be absolutely inaccessible, and the search for them meaningless. . . . Everyone knows that in positive explanation, even when it is most perfect, we do not pretend to expound the generative *causes* of phenomena, as that would be merely to put the difficulty one stage further back, but rather to analyse the circumstances in which the phenomena are produced, and to link them to one another by the relations of succession and similarity.[15]

The positive philosophy, then, attributes a distinctive series of characteristics to scientific knowledge. The first is that science takes as its object phenomena or general relations between phenomena. 'Phenomena', for empiricists, are external 'appearances', immediately given in sense-perception. It follows that Comte adheres to the familiar empiricist thesis that scientific knowledge must be based on sensory observation, its scope and limits being determined by the scope and limits of sense-experience. Comte, like many of his predecessors, did not distinguish very clearly between the claims that knowledge must have its source in sense-experience and that it must be testable by appeal to sense-experience. Sometimes it seems he has the one in mind, at other times the other, so that it may be assumed he would have assented to both.[16]

The second characteristic of knowledge in the positive state concerns the form of the statements which constitute it. These are not statements of particular facts (though they may be derived by inductive generalisation from them) but are statements of universal laws. They state the necessary and invariant relations between classes of phenomena. A phenomenon, or a class of phenomena, is scientifically explained when the law governing its occurrence has been discovered. As science advances, phenomena and the laws governing them are subsumed under progressively smaller numbers of increasingly general laws. A corollary of this conception of scientific explanation is that science involves the abandonment of any search for the unobserved causes or generative mechanisms underlying observed phenomena. It also involves abandoning the search for 'final causes' – that is to say, for explanations in terms of 'goals' or 'intentions'. Explanations of these types are rejected by Comte as metaphysical or theological and are, rather confusingly for the modern reader, termed 'causal' explanations. The type of explanation which Comte advocates instead of causal explanations is precisely the type which now is recognised as the paradigm of causal explanation. On this conception (about which I shall have more to say in chapters 3 and 4) the 'cause' of a phenomenon is an observable 'condition' or 'circumstance' invariably accompanying or preceding the phenomenon (or phenomena of that type) and never occurring without the production of the phenomenon in question. This conception of causal explanation is a plausible account of some well-known examples of scientific explanation. The heating of a metal bar is a necessary and sufficient condition for it to expand and so is properly called its 'cause'. The increase in pressure on a constant mass of gas at constant temperature is the 'cause' of a decrease in its volume, and so on. But what is to be said about causal explanations of these phenomena in terms of the atomic theory of matter? The relations between the temperature and volume of a metal bar, and those between the pressure and volume of a mass of gas can both be explained in terms of the properties and, in particular, the states of motion, of their molecular constituents. The changing states of motion of these unobservable particles may also be said to be 'causes' – generative causes – of the observed, or 'phenomenal' changes in macro-properties such as temperature, volume, pressure and so on. Although Comte accepted such explanations as scientific it is not at all clear that he was consistent in so doing. The conception of cause which they involve should strictly speaking have been rejected by Comte as metaphysical, and such explanations cannot obviously be reduced to explanations in terms of general laws governing phenomena. Similarly, this conception of scientific knowledge commits Comte either to the outright rejection of teleological explanations (i.e. explanations in terms of aims and intentions) and functional explanations in physiology and sociology or to some attempt to show that they are really no more than his favoured type of causal explanation in a logical disguise. This is a problem Comte never adequately tackled. Finally, the limitation of the object of scientific knowledge to observable 'phenomena' entailed important restrictions on the scope of human knowledge in Comte's conception of it. For instance, he was convinced that astronomy could never study the chemical composition, mineralogical structure or living organisms belonging to the 'stars'.[17] This was because astronomical observation was restricted to visual observation alone. Such a restriction of the scope of scientific knowledge is a persistent danger for positivist and empiricist philosophies of science. Of course, no one has gone so far as to restrict knowledge to the content of what is actually observed, but Comte came close to this in seeming to restrict knowledge to what 'could' be observed in the sense of 'immediately technically possible' observation. The different senses of 'possible observation' have, since Comte's day, given positivists serious difficulty in their attempts to distinguish between what can and what cannot be tested by some 'possible' observation.

It follows, then, that the Comtian conception of scientific explanation must be regarded either as excluding from the status of 'scientific' explanation a whole range of explanations which are and were widely accepted as scientific or as representing all of these types of explanation in a very defective and inadequate way. It also follows that if applied in a rigorous way as a guide to the production of new scientific knowledge Comte's conception of the nature of scientific explanation would be quite disastrously restrictive.

A further corollary of the conception of scientific knowledge as consisting in the discovery of general laws governing phenomena is the assertion of a close logical connection between explanation and prediction. Comte goes so far as to make rational prediction a criterion of scientific knowledge ('Yet without such prediction there is no science properly so called').[18] The link here, of course, is that predictive success or failure is the means by which the general laws which license the predictions are tested. 'Knowledge' which yields no predictions is not testable and therefore not true knowledge. But this connection of prediction with explanation has still more significance for Comte: it provides the basis for the all-important link between science and 'art' or, perhaps, what we should call 'practice' or 'technique'. There are two distinct types of such relationship for Comte. First, we may modify our actions in the light of foreknowledge of some future unalterable event – e.g. evacuate homes or reinforce sea walls in the light of a prediction of high tides – on the basis of astronomical knowledge. Second, we may deliberately intervene to alter 'conditions' or 'circumstances' and so bring about desired effects. As Comte understood, these two types of relationship between science and technique ultimately derive from differences in the scale and type of system concerned. Human intervention is powerless to modify astronomical systems, whereas physiological and social systems are eminently modifiable. Whereas prediction alone is the criterion of success in astronomy successful modification of outcomes is the main criterion in physiology and sociology. It is this relationship between science and 'art' in the case of sociology which takes the main weight of Comte's political project, and I shall return to it a little later.

Yet another of Comte's theses on the nature of scientific knowledge is linked with the concept of general law. This thesis is that of the unity of the sciences. Comte is cautious in the notion of unity he proposes, though:

> In assigning to positive philosophy the aim of reducing the totality of acquired knowledge to one single body of homogeneous doctrine, relatively to the different orders of natural phenomena, I have no intention of making a general

study of these phenomena as the diverse effects of one single principle, as subject to one and the same law.[19]

For Comte, then, the principle of the unity of science does not require that all knowledge be presented as deducible from a single law. The only plausible candidate was Newton's law of gravitation, which did already allow of the deduction of the laws of planetary motion, of free fall near the earth's surface and, in a suggestion of Laplace, even of chemical phenomena. But Comte regarded such aspirations as not only premature, but also not particularly valuable even if achieved. For practical purposes the division of intellectual labour in the various sciences would have to remain fundamentally unchanged. The rather more modest unity to which Comte does aspire is unity of method and homogeneity of doctrine. By unity of method Comte seems to have meant that the general characteristics of the 'positive state' apply to *all* of the sciences once they reach this state, although at a lower level of generality there will be differences of method between the individual sciences. For example, although observation is the necessary source of all scientific knowledge, Comte distinguishes three sub-species of the general category 'observation'. These are 'observation', narrowly conceived, experimentation, and comparison of types. These different forms of observation are differentially appropriate and important in the different sciences. The notion of 'homogeneity' of doctrine is not clarified by Comte but at least it means, presumably, that the laws of the different sciences if not actually mutually deducible would nevertheless not contradict one another.

On one final characteristic of the 'positive state' Comte is in line with his empiricist predecessors and successors. The distinction between analytic statements ('relations of ideas') and synthetic ones ('factual' statements) is not obviously exhaustive. It does not provide any obvious way of classifying statements such as express aesthetic evaluations, or moral and political judgments. Empiricists have, in general, been restricted to two alternative ways of treating value judgments. Either they are regarded as a species of disguised factual statement (the Utilitarians, for instance, proposed the programme of representing all moral judgments as statements about quantities of happiness or pleasure) or they must be regarded as non-cognitive, perhaps even as literally meaningless (as mere expressions of feeling or attitude). Comte belongs to the latter tradition. For him, positive science must neither 'admire nor condemn' the facts, but simply regard them as objects of observation. This notion that science must remain neutral on questions of value, or sacrifice its claim to the status of science, remains one of the most strongly held values of empiricist philosophers and of many scientists, too. But it also remains the object of strong controversy and we must return to it.

Comte's sociology

To conclude this chapter I shall enter into some of the controversy surrounding Comte's attempt to put into practice his intellectual project of a sociology conforming to his notion of the positive method. First, the status of the class of phenomena which sociology takes as its object. All living beings present 'two distinct orders of phenomena' – those pertaining to the individual, and those pertaining to the species. This distinction is of particular importance in the case of social species such as man. The second order of phenomena – those pertaining to the species, social phenomena – are more complex and particular than, and are also dependent upon the individual phenomena. But it doesn't follow that social physiology is merely an appendix of individual physiology (as St Simon held), nor that the 'collective study of the species' can be treated as a deduction from the study of the individual (as in Enlightenment political philosophy and classical political economy). The interaction of individuals and the action of each generation upon its successor are the sources of a modification of the effects of the laws of individual phenomena. This modification is responsible for the autonomy of social phenomena, and its social conditions are the primary concern of sociology. 'Thus social physics must be founded on a body of direct observation proper to it alone, always having regard to its intimate and necessary relation to physiology.'[20]

Once having delineated, to his satisfaction, the proper field of sociology, Comte seeks to apply to it a 'fundamental distinction' which he derives from the other sciences – especially biology. This is the distinction between the 'static' and 'dynamic' treatment of phenomena. In fact, Comte's use of the distinction in no sense corresponds to its use in other sciences, but it is nevertheless an important distinction. Social statics has as its objective the study of the constituent parts of the different forms of social order and their mutual relationships, abstracting as far as possible from their 'movement' or development. The laws proper to social statics are 'laws of co-existence'. Social dynamics has as its objective the discovery of general laws governing the overall development of human societies and ultimately of the human species itself. The law of three stages which I have already discussed is a leading law of social dynamics. The laws proper to social dynamics are 'laws of succession'. It is in this distinction that is to be found yet another formulation of Comte's central political project. The principal metaphysical and theological traditions of social thought which Comte's attempt at a positive social theory are meant to supplement were Catholic and monarchistic reaction and the persistent 'negative' political philosophy of the Enlightenment. Rid of its theological or metaphysical shell of the 'divine right' or the 'sovereignty of the people' each of these traditions of thought has a rational kernel. Conservative thought rightly insists on the necessity of social order, but seeks in vain for a return to an obsolescent form of social order, whilst the philosophy of the Enlightenment rightly insists on progress but wrongly conceives of progress as exclusive of order. Hence the threat of anarchy and revolution. Comte, on the other hand, advocates the positive study of order in the social statics, and of progress in the social dynamics, the consequence of which will be a reconciliation of the principles of progress and order: orderly progress.

Several important criticisms of Comte, and of the whole positivist programme for the social sciences, have to do with the notion of the law-governed character of social phenomena, and in particular with Comte's distinction between two sorts of sociological laws. Some of these criticisms are directed from philosophical standpoints systematically opposed to the positivist one (I have, in a preliminary way, referred to these collectively as 'humanism') and so will be more appropriately dealt with in connection with their philosophical source. But other criticisms come from within the empiricist tradition and I shall deal here with several of these, as advanced by the contemporary philosopher Karl Popper. The first criticism is that Comte's whole conception of an analogy between the application of social knowledge in political change, and the application of physical knowledge in industry, warfare, trade, etc. (hereafter referred to as 'social engineering') is vitiated by Comte's defective concept of a 'law of succession'. Popper's criticism is also (mis)directed against Marx, on the (mistaken) view that Marx, too, held a conception of history as a necessary sequence of stages.

Popper's underlying political project has a close affinity with Comte's own; it is to demonstrate that scientific knowledge can form the basis for piecemeal social reform (this, indeed, constitutes the analogue in the social sciences for natural scientific experimentation) but never for the advocacy of revolutionary transformation. Thus Popper distinguishes between 'piecemeal' and wholesale or 'Utopian' social engineering,[21] arguing that the former is essential to the development of scientific knowledge of society whilst the latter is simply logically incoherent. Popper thinks he can detect the advocacy of the latter in Comte, as well as in Marx, and so Comte becomes a prime target.

To sustain his argument Popper requires two distinctions. First, he points out that there is a difference between trends and laws.[22] The statement of a trend simply summarises a series of facts or observations, recording a directional variation in some parameter. For example, Weber asserted the existence of a 'trend' for institutions in modern society to become more and more bureaucratic, and for bureaucratic modes of organisation to be adopted by progressively more institutions. More simple cases are such trends as rising or falling death rates, birth rates, unemployment rates, etc. Trend statements are categorical (i.e. unconditional), particular, and do not license predictions. That it has been getting warmer for the past few days, or that the balance of payments deficit has been increasing for the last few months is not, of itself, any basis for predicting that it will continue to get warmer, or that the balance of trade will continue to get worse.

By contrast, the statement of a law is conditional and universal. The law that metals expand when heated is, when fully expressed, a statement to the effect that all metal objects, if heated, expand. Although the evidence for the truth of the law may be particular observations of the behaviour of particular pieces of metal, the law itself does not assert that any particular piece of metal actually has been heated or is being heated. It merely states what would happen whenever this condition was fulfilled. Knowledge of laws, unlike knowledge of trends, can form a scientific basis for prediction. If it is known that all metals expand when heated then it can be predicted that if this particular piece of metal is heated, then it will expand.

Popper also distinguishes two types of scientific prediction.[23] One sort, which he calls 'prophecies', are of events 'which we can do nothing to prevent'. Examples are predictions of the occurrence of typhoons, comets and eclipses. The other sort, which he calls 'technological predictions', form the basis of engineering, and inform us of steps we should take in order to achieve certain results. These predictions concern physical, chemical, social systems, etc., which allow of human intervention to alter the circumstances in which effects are produced so as to modify them in accordance with our intentions. It should be obvious that Popper's distinction corresponds exactly to Comte's distinction between the two types of relationship between science and 'art'.[24]

Popper's argument is that theorists like Comte, Mill and Marx (in Popper's controversial interpretation), in claiming to discover laws of development or progress in society, in claiming to distinguish successive stages through which all societies must inevitably pass, begin by observing (often accurately) trends of various sorts, but go on to make predictions on the basis of these trends as if they were laws. But, worse than this, they make unconditional predictions, whereas even laws license only conditional predictions. Such unconditional predictions, or 'prophecies', are, then, devoid of any scientific basis whilst the notion of 'law of development' on which they purport to be based is logically incoherent. If follows that the revolutionary project of 'utopian social engineering' is deprived of its apparent scientific backing in the notion of such inevitable successions of social orders.

But there is a serious flaw in the argument. Popper uses the term 'prophecy' equivocally. It began as a prediction of an event which we can do nothing to prevent, but ended as a prediction of an event which will happen 'no matter what', independently of any conditions.[25] Clearly, for example, an astronomical prediction is a prophecy in the first sense, but not in the second. This equivocation vitiates Popper's argument. Much of the force of the argument derives from the absurdity of the idea of an 'absolute trend' leading inexorably and unconditionally to some end-state. However, if Marx's prediction of the end of capitalism, or Comte's prediction of the emergence of a new scientifically ordered society are understood as prophecies in Popper's original sense they lose their appearance of absurdity. If they are regarded not as predictions about what will happen unconditionally, but as predictions about what cannot be prevented by deliberate human intervention in history – that is to say, as statements about the limitations of what Popper calls piecemeal social engineering – then they may be false, but at least they are not obviously absurd. Not only was this precisely Comte's objective (i.e. to set limits to political reform and discredit 'negative' theories of revolution) but Popper, unbeknown to himself, apparently, is entirely in accord with him. Popper's notion of piecemeal social engineering and Comte's notion of social engineering are identical. For both writers they are the social science analogue of experimental testing of theories in the natural sciences, and an important implement of social progress.

As I shall argue later, the conception of experiments as a means of testing theories is a defective and over-simple representation of the role of experimentation in the natural sciences.[26] Both Comte and Popper presuppose it. But their conception of social reforms as a means of testing social theories is even more questionable. Comte is quite explicit about the political authority which his priesthood of sociologists would have, and makes no attempt to disguise the political significance of this. Popper simply fails to pose the crucial questions of the nature of the social institutions through which the social experiments (reforms) required by the sociologists would be proposed and implemented, and whose interests they would serve. But the political character of his proposals can nevertheless be established by considering what is presupposed in them. For social reforms to serve as a test for social theories, there must be an identity between, on the one hand, the political problems of those who have the power to implement reforms as a means of solving those problems and, on the other hand, the theoretical problems of the sociological theorists. To advocate that sociological theory be, in this respect, an articulation of the political problems of a ruling group is to accede to a conception of sociology as a ruling ideology, or as a variant of such a ruling ideology. Popper's examples of the urgent practical problems which social engineering is to tackle, and his examples of the 'technological laws' which would be set to work in solving them both reveal a political and ideological link with a definite interest. The 'most urgent practical questions of the day' include the possibility of controlling trade cycles (not eliminating them!) and 'how to export democracy to the Middle East' (Popper's book appeared in 1957),[27] whilst available technological laws include 'You cannot have full employment without inflation' (intended as a universal law of human society, and not one restricted in scope to the capitalist mode of production).[28] Quite generally, those positivists who think of the relationship between theory and practice in this way simultaneously assert and deny the scientific status of sociology. Their position is internally contradictory.

There are two arguments of subsidiary importance which Popper directs against the ideas of laws of succession and 'utopian social engineering'. The first is that the evolution of society (or of life on earth) is a unique historical process.[29] Its description is a singular historical statement, lacking the generality required for the statement of a law. This is, clearly, a powerful objection to Comte's laws of succession in their ultimate application to the whole of human society. That the history of the human species is to be understood as *one* history is a central Comtean doctrine. However, Comte's application of the law of three stages to 'each of our leading conceptions – each branch of our knowledge' is not so susceptible to Popper's criticism. Here Comte merely claims that several discrete histories are subject to a single general law. The second of Popper's arguments is directly concerned with 'utopian social engineering'. Such revolutionary projects, he claims, have as their objective a re-ordering of the totality of social relations. The 'totalities' which are proposed as objects of scientific knowledge, and as objects of political transformation by 'utopian social engineers' cannot, argues Popper, logically be objects of either. This is because all observation and description must be selective, whereas the utopian notion of totality involves 'all the properties or aspects of a thing, and . . . all the relations holding between its constituent parts'.[30] Popper's conception of a 'real world' consisting of an infinity of aspects and relations from which we make a 'selection' for scientific observation and description is epistemologically suspect, and we shall have occasion to discuss it further in the context of Weber's methodology. Fortunately it is not necessary to do so here, since Popper is so clearly attacking men of straw. Neither Marx nor Comte (nor, for that matter, the theorist Popper refers to most in this connection,

Karl Mannheim) holds to such a conception of totality. The social 'totality' is, for them, grasped principally through a set of fundamental and distinctive characteristics (the system of property, the type of state, the predominant 'mode of philosophising', etc.). The transformation of a social totality in respect of these fundamental characteristics is held to be a condition of transformation in other respects because of the causal primacy of the 'fundamental' characteristics. None of this entails or presupposes the mystical conception of totality which Popper criticises.

A final criticism of Comte's version of positivism is implicit in Popper, but not actually expressed by him. Popper's view is that general laws governing human social behaviour are possible – he even gives some candidates for the status. But he outlines – as a 'historicist' doctrine – an argument which he (presumably) would accept as fatal to this view if successful.[31] The 'historicist' argument is that there are no universal uniformities in social life, but merely uniformities which characterise only some societies, and then only for limited periods of time. Such uniformities are not laws in the scientific sense. Popper's position seems to be that if the social studies were, indeed, limited to the discovery and characterisation of such uniformities of limited scope, then this would rule out the possibility of scientific sociological laws, but that fortunately this conclusion may be avoided since there are, after all, some universal uniformities.

Now, if Popper is right in this, then he has a very strong argument against both Comte and Marx. Both of these 'historicists' (in Popper's idiosyncratic use of this term) held that there were scientific laws (laws of 'co-existence' in Comte's sense) which were limited in their application to certain epochs and to certain types of social formation. This is what Comte seems to have meant by his claim that knowledge in the positive stage was 'relative' rather than 'absolute'. Such knowledge states the existence of laws of co-existence peculiar – or 'relative' – to each social type. The objection to this is clear: a general law asserts a universal relation between phenomena. It is supposed to hold good independently of restrictions of space or time, and so a 'law' of restricted scope cannot be a general law.

This objection can be answered with the help of an example which brings out the logic of the situation rather more clearly than any drawn from Comte's own work. This is the example of Marx's general law of capitalist accumulation, to the effect that, in capitalist society, the increasing productiveness of labour leads to greater insecurity of employment. Marx states the law as follows:

> The law by which a constantly increasing quantity of means of production, thanks to the advance in the productiveness of

> social labour, may be set in movement by a progressively diminishing expenditure of human power, this law, in a capitalist society – where the labourer does not employ the means of production, but the means of production employ the labourer – undergoes a complete inversion and is expressed thus: the higher the productiveness of labour, the greater is the pressure of the labourers on the means of employment, the more precarious, therefore, becomes their condition of existence, viz., the sale of their own labour-power for the increasing of another's wealth, or for the self-expansion of capital.[32]

Marx goes on to argue that some other economic writers have confused this antagonistic character of capitalist accumulation with analogous but 'essentially distinct' phenomena of pre-capitalist modes of production, and so come to regard it as a 'general natural law of social wealth'. Marx's law can be loosely paraphrased as: under capitalist relations of production, an increase in the productiveness of labour leads to an increased competition between labourers for a (relatively) diminishing number of jobs.

When Marx denies that this is 'a general natural law of social wealth' he is denying that an increase in social wealth always and everywhere leads to an increase in the precariousness of the labourer's employment. He is, therefore, apparently susceptible to our Popperian argument in just the same way as Comte. But it is clear from the quotation that Marx is not arguing that there is something special about certain places and times which renders the law applicable. The law applies under certain specifiable conditions – social systems dominated by capitalist production relations – which may or may not be actually satisfied in various places or times. The law – like any other law – is conditional in form; it claims only that if certain economic relations prevail, then certain consequences follow. It makes no categorical claim about the general distribution of those economic relations and so cannot be falsified by the existence of economic forms of society in which capitalist relations of production, and hence capitalist accumulation, do not occur. Independently of the question of its truth or falsity, there is nothing about the form of Marx's 'general law of capitalist accumulation' which renders it unacceptable as a general law. The same applies to Comte's laws of co-existence. As we shall see, many natural-science laws are similarly restricted in scope. Some, indeed, do not apply to any actual or realisable state of affairs at all, but characterise the behaviour of 'ideal' gases, 'perfectly' elastic particles, and so on.

Finally, it is necessary to turn to the by now rather heavily worked issue of value-neutrality. Comte's commitment to value-neutrality as a general characteristic of the scientific method gets further backing with respect to sociology from his relativism. Just as each form of social order has its own kind of unity, its own 'method of philosophising', and its own laws of co-existence, so the successive epochs 'can never be commensurate with one another, as far as individual happiness is concerned . . .'.[33] One of the most powerful attacks on Comte's – and the general positivist – claim to value-neutrality has come from the Hegelian Marxist philosopher, Herbert Marcuse. The core of Marcuse's position is that the central doctrine of positivism commits the positivist social theorist to the rejection of a critique of the existing social order, and so to political conservatism and the abandonment, in practice, of the pose of neutrality.

The standard of adequacy which Marcuse demands of any set of concepts for analysing a particular social order is that it include at least some concepts which are historical and transcendent. That is to say, any adequate analysis of a social order must be capable of understanding it in the light of what it emerged from and, more especially, in the light of its future potentialities. This is the notion underlying Marcuse's own way of using Comte's distinction between positive and negative philosophy. The philosophy of the Enlightenment was negative in that it 'tested human practice by the standard of a truth transcendent to the given social order, the standard represented by a social ordering that did not exist as a fact but as a goal'.[34] That is to say, the Enlightenment philosophers began with a notion of a 'true' human society which embodied in its institutions the values of reason and freedom, and it was in terms of this idea that they were able to condemn the 'facts' of eighteenth-century society as irrational and oppressive.

By contrast, positive philosophy has as its avowed aim the subordination of reason to the facts of social life. Whilst for the negative philosopher social reality is measured by the standard of human reason, the positive philosopher measures human reason by the standards of the prevailing social order. By insisting on deriving scientific concepts from the observable 'facts' of social life, Comte and other positivists reject the possibility of any radical critique of the existing order. 'As a result,' Marcuse concludes, 'the conceptual interest of the positive sociology is to be apologetic and justificatory.'[35] Both the negative philosophers and the positivists have value-commitments: the one against, the other for, the existing order.

There are two rather obvious difficulties in Marcuse's position. One concerns the epistemological status of the 'transcendent' concepts, and standards of reason and 'truth' with which the negative philosopher criticises the prevailing social order. Are they in some sense cognitively superior to the concepts of the positive philosopher (if so, in what sense and in what respect?) or do the positive and negative philosophies reduce to conflicting ideologies with no independent standard of rationality? The second concerns the gap between the positivist epistemologist and the positivist sociologist. I shall attempt to argue in the next chapter that the positivist conception of the relationship between experience and theoretical concepts in science is not just inaccurate, but logically incoherent. If this is so, it follows that the attempt to construct social theory in accordance with the positive method must necessarily fail. Thus when contemporary empiricist commentators express disappointment at Comte's failure to apply his own method in his substantive sociology, they set Comte an impossible standard. What is at fault is not Comte's application of the method, but the positivist theory of knowledge itself. But simply to admit the possibility that Comte's social theory may not have been in accord with his epistemology is sufficient to show that Marcuse's argument is not conclusive.

However, that Comte's social theory, and indeed the whole complex of his history and philosophy of the sciences together with his sociology, is the articulation of a political project has been a central theme of my own analysis of Comte's work. There is a link, in my view, between the positivist epistemology and conservative social theory, but the link is not the close, logical one which Marcuse claims to have established. The link can, I think, only be established on the basis of some substantive propositions of social theory. One of these propositions is that the common-sense thought in terms of which the social theorist, like other members of his social class or stratum, understands his own position in society and his relationships to others has embedded in it categories which both disguise and justify certain aspects of the existing social order.[36] If this assumption is accepted then it follows that sociology can only escape its 'apologetic and justificatory' character to the extent that it breaks with such common-sense concepts. If it is further assumed that one of the effects of the positive philosophy upon substantive sociological practice (though not strictly an application of it) is a tendency to look for observational or experimental support or counter-evidence for general laws, at the expense of critical analysis of the concepts in terms of which the laws are expressed, then the critical rejection of common-sense ideology would not be decisively achieved. As we saw, Comte's social thought was a rather uneasy combination of the principal conceptions of the two leading variants of the ruling ideology of his time: aristocratic and bourgeois.

3 The natural sciences: I. Contempory positivism and the concept of explanation

As I suggested in chapter 1, the central issue dividing the main schools of thought on the relationship between philosophy and the social studies concerns the applicability of the methods and forms of explanation proper to the 'natural' sciences in the 'social sciences'. In the name of the unity of science the positivists have argued for an extension of the methods and forms of explanation developed in the natural sciences into the social sciences, and have generally refused to recognise a difference of principle between the approaches appropriate to the two fields of enquiry. By contrast, 'humanists' of several varieties have argued that such an extension of natural science methodology and standards of explanation is inappropriate and conceptually confused. Typically, the 'humanists' argue this on the basis of their belief in the distinctive character of the object of social knowledge, or understanding (its 'phenomena' pre-empt the would-be scientist by producing explanations of themselves, are intentional, meaningful, rule- rather than law-governed, etc.).

One of the central arguments of this book is that this dispute, in setting the terms for most (though not all)[1] contemporary debate in the methodology of the social sciences, operates as a logical strait-jacket which prevents the posing of important questions necessary to the development of this field.

One method of breaking out of this straitjacket is to question a contention of the positivists which is not (or not thoroughly) challenged by the 'humanists'. This is that, in its main outlines, the positivist conception of the natural sciences is adequate.[2] If, however, the positivist conception of science is inadequate even as an account of the natural sciences, then nothing whatsoever about the fundamental unity or division between the social and natural sciences will follow from a humanist demonstration that the social studies 'cannot' become sciences in the sense of the positivist model of the natural sciences. Because the 'humanist' criticism of positivism is primarily criticism of it as a source of social-science methodology, and not as a philosophical theory of science in general, such criticism is marred by a confusion between objections to positivist epistemology as such and objections to its extension in characterising and informing a particular research-field. This has implications which go beyond the mere attribution of a lack of rigour to such humanist positions. Characteristically the humanist is led to suppose that the epistemological problems and methodology of the natural sciences can be put aside as of no relevance to the development of an adequate methodology in the social studies, and may even be led to complete epistemological scepticism or agnosticism. I shall attempt to demonstrate this a little more fully later on.[3]

An important part of the approach which I hope to outline and defend in the rest of this book is that a necessary condition of the development of an adequate social-science methodology is selective and critical discussion of both formal and substantive natural-science analogues of problems in the social sciences. Clearly this approach is ruled out both by the 'humanist' insistence on the fundamental division of the natural from the social sciences, and by the positivist conception of social-science methodology as simply an 'application' of an epistemological theory of science 'in general'. Underlying these positions, of course, are three incompatible conceptions of the unity and diversity of the sciences.

It is relevant to my argument, then, to present criticisms of the positivist conception of the natural sciences and to attempt to develop an alternative theory. For this reason I make no apology for devoting the present chapter and the next to an exposition of the main lines of development of positivist philosophy of science (including some closely related empiricist theories) in the twentieth century, together with an assessment of the achievements of anti-positivist (and, more generally, anti-empiricist) philosophies of the 'natural' sciences. I do not hope to give a critique in the fullest sense of the term of positivist philosophy of natural science. This is partly because of the so far predominantly negative character of the anti-positivist achievement. Although the main lines of philosophical objection to positivism are already clear and well established no adequately articulated alternative has yet appeared. Nevertheless, enough of a coherent and viable alternative exists to provide the main guidelines for further historical and philosophical research.

Twentieth-century positivism: logical empiricism

Origins

The distinctive twentieth-century form of positivism, 'logical empiricism' or 'logical positivism', is most closely associated with a group of philosophers active in the 1920s in Vienna – the 'Vienna Circle'.[4] Their philosophical doctrines clearly belonged to the broad tradition of radical empiricist philosophy stemming from Hume, though they were responsible for some important innovations. Their epistemology was to a considerable extent a response to the double revolution in physics (relatively theory and quantum mechanics) which had taken place in the first decades of the twentieth century, whilst it shared the preoccupations and utilised the techniques produced by the advancing science of mathematical logic and the theory of meaning.

Logical atomism

Of some importance in this respect was the philosophy of linguistic analysis associated with the names of Russell, Moore and Wittgenstein in Britain. For Russell and Wittgenstein, particularly, the successful use of analytical techniques in solving problems in the theory of meaning led to a whole-scale philosophical programme known as 'logical atomism'.[5] Central to this programme was the notion that the statements of everyday and scientific languages are compounds of simpler statements and concepts, into which they may be resolved by the provision of definitions. For instance, the definition 'Man = dfn. featherless biped' licenses the replacement of 'All men are mortal' by 'All featherless bipeds are mortal' without change of meaning. In this case a compound concept 'man' is split up with the help of a definition into the 'simpler' constituent concepts 'featherless' and 'biped'. But these concepts, in turn, can be defined and so split up into yet simpler concepts, and so on *ad infinitum*. According to the logical atomist programme the ultimate products of analysis are 'simple' propositions whose constituent concepts are incapable of further analysis by definition, and whose meaning must be acquired ostensively – that is to say, by some unexplained process these ultimate propositional constituents must be linked or hooked on to extra-linguistic elements to which they refer. For these elementary signs, their meaning is their reference. The meaning of all compound sentences is ultimately dependent upon these ostensive links between the simplest constituents of language and the simplest constituents of the world (or, perhaps, the simplest constituents of the describable world). To claim that the statements of ordinary language or of scientific language can be resolved by analysis into simple propositions without change of meaning is to say that they are 'reducible' to them. Conversely, to say that elementary propositions can be compounded to yield everyday and scientific statements is to say that the latter are 'logical constructions' out of the former. Sometimes, speaking somewhat more loosely, it is said that the objects and properties referred to in scientific and common-sense speech are 'logical constructions' out of the elementary referents of elementary propositions. The philosophical programme of reducing statements to their elementary forms faced some rather serious problems. For instance it involved the replacement of all referring expressions which depend upon context for their successful use ('this drawer', 'that dial', etc.) by descriptions in general terms. But it can be shown that no description in general terms, no matter how complex, can ever secure uniqueness of reference.[6]

Observation statements

However, it is fortunately unnecessary to demonstrate the impossibility of the logical atomist programme since it is now largely of historical interest only. And its historical interest lies in the metaphysical interpretation (they would have rejected this description) which the logical empiricists give to the elementary referents of the atomists' elementary propositions. Whereas Wittgenstein, in particular, had maintained a judicious silence as to the constitution of his elementary 'objects', confining himself to their formal properties only,[7] the logical positivists identified them with the ultimate constituents of sensory perception, 'sense-data'. The elementary propositions were, therefore, statements which merely recorded sense-impressions. The special characteristic of such statements, as we saw in the work of earlier empiricists, was supposed to be their incorrigibility. The claim that I am now seeing a sparrow through my window is obviously fallible (it could be a dusty blue-tit, what I take for a window could be a cunningly placed projection-screen, or I may, after all, be only dreaming that I sit here staring desperately out of the window, trying to think up an example). But the claim that there is a moving grey and brown bird-shaped patch in my visual field isn't fallible, since it makes a claim about my own 'private' experience only, and so cannot be shown to be false by any of the standard methods (fetching the binoculars, looking up the bird-book, searching for the projector, waking me up, etc.). So it seems that here is a class of statements – statements which merely record sense-data of this sort – which are indubitable, and so ideally suited to form the basis for a reconstruction of knowledge on a secure foundation. In particular, for the logical empiricists they held out the promise of a firm core of scientific knowledge which would be proof against any future scientific revolution on the scale of that which had recently overthrown the Newtonian theoretical system.

Operationalism and verificationism

The certainty of any set of propositions, or any scientific system could be demonstrated, the logical empiricists thought, provided only that it could be reduced, or shown to be a logical construction out of true observation statements. This type of analysis also provided the setting for a new theory of meaning: the meaning of any sentence was the set of possible observations sufficient to demonstrate its truth. Put more elegantly: the meaning of a statement is its method of verification. In this form, the logical empiricist theory of meaning had close affinities with that of the American philosopher and physicist P. W. Bridgman. In his earlier work Bridgman put forward a theory of meaning such that the meaning of any scientific concept was identical with the set of operations required to determine the values of the referent of the concept. Thus the concept of length is no more and no less than the set of operations by which length is measured. This seems to have the difficulty among others that, for example the concept of temperature, as measured by the expansion of a mercury column, is a different concept from the concept of temperature as measured by changes in electrical conductivity or by changes in the pressure exerted by a gas. Also the operationalist theory of meaning requires that the meaning of any empirical concept be exhausted in some finite set of operations, whereas the development of scientific knowledge involves the progressive introduction of new techniques for measuring the properties referred to by existing scientific concepts in a way that is not specifiable in advance.[8]

Analogous difficulties attend the strict form of the verification theory of meaning, and the history of logical empiricism since the twenties has consisted in a series of revisions which have progressively weakened the requirement of empirical testability. One such revision involved a shift from the verification theory of meaning, as sketched above, to a verification criterion of meaningfulness – a putative statement is meaningful if and only if it is either analytic (or logically false) or conclusively verifiable, the verifiability of a statement being interpreted as its equivalence to some finite set of statements recording possible observations.

There are three distinguishable kinds of problem with the verification criterion understood in this way, and logical empiricists have devoted great theoretical ingenuity to the attempt to overcome them. The first sort of problem concerns the 'logical construction' of statements about material objects, their masses, shapes and other properties out of observation statements. It very soon became obvious that this programme was unrealisable. No amount of statements describing actual or possible sensations could ever be strictly equivalent to a statement describing a material object. The statement, 'The sparrow is cleaning itself' involves a claim about the real world which goes beyond what is contained in any finite set of descriptions of patterns on a visual field, even if these are added to by descriptions of tactile, auditory and other sorts of sensation. Any finite conjunction of such statements could be true, consistently with the falsehood of the statement about the sparrow. The difficulty is compounded when the attempt is made to produce logical constructions of statements about objects which, whilst having an important role in science, are even further removed from immediate sensation than sparrows, such as molecules, protons, viruses, etc.

Phenomenalism

The positivist has two alternatives. One is to offer a re-interpretation of propositions about sparrows, metals, protons and viruses such that although they appear to be statements about categories of existing things they should strictly speaking be construed as a convenient shorthand way of summarising statements about sense-contents. This position is known as phenomenalism and, as we shall see, it implies a drastically impoverished conception of scientific explanation. Apart from this, philosophical analyses of the function of concepts like 'sensation' and 'experience' in actual discourse demonstrate that they do not denote some logically private entity, as the phenomenalist supposes. The later work of Wittgenstein contains arguments which purport to show that words with such a function could form no part of any actual language.[9] There are also arguments to the effect that any language in which it is possible to speak about 'sensations' and 'experiences' must also be a language in which it is possible to make reference to more basic particulars, such as material objects, which are located in space and time.[10] 'Material-object' statements, so called, could not, if these arguments are valid, be in general construed as inferences from statements describing sensations. The logical priorities are in the reverse order.

Confirmationism

The alternative stratagem for the positivist is to concede the impossibility of the programme, and either treat material-object language as providing the observational basis of science or insist on the need for some relationship between observation statements and all other statements accepted as meaningful, though allowing that this relationship may be weaker than logical equivalence. If it is conceded that statements about manometer readings, cloud-chamber tracks, marks on photographic plates, etc., form the observational basis of science then this entails the abandonment of the initial rationale of the positivist enterprise. Observation was to be the neutral arbiter which pronounced finally on the truth or falsity of theories. It was to be this which gave science its special claims to provide knowledge, justified the claim of scientific knowledge to be capable of progress, and to be the very paradigm of rational knowledge. So long as observations were thought of as recorded in indubitable elementary propositions this seemed a realisable prospect, but statements about manometer readings and cloud-chamber tracks are as fallible and contestable as any other: the whole prospect of giving to scientific knowledge a firm foundation begins to fade.

The acceptance of a looser relationship than logical equivalence between observation statements and material-object, not to mention theoretical statements turns out to pose yet another set of problems. These are the problems which constitute the second sort of difficulty with the verification principle.[11] Even for statements about particular material objects (particular sparrows or manometers) no finite set of actual or possible observations (= sense-data) could conclusively verify (= verify beyond logical possibility of mistake) them. If the positivist maintained this form of the verification principle, then he would have to rule out as meaningless particular statements about physical objects. He would also have to rule out universal statements (including general laws) and statements about theoretical entities. The problem, then, is to relax the verification criterion so as to allow such propositions as meaningful, yet to exclude 'metaphysical', religious and other types of cognitively unacceptable statement (notice the circularity of this procedure – the positivists began with a criterion which was supposed to provide a way of telling the difference between the meaningful and the meaningless, but when it is applied the results do not accord with the intuitions of the positivist, and so he alters the criterion in the hope of getting results which do conform to his intuitions). This attempt to relax the verification criterion by just the right amount led to attempts at formulating a notion not of empirical verification, but of empirical confirmability. For a proposition, or putative proposition, to count as meaningful it ought to be possible to specify a possible observation which would at least count in favour of the truth of the proposition. For an example of the logical mess to which this can lead, see A. J. Ayer's classic positivist text *Language, Truth and Logic*, pp. 35–9, and the introduction to the second edition. Another, related difficulty concerns the precise meaning of 'possible observation'. If 'technically possible' observation is meant, then speculation as to the view from Mars is not meaningful since it is at present technically impossible to have such views (the positivists' favourite example used to be statements about the other side of the moon!). If physically possible is meant, then speculation about happenings which run counter to current physical theory are ruled out as meaningless. This would be to rule out precisely those examples of reasoning which are responsible for the advance of science: Einstein's discussion of the Michelson–Morley experiment which gave birth to the special theory of relativity was precisely to treat it as an event which was impossible in terms of current notions of physical possibility. This seems to leave only the option of 'logically possible' observation which, in turn, renders the verification principle so weak as to allow almost anything to count as a meaningful statement. But even if some such formulation of the verification criterion did achieve the right inclusions and exclusions for the positivists' intuitions, it would still represent an enormous concession on their part. Science could no longer be represented as resting upon an indubitable observational basis.

The third[12] set of difficulties associated with the verification principle has to do with the status of the principle itself. First of all, what is it that the criterion is applied to? Clearly the positivist is not entitled to say that the criterion distinguishes meaningful from meaningless statements, since a 'meaningless statement' is just not a statement at all. Ayer's device of speaking of 'putative statements' doesn't get around the problem either, since in order to tell whether a 'putative statement' is or is not verifiable we first need to understand it. But if it can be understood, then surely it is meaningful? Some prior notion of meaningfulness is presupposed in the very application of the verification principle. This is related to another difficulty. Does the verification principle itself satisfy the verification criterion of meaningfulness? Ayer's answer to this question was that the verification principle was not an empirical proposition at all, but a definition of what is meant by saying that a proposition is meaningful. The not surprising response to this was that there are many meanings of the term 'meaningfulness' not captured by Ayer's principle, and so it is either a mistaken report on actual usage, or a stipulative definition reflecting only Ayer's own predilections as to the use of the term, and carrying no particular compulsion for others.

Thus the major departure of logical positivism from earlier forms of positivism, namely its claim to rule out (non-analytic) non-empirical statements not just as 'unscientific' but as actually meaningless was gradually abandoned. The verification criterion became a test of empirical (as distinct from ethical, aesthetic, etc.) significance – i.e. a criterion of demarcation between the scientific and non-scientific.

The modern positivist conception of scientific explanation

Having briefly surveyed the general features of the logical positivist theory of knowledge, and examined some of its internal difficulties, it is necessary to consider in more detail some of its specific achievements in the philosophy of science. Here, as with the verification criterion, the positivist characteristically takes key concepts such as 'explanation', 'law', 'theory', etc., which have a rough-and-ready use in science and discussion about science, and presents an 'explication' of these concepts, an 'explication' being a stipulative definition, a recommendation that the term in question be used in a slightly different, but more precise way than hitherto.

The first such explication with which I shall deal is the positivist conception of a scientific explanation. This conception is commonly referred to as the 'covering law' or deductive-nomological conception of explanation,[13] and is merely an elaboration of the basic pattern of explanation which I discussed in connection with Comte's work. As its names suggest, this conception of what it is for some set of statements to constitute an explanation is almost entirely a question of the formal properties of the statements and of their mutual relationships. When fully stated, all explanations take the form of valid deductive arguments with the description of the event to be explained (the 'explanandum') as the conclusion drawn from premises ('the explanans') which include one or more universal laws (hence the 'nomological' or 'covering law' model).

The rationale for this conception of explanation can be readily demonstrated with the help of examples. Generally speaking, explanations of events take the form of a reference to some prior event which is designated the 'cause' of the event to be explained. A plane crash is explained as a result of engine failure coupled with pilot error; the expansion of a metal rod is explained by the heat of a Bunsen burner. But the positivist rejects all thought of mystical, unseen connections between discrete events, so how can one event be said to explain some quite distinct later event? And why should this event be selected, rather than some other? The positivist answer to these questions is to say that explanations like this are incompletely expressed. It is only in virtue of taken-for-granted background assumptions that the mere reference to a prior event can be explanatory. It is only if we are aware of a general association between pilot error and engine failure, on the one hand, and plane crashes, on the other, that mentioning one or the other as the 'cause' of a particular crash is explanatory. Similarly, it is only if we are aware of a general relationship between changes in temperature and changes in the length of rods of metal that reference to heating as a 'cause' of this particular measured expansion is explanatory of it. To explain an event, then, is to present it as an instance of a universal law to the effect that always if events of the same type as some specified prior event occur, then events of the same type as the explanandum-event follow. To explain an event is to subsume it under a universal law.

The structure of an explanation can, then, be set out in the form of a simple deductive argument as follows:

Premises { Always, if A occurs then B occurs (law)
A occurred (antecedent condition)

Conclusion: therefore, B occurred (explanandum-event)

Of course, many explanations will be more complex than this, including a conjunction of several laws, and asserting the combined occurrence of several antecedent conditions, but such complexities raise no important difficulties of principle. In the case of the plane crash, my supposed explanation, fully expressed, would give content to the above formal structure as follows:

Law: always, if pilot error is combined with engine failure then a crash occurs.
Antecedent condition: both pilot error and engine failure occurred

Explanandum: therefore, a crash occurred

Explanation and prediction

Now, one obvious strength of this model of explanation is that it makes plain the relationship between explanation and prediction which, as we saw in chapter 2, is central to the positivist conception of the relationship between scientific knowledge and its practical application. Just as the combination of general laws and statements of antecedent conditions enables the description of an event to be deduced, and enables the event to be explained, so exactly the same combination of premises, if known prior to the occurrence of the event (or prior to the knowledge of its occurrence) would generate its prediction. Scientific prediction and explanation have an identical formal structure. The description of an event to be explained or of an event to be scientifically predicted constitutes the conclusion of a deductive argument including at least one universal law amongst its premises. This thesis, which follows from the positivist conception of scientific explanation, is known as the thesis of the symmetry of explanation and prediction. The covering-law conception of explanation also yields a simple and impressive account of the testability of explanations on this basis. Explanations can be confirmed or refuted by their success or failure in generating predictions.

Scientific laws

Before going on to discuss criticism of this notion of explanation it will be necessary to go into a little more depth concerning the nature of universal laws. One immediate problem concerns the difference, if any, between accidental generalisations and genuine 'nomological' laws. In other words, the difference between conjunctions of events type A with events of type B which are merely accidental, and conjunctions of events which constitute a causal law. For instance, it may so happen that all the books on my bookshelf have red covers, and a generalisation to this effect could yield an argument of the same form as that demanded by the covering-law conception of explanation:

All books on my shelf are red
This is a book on my shelf

Therefore, this book is red

Why won't this do as a scientific explanation? It is very hard to see how Hume or Comte could have adequately answered this question, since for them laws were just observed regularities in phenomena. But modern positivists have attempted to provide criteria for distinguishing such accidental generalisations from genuine laws, as might be expected, by reference to their logical characteristics. One criterion is that a universal statement is a law only if it licenses the prediction of some event not included in the evidence for it. The idea here is that the content of a law somehow 'goes beyond' its evidential basis. This criterion obviously excludes my red books example from the status of an explanation. But there are other universal statements – which we might call empirical or rule-of-thumb generalisations – which are not laws and yet are still not excluded by this criterion. Examples might include 'all swans are white', 'all men are greedy' and 'all mammals have legs'. Such generalisations are thought to be true – or have been thought to be true – on the basis of extensive observation, but are not scientific laws as are Newton's laws of motion, the ideal gas equations, and the inverse square law for electro-magnetic radiation. A second criterion is required to exclude these from the status of scientific laws. According to this criterion a universal statement is a law only if it enables the deduction of subjunctive or counter-factual conditionals. Thus, to return to the example of the metal rod, the universal statement connecting changes in temperature of metal rods with their length satisfies this condition since it justifies claims about what could have happened if the rod had been (contrary to what did happen) cooled, or heated to twice the temperature. Empirical generalisations do not justify such counter-factuals, and so are excluded from the status of scientific laws. The trouble with this account of scientific laws, though, is that it gives the positivists a difficulty analogous to the problem of 'logical construction' of material objects from sense-data.

If a scientific law by definition makes a claim which goes beyond the evidential or observational support it has, then the positivist is hard put to it to explain how belief in the truth of general laws can ever be justified. To say, as some positivists have, that the drawing of inferences from general laws which go beyond their evidential base can be justified in terms of support given to laws by the possibility of deriving them from higher-level, more general laws, is either to make an important concession to rationalist epistemology or simply to push the problem one step further back. The positivist still has to explain the origin of the support for the higher-level law.

Statistical laws

There remains a further type of general statement which figures in scientific explanations which is recognised by most positivists not to be covered by the above account of scientific laws. These statements – statistical generalisations – are common in the social sciences, and so a word about them here might be in order.[14] We can very simply characterise such statements as having the form: '*N* per cent of As are Bs' in contrast to universal laws whose form is: 'All As are Bs'. We can distinguish three different ways in which statements of statistical or 'probabilistic' form commonly occur in scientific explanations. First, they may refer to the statistical relationships between kinds of events or phenomena in a particular sample. It may be found, for example, that of a particular sample of car workers, 70 per cent voted Labour in the 1970 general election. Any scientific interest such a generalisation might have depends on its status as evidence for some generalisation not restricted in scope to any particular sample.[15] It may together with other evidence be regarded as, for instance, growing inductive support to statistical laws (or even universal laws)[16] relating class membership, working conditions, income levels, or whatever, to voting behaviour. Unless statistical generalisations referring to samples do relate in this way to generalisations not so restricted, they are analogous in logical status to 'empirical generalisations' as discussed above.

A second type of occurrence of statistical generalisations is as first approximations to laws of universal form. A simple medical example might be '*N* per cent of people who are in contact with a sufferer from the common cold themselves contract the disease'. The scope of this generalisation is not restricted to any particular sample. It asserts that whenever the antecedent condition (contact with a sufferer) is satisfied the consequent (contraction of the disease) will follow in *N* per cent of cases. Such statistical generalisations do not always involve a causal connection, and where they do the events, processes, etc. of the kind mentioned in the antecedent condition may not be causal factors in the production of those mentioned in the consequent. Both, for example, may be causally related as effects of some other cause or complex of causes which are not referred to in the law. But the example I have chosen can be regarded as a first approximation to a causal law, and events of the kind referred to in the antecedent of the law would generally be counted as 'causes'. A further analysis of this example, then, will help in getting clearer about the positivist concept of cause as it applies to such cases. According to the positivist paradigm of explanation, catching a cold has not been explained until it can be subsumed under a universal law, and so the stratagem for dealing with such cases as this will be to search for other conditions which are correlated with the catching of colds in the hope that these can be combined with the one already established so as to yield a universal law. Thus it might be discovered that a higher proportion of contacts get the disease if the sufferer is at some stages of development of the disease than at others. Another relevant variable may be the type and duration of contact, and yet another the physiological state of the contact, his or her previous medical history, etc. Ultimately, these might be combined to form a universal law with a multiplicity of conditions contained in its antecedent clause. 'Always, if a person with low resistance has sustained and close contacts with a sufferer in the early stages of development of the common cold, that person contracts the disease.' If qualms about how to define terms like 'resistance' and how to measure degrees of it or classify types of contact are temporarily waived, this seems to be a reasonably promising way of showing that such statistical laws form part of incomplete explanations only, and remain to be reduced to universal laws by further investigation. However, a certain revision of the positivist conception of 'cause' is required by this type of solution. So far, the 'cause' of a phenomenon has been specified as an event of a type universally connected with the phenomenon which is its 'effect'. Often, it has also been held that for such an event to be a 'cause' in the fullest sense, the 'effect' must never occur in the absence of it. Another way of putting this is to say that a cause is an event (process, state, etc.) which is both empirically necessary for the occurrence of its effect, and empirically sufficient. Now, in the above example, contact with a sufferer is neither a sufficient condition for getting a cold (i.e. *ex hypothesi*, in 30 per cent of cases contact does not have this effect) nor a necessary condition (one can catch a cold without being in contact with a sufferer, e.g. in medical experiments where persons are injected with cold virus), and yet contact may still be spoken of as the 'cause' and as 'explaining' many particular cases of the disease. An ingenious solution of this problem, whilst retaining the main features of the positivist concept of cause, is to say that a 'cause' is a necessary part of a combination of conditions which are jointly sufficient for the production of an 'effect' which, however, may also be produced by some other set of conditions (i.e. a cause is an Insufficient but Necessary part of an Unnecessary but Sufficient condition – or 'INUS' condition).[17] This allows 'contact with a sufferer' to count as a causal condition and, though conceding that not all causes are necessary and sufficient conditions, manages to give an account of causality in terms of necessary and sufficient conditions.

But there is a third type of occurrence of statistical generalisations which, it is often held, cannot be treated in this way as first approximations to universal laws. These are generalisations about the behaviour of aggregates when there is a supposed indeterminateness in the behaviour of their individual constituents. The phenomena of radioactive decay provide an example. Radioactive isotopes are said to have a 'half-life' of some specified period – let us say t minutes. This implies that, for any sample of such an isotope, approximately half of its constituent atoms will undergo radioactive decay in any period of t minutes. Now there is no way of predicting, for any one atom, precisely when it will decay. All that can be said is that there is a probability of 0·5 that it will decay within any period of t minutes. More importantly it may be that the character of subatomic phenomena is such that no universal law governing radioactive decay, such that it can be predicted in the case of specified atoms, will ever be discovered. Such statistical laws, then, would remain the best that science could (in principle?) achieve in this field.[18] It would have to be conceded that some explanations in science are not reducible to the deductive-nomological form. One of the least dogmatic of contemporary positivists, Carl Hempel, seems to accept that this really does have serious consequences for the universality of the deductive-nomological model. For him, statistical explanations license only inductive inferences of the phenomena they are meant to explain.[19] Such explanations, then, have a different form from the deductive-nomological:

N per cent of As are Bs
There is an A
════════════════ (with probability *N*)
Therefore B

The double line represents the fact that a non-deductive inference is involved here, and that B is inferred only with a certain degree of probability. Now, Hempel is unclear on this, but it seems that he makes more of a concession than he strictly needs to. First of all, the inference that B will occur is not an inductive inference. At this point Hempel seems to confuse what he clearly distinguishes elsewhere: probability construed as 'statistical frequency' and probability construed as a relation between inductive evidence and a generalisation which it is said to support. The likelihood, in the above example, of any particular A being a B is at least in part a question of the statistical frequency with which As are Bs. It is not a question of the extent of the existing evidence for the assertion that *N* per cent of As are Bs. In fact, it is quite possible to revise the explanatory schema to render it properly deductive:

N per cent As are Bs
This is an A

Therefore there is a probability of *N* per cent that it is a B

Thus, if it is conceded that explananda may include not only events but also probabilities, then statistical explanations may be represented as deductive in form. Also, although statistical laws are not, by definition, universal laws, they share many of the characteristics of such laws (e.g. licensing the deduction of counter-factuals, going beyond the evidence for them, etc.). The uses of statistical generalisations in the sciences, then, require relatively little modification of the deductive-nomological model of explanation.

Functional explanations

There are, however, some difficulties with the deductive-nomological account of explanation which are less easily dealt with. One has been mentioned already. It is that some sciences make extensive use of explanations involving the concept of function, and describe processes as directed towards some 'goal' or end-state. Apparently, such explanations are not deductive-nomological in form. Here, the positivist stratagem is to show that in so far as such explanations are genuinely scientific, they are, after all, reducible to the deductive-nomological form. Although functional explanation plays an important part in the social sciences I have insufficient space to follow this argument further at this point.[20] Some further reference to functional explanations will be found in chapters 5 and 9.

The symmetry of explanation and prediction

A second objection is that the symmetry of explanation and prediction which is an implication of the deductive-nomological model of explanation is by no means universal in the sciences. Functional explanations, for instance, are conceded by the positivists to be scientific explanations and yet they have little or no predictive power.

Paradoxically, Hempel's reduction of functional explanations to the deductive-nomological form has the consequence of attributing to such explanations in their reduced (i.e. deductive-nomological) form very weak predictive power.[21] Also, it is frequently claimed that the theory of biological evolution is explanatory of the origin of new organic species, but has never been used to predict the emergence of any new species.[22]

The history of the sciences also seems to yield many examples of predictive success not accompanied by any explanatory power. Many scientific theories (such as Ptolemaic astronomy) which are now out-dated and accepted as false had and still do have a record of high predictive success. The positivist's response would no doubt be that he is concerned with the formal characteristics of explanations and not their truth or falsity. Moreover, the deductive-nomological model can show how it is that predictive success is consistent with explanatory falsehood: true conclusions can be validly deduced from false premises. No matter how large a finite class of true predictions is generated from a universal law it is always possible that it is false, and that the next prediction will fail.

But there are still other examples of computational systems which generate accurate predictions and yet do not even stand as candidates for the status of 'explanations'. A valuable example, described by Rom Harré, is the system of astronomical prediction developed by the Babylonians.[23] The Babylonians were able to predict astronomical phenomena on the basis of numerical computations which appear to have borne no relation to any physical model of the universe. Yet another type of example in which there is substantial predictive power without explanation is medical prognosis. General medical knowledge of the developmental stages of different diseases enables the prediction of future states of the patient on the basis of present symptoms. Thus, the diagnosis of coronary heart diseases or of cancer on the basis of symptoms will yield a prognosis about the future development of the disease, but the symptoms cannot be said to explain these future developments.

Explanation, causality and 'conceptual schemes'

These apparent counter-examples are not decisive against the positivist conception of explanation. They are, however, indications that something is amiss. A further indication of what this 'something' is may be gleaned by consideration of just what 'explanation' amounts to on the deductive model. Somehow the occurrence of an event is supposed to be explained by subsuming it under a general law – by, in other words, saying that the event was to be expected since, in such circumstances, such events always occur. An impoverished account of what science aims at, surely? It seems that part of what is wrong, at least, is that any adequate conception of explanation must do more than specify a few elementary formal characteristics. These formal characteristics, it appears, may be shared by non-explanatory schemata.

To get a clearer idea of just what is missing from the positivist account, it will be helpful to return to the common-cold example which I made use of above. I began with the statement of an imaginary statistical correlation, and went on to suppose how this statistical law could be converted into a universal law by the discovery of new conditions related to the catching of colds. But there are problems with this account. How is one to tell when all the relevant conditions have been gathered (i.e. that the law really is in its final, universal form)? Perhaps, unnoticed by the investigator, all of his cold-sufferers wore gold rings on their fingers. Perhaps, unknown to the investigator, the removal of the rings would have rendered the cold non-infectious. A vital necessary condition for catching colds would have been left out of the statement of the supposed universal law. And how could the investigator have justified restricting his research for further conditions in the way that I presented him as doing (to physiological states and histories of 'contacts', type and duration of contact, stages of disease, etc)? Why not investigate the positions of the planets, the rate of inflation, or the state of the tides? The answer, surely, is that the statement of the original law, and the selection of possibly relevant conditions for amplifying it, both make certain logical presuppositions. These are that a certain set of concepts ('contagion', 'infection', 'disease', 'common cold', 'person', 'physiological state', etc.) is adequate for grasping the phenomena under investigation, that these concepts designate and provide criteria for recognising kinds of 'things', 'processes', 'events', etc., between which certain general types of interaction are conceivable and others not (not conceivable within this particular framework of concepts, that is). Explanations, then, presuppose a conceptual framework in terms of which to identify and classify the general types of things in the universe (or rather, that aspect of it which forms the object of the particular science in question), and which specifies the general types of causal interaction which can take place between them. The inductive inference that all the relevant circumstances had been included in the universal laws governing the catching of colds could only be justified on the assumption of the adequacy of some such conceptual scheme. Similarly the restriction of the scope of the investigation which generated the universal law could only be rationally justified on the basis of a conceptual scheme which was the source of a hypothetical causal mechanism (or possibly several) which in turn generated criteria of relevance for the investigation. In this example the causal mechanism upon which the construction of the law was premised was the germ-theory of disease. But there certainly have been epochs in which the appropriate conceptual scheme would have demanded investigation of planetary positions. Precisely such causal relations between astronomical events and the fortunes – including their illnesses – of individuals on earth were postulated in medieval astrology.

The source of certain difficulties in the positivist conception of causality is now revealed. In particular the difficulties of distinguishing symptoms from causes, and of distinguishing causal laws from other types of law, arise from the attempt to reduce the concepts of cause to those of necessary and sufficient conditions. Sometimes, it is true, necessary and sufficient conditions are referred to as 'causes', but this is so only where such conditions are supposed to be related to, or form part of a generative causal mechanism.[24] The identification and description of such mechanisms depends, in turn, upon the utilisation of a conceptual scheme of the type described above.

A further set of difficulties arises for positivism from the account of the empirical testability of scientific laws in terms of predictive success or failure, and the erection of this feature of scientific explanation as a demarcation criterion for science. However, these difficulties are most appropriately delayed until a further element in the positivist philosophy of science has been discussed. I suggested above that to explain an event by saying it was to be expected in the circumstances is hardly to explain it in a sense that does justice to the achievements of science. The justified response of the positivist might have been that I had omitted an important feature of the positivist account of science: its contribution to the discussion on the nature of scientific theories.

4 The natural sciences: II. The positivist conception of scientific theory and its competitors

In the present chapter I shall continue my exposition of the positivist philosophy of natural science with an account of its conception of the nature of scientific theories. I shall confront this conception with a series of anti-positivist objections and finally sketch very briefly some of the non-positivist alternatives. Although I shall not make the connections explicit at this stage attentive readers will detect many of the most characteristic arguments of contemporary 'humanist' critics as to the distinctive character of the social studies in the mouths of anti-positivist philosophers of the natural sciences.

The hypothetico-deductive account of scientific theories[1]

The most widely accepted positivist conception of theories is known as the 'Hypothetico-Deductive' conception; 'deductive' because, like the positivist account of explanation, it represents theories as deductive systems, and 'hypothetico' for reasons which will become clear later. For convenience I shall speak of the 'H–D' account from now on. The requirement for theory arises, the positivists argue, when empirical laws covering a given field of phenomena have already been established. So, to use a favourite example of the positivists, let us suppose that universal laws governing the relations of pressure, temperature and volume in gases have been established by investigation. It is now possible to explain, e.g., the expansion of a particular sample of gas at constant temperature in terms of a reduction in the pressure exerted on it, in virtue of a universal law relating these variables (Boyle's Law). But this need not be the end of the matter. Why, it may be asked, are pressure, volume and temperature related in this way? In accordance with the positivist conception of explanation, the answer to this question will involve subsuming Boyle's Law (and, possibly, other laws governing related phenomena) under another, higher level universal law from which it can be deduced. In this way, as the capacity to give scientific explanations in any particular field 'deepens', knowledge takes on the form of a hierarchy of increasingly general laws, the lower level laws being deducible from the higher level. The highest level laws are thought of, in this way, as the axioms and postulates of a deductive system. Among them are statements of quantitative relations between variable terms, and from them can be deduced 'theorems' which ultimately yield quantitative relationships between variables which have an 'observational' interpretation – such as the variables of Boyle's Law. Generally, although this is not regarded by positivists as an essential aspect of theories, the mathematical variables involved in the highest level laws will be interpreted as referring to properties of unobservable entities which in some sense are supposed to lie 'behind' or 'under' the observable phenomena which this whole deductive structure – or 'theory' – is supposed to explain. Concepts which specify the unobservable processes, properties and entities postulated in the theory are termed 'theoretical' concepts and are distinguished from 'observational' concepts which specify things and properties which are directly observable and measurable. An immediate difficulty now emerges for this deductive conception of scientific theories. Statements belonging to the theory involve the use of technical, theoretical concepts, whereas the empirical generalisations which they are supposed to explain are expressed in terms of 'observational' concepts. How, then, can the latter set of statements be deduced from the former? The answer, on the H–D account, is by means of the introduction of statements linking observational with theoretical concepts. These statements, sometimes called 'bridge-principles' or 'correspondence rules', express functional relations between 'theoretical' variables and 'observational' variables, and so can be combined with purely theoretical statements to license the inference of statements at the observational level.

An example: the kinetic theory of gases

Figure 1 is an attempt to represent the internal structure of the kinetic theory of gases along these lines. The statements of the theory belong to three main 'levels' – the theory proper, the level of observation, and the intervening level of bridge-principles which serve to link theoretical terms such as 'speed', 'mass', 'kinetic energy of molecules' with observational terms such as 'pressure', 'volume' and 'temperature'. The statements of the theory embody an analogy between molecules, as the ultimate constituents of gases, and material particles whose motions are governed by Newtonian laws of motion. Upon this is superimposed yet another analogy between the

Theory

1 Gases are composed of molecules.
2 These molecules are in constant motion, and collide with one another and the walls of their container.
3 The total volume of the molecules in a given sample of gas is negligible compared with the volume of the gas.
4 Molecules exert no force on one another except at collision.
5 Molecular motions and interactions obey the laws of classical mechanics.

Bridge-principles, or correspondence rules

(a) Pressure $= F_1$ (mass, concentration, mean speed of molecules).
(b) Temperature $= F_2$ (mean kinetic energy of molecules).
(c) Rate of diffusion $= F_3$ (mean speed, concentration and diameter of molecules).
(d) etc.

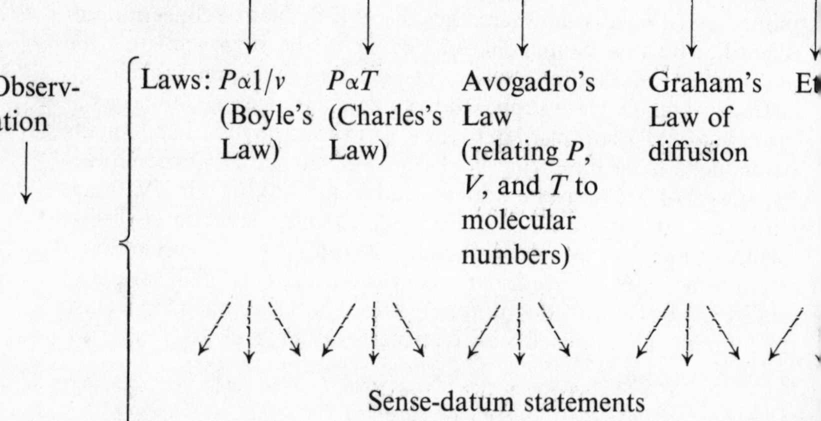

Key

'F' means 'function of', in the sense that terms so related have a definite quantitative relationship to one another such that from known values of one, corresponding values of the other can be calculated.
'P' is short for 'pressure', 'T' for 'temperature', 'V' for 'volume', and 'α' for 'is proportiona
Arrows represent the direction of deductive inferences. Arrows drawn with broken lines indicate a further set of inferences which are insisted upon by strict positivists and phenomenalists.

Figure 1 The Hypothetico-Deductive account of scientific theories: The kinetic theory of gases as an example

statistical behaviour of large numbers of these molecules and the macro-level properties of the gas which are characterised by laws such as Graham's, Boyle's and Charles's. The bridge-principles in this case express quantitative relations between the statistical properties of swarms of molecules and macro-properties such as pressure, temperature and diffusion-rates. This analysis of the structure of the theory has the merits of demonstrating how the observational laws (Boyle's, Charles's, etc.) are explained by deduction from statements of the theory, how theories can be tested (by their predictions at the observational level), how they can relate previously unrelated laws (observational laws governing pressure, volume and temperature, viscosity, diffusion-rates, thermal capacities, etc. are now linked as implications of a single deductive system), and how they can generate new knowledge (inferences from the theory may include hitherto unobserved regularities at the observational level).

The status of theoretical entities: realism versus phenomenalism[2]

Despite this apparent strength, the H–D account has come in for some serious criticism in recent times. One of the central problems concerns the status of the hypothetical entities postulated by the statements of the theory. Since these are, by definition, not objects of observation, strict positivists and phenomenalists attempt to treat them as 'logical constructions'. For them, the use of an analogy with swarms of material particles may be a useful psychological prop for the scientist. It may also serve as a heuristic device in the generation of new hypotheses, and be helpful in teaching the theory. But from the point of view of the internal logic of the theory and its explanatory power the material analogy is quite dispensable. Above all, the tempting supposition that there really are molecules which behave as specified by the interpreted statements of the theory must be regarded as either 'cognitively meaningless' or, at best, unscientific. A theory, on this view, is a deductive system for the generation of propositions at the observational level. The material analogies which may or may not be associated with 'interpretations' of its most fundamental propositions have no bearing upon its explanatory power or scientific status. This 'instrumentalist' conception of scientific theories is the only one strictly available for verificationists and phenomenalists, since statements about molecules understood literally as statements about unobservable entities are neither conclusively verifiable by observations, nor are they logically equivalent to any finite set of observation statements. For those who adopt such a philosophical position, the addition of yet a new 'level' of reality beyond the 'material object' level adds to the problems they already face in interpreting statements about material objects themselves in terms of statements about sense-data.

Such 'instrumentalist' interpretations of scientific theories are not the exclusive property of radical empiricists such as positivists and phenomenalists, however. Conventionalists, such as Duhem and Poincaré (who reject a central doctrine of empiricism – the possibility of 'theory-neutral' observation statements), have also argued, on somewhat different grounds, that theories are simply elaborate deductive devices for 'representing' and anticipating experience.[3] Such an interpretation of scientific theories led the physicist Mach to deny the existence of atoms, and should have led Comte to the same conclusion, given his conception of scientific laws as expressing relations between phenomena.

Instrumentalism carries with it a distinctive account of the status of bridge-principles. They must be regarded not as statements of empirical relationships between micro-level processes and macro-level regularities, but as partial definitions or rules of inference. This has the implausible consequence, in the case of the kinetic theory of gases, of representing the nineteenth-century achievement of a dynamical explanation of thermal phenomena not as the production of new knowledge about the world, but as a mere revision in the definitions of certain physical concepts. Another argument against instrumentalism is given by Hempel,[4] who argues that the distinction between theoretical and 'observable' entities is arbitrary and transitory, and so cannot form the basis of any rational decision as to what to count as 'existing'. Thus, the wiring of some circuits may be visible, but what if some wire is so thin that a microscope is required in order to see it? Are we to say that since the interpretation of what is seen through a microscope depends on acceptance of the optical theory on the basis of which it is constructed, wire which can only be seen with a microscope does not really exist? Viruses, molecules, atoms, protons, etc. differ only in degree from this case and from one another, Hempel continues, and so what is the justification of restricting existence claims to only some of these, and not to others?

Plausible mechanisms

A somewhat different line of argument against instrumentalism is merely an extension of the main argument which I outlined above[5] against the deductive concept of explanation. To subsume a phenomenon or a law from some higher-level law or combination of them is not of itself to explain anything. Certainly the deduction of values for several important macro-properties of gases which were in close agreement with observed values played a large part in the elaboration and establishment of the kinetic theory of gases. But the physical analogy which postulates an underlying mechanism for these observed phenomena cannot be treated as merely accidentally and inessentially involved in the selection of only certain relevant and successful inferences from the infinite range of possible ones which could be drawn from any set of uninterpreted axioms and postulates. Historically speaking, criteria of adequacy for scientific explanation have always involved more than purely formal considerations. Although conceptions of what counts as a plausible mechanism have changed (it is, for instance, unclear whether the present state of the theory of the mechanism underlying electromagnetic radiation will give rise to further development of a 'more plausible' mechanism, or to a change in criteria as to what counts as a 'plausible' mechanism) all branches of scientific enquiry have required conformity to some notion of plausibility. Such notions of plausibility are not exhaustively representable in formal terms (absence of contradiction, etc.) but nevertheless have an indispensable role in scientific reasoning, particularly in providing the structural conditions for the growth of scientific knowledge. For example, given the implausibility of Darwin's own hypothetical mechanism – pangenesis – for organic inheritance the acceptability of the theory of evolution itself came to turn upon the production of a more plausible one. This, in fact, had to await the recovery of Mendel's work and the development of genetic theory. Another example was the difficulty faced by heliocentric astronomy in the absence of any coherent alternative to Aristotelian dynamics during the latter part of the sixteenth and early seventeenth centuries. The problem of adequately specifying the mechanisms of planetary motion on the heliocentric hypothesis came to define the terms of reference for the development of classical mechanics until it was (with some qualifications) achieved in Newton's *Principia*. Even then the law of universal gravitation continued to be regarded as unsatisfactory since it seemed to rely on a form of interaction which was implausible in terms of the conception of physical plausibility which was dominant at that time (no action at a distance). Accordingly Newton and others continued to speculate about possible mechanisms underlying gravitational attraction which did conform to contemporary criteria of plausibility.

Concepts of cause

Finally, the instrumentalist conception of theories involves the rejection of at least one important conception of causality, which I began to discuss in the context of my criticism of the deductive conception of explanation: that is, the 'underlying' or 'generative' mechanism conception of cause, as against the positivist conception of causality as 'constant conjunction' or 'necessary and sufficient condition'.[6] Clausius, one of the originators of the kinetic theory of gases, described the relationship between molecular motions and pressure like this: 'the pressure of the gas against a fixed surface is *caused* by the molecules in great number continually striking against and rebounding from the same'[7] (my emphasis). This suggests an interpretation of at least some of the bridge-principles involved in the kinetic theory not as definitions or rules of inference but as causal laws. This would, indeed, be consistent with a realist interpretation of the theoretical statements describing molecules and their relationships. One important feature of the concept of causality involved here, and one which is especially relevant to the discussion of causality in the social sciences, concerns the independent identifiability of cause and effect. On the classical empiricist ('Humean') conception of causality, a cause must be identifiable independently of its effect (this is supposed to follow from the contingency of the causal connection). But where unobservable entities and their behaviour constitute the causal mechanism which generates observable, macro-level happenings and relationships, the unobservable entities themselves are not identifiable or even specifiable independently of the phenomena they are supposed to cause.

Empirical testability

Although these arguments against the instrumentalist interpretation of scientific theories have considerable force against the most radical forms of positivism and empiricism, they are far from decisive as objections to the Hypothetico-Deductive account of theories when it is combined with a much less stringent conception of empirical testability. Hempel, for instance, with a relatively weak, 'confirmationist' conception of testability is able to fully reject instrumentalism and accept the existential character of statements about viruses, molecules, etc. But it is important to recognise the extent of this concession. Hempel, along with many other contemporary empiricists, does not insist on reduction to sense-datum language. This means that cloud-chamber tracks, thermometer readings, absorption lines in spectra, etc. are now allowed to count as objects of observation. This has, as we shall see, important consequences, and involves a great retreat from the idea of sense-datum statements as the indubitable basis of knowledge. Further, statements about in-principle unobservable existents are allowable as scientific. Such statements are clearly confirmable only incompletely and indirectly. Also, the acceptability of such statements includes a whole new class of statements – existential hypotheses – about which classical empiricist theories of science had almost nothing to say. A scientific theory must be conceded to consist, at least in some cases, of universal laws governing phenomena, together with existential hypotheses about the general kinds of things whether observable or not which exist in the universe. Further analysis of the example of the kinetic theory yields another difficulty for the empiricist conception of a universal law itself. This emerges once it is recognised that the basic assumptions of the kinetic theory, and hence the laws deduced from them, are not precisely true of any actual gas. The theoretical statements are simplified abstractions from the model of the internal structure of an actual gas, and strictly speaking observational laws such as those of Boyle and Charles hold only for 'ideal' gases for which these simplifications were, *per impossibile*, true. Monatomic gases at relatively low pressures approximate very closely in their behaviour to the ideal gas laws, but where there are several atoms in each molecule, where molecular shape deviates considerably from the sphere and where there are relatively great intermolecular attractions the empirically observed behaviour of gases deviates further from the ideal gas equations. In some cases this can be dealt with by adding auxiliary assumptions to the basic theory, but in others recourse has to be made to quantum mechanics. However, the main point to come out of this analysis is that some laws, at least, are not laws relating phenomena, but are abstract relations to which phenomena may approximate only more or less closely. Similarly, some existential hypotheses may refer (or purport to refer) to particular existents, whilst others refer to abstract entities such as 'ideal gases', 'point masses', etc. The very notion of empirically testing statements such as these is logically absurd, yet they have an essential place in scientific theorising.

But even for theories which do not involve reference to such 'abstract entities', there are difficulties with the criterion of empirical testability. The point of the empiricist demarcation criterion is not simply to find some characteristic which is both common and peculiar to scientific statements and theories. It is also to account, in some sense, for the special cognitive authority of scientific theories. Empirical testability seems to fulfil this requirement very satisfactorily. Contemporary scientific knowledge is represented as the sum of all those propositions which have survived generations of repeated confrontations with reality. Empirical testability is the mark of the openness of claims about the world to revision under the impact of the world itself. The importance to the empiricist conception of scientific knowledge of the availability of a class of theory-neutral observation statements is now quite clear. But before going on to discuss this requirement of the empiricist theory of scientific knowledge, a further discussion of the options open to the empiricist in accounting for the relationship between observation statements and theory statements is in order.

Confirmationism and falsificationism

Hempel, and other empiricists who reject strict verificationism, are faced with the problem of constructing a concept of 'empirical confirmation' which is weaker than strict verification, but still sets some limit on what can count as scientific. It is recognised that no matter how many implications of a theory are discovered to agree with observation, it is still logically possible that the next prediction will not be borne out. There is no logically valid argument which justifies the attribution of truth to the statements of a theory on the basis of confirming evidence. Any theory makes a claim which goes beyond its evidential basis, and more than one possible theory may account for any finite set of observations. The widespread recognition of this has led to two broad responses. The first is to make use of a rather suspect application of mathematical probability theory to assess the degree of confirmation afforded to a scientific theory by a given extent of observational support.[8] The obvious difficulty with this is that since even for a single law there is an infinity of possible confirming or counter-instances, no matter how many confirming instances have been recorded they still, expressed as a proportion of possible instances, give only infinitely small 'probability' to the law. There are, of course, much more sophisticated attempts to apply the same principles and avoid this outcome, but as of now the prospects of a satisfactory outcome do not look good. Alternatively, the empiricist may concede that there can be no adequate account of testability in terms of either verification or confirmation, and pose openness to refutation by empirical evidence as a demarcation criterion.[9] This is initially more promising since it can be expressed in terms of a logically valid argument. Although no amount of evidence is sufficient to conclusively verify a universal law, one counter-instance is enough to conclusively falsify it. One case of a metal which contracts when heated is sufficient logically to falsify the law that all metals expand when heated. Adoption of falsifiability as a demarcation criterion has the advantage that it can represent the rejection of hypotheses as decided on the basis of logically valid arguments, but perhaps the disadvantage of entailing a rejection of the picture of science as a 'search for truth'. It is, rather, a search for falsification; the best that we can say of what now passes for knowledge is that we have not so far been able to demonstrate its falsity. But if this depicted, even as a 'rational reconstruction', the actual mechanisms by which scientific hypotheses are selected and rejected, then surely every schoolchild has refuted some of the most fundamental scientific laws? Surely contemporary science should be called to explain its dogmatism in continuing to believe in such demonstrated falsehoods? Kuhn, arguing on the basis of his historical analyses, claims that all theories are, from their inception, faced with apparent counter-instances. Far from leading to the immediate rejection of the theories, they provide the routine puzzle-solving work of scientists throughout periods of normal science. Unfortunately for the neat logic of falsification, there are several 'conventionalist' strategies by which a theory may be defended against apparent counter-instances. The experiment or observation which seems to yield a result contrary to theory-based expectations can only do so on the basis of some interpretation of those results. A theory under test may be defended by offering re-interpretations, by questioning the technique of the experimenter or the theory of his instrumentation, and so on. Alternatively, the interpretation of the results may be accepted and one or another type of protective modification of the theory itself adopted. Theory-based expectations never presuppose the truth of only one law. Always it is a conjunction of several laws that is 'falsified', and so the logic of the situation licenses some choice as to which law is rejected or modified. Modifications may include adding to the initial conditions specified in the law, or restricting the scope of the law (as, for example, in the cases of Newton's laws which are restricted to relative velocities which are low compared with the speed of light). Finally, *ad hoc* hypotheses may be added to the theory so as to alter the theory-based expectations in the required way. Disreputable as these 'tricks' may seem, the history of science is full of examples, and there are reasons for thinking that they are indispensable to scientific thinking. Also, of course, statistical laws and existential statements which, as we have seen, form part of many scientific theories cannot even be represented formally as falsifiable by a single instance. Mere failure to find something which is claimed to exist can never conclusively prove its non-existence. Similarly the discovery of a sample of a population with a distribution of properties different from that asserted of the whole population can never conclusively disprove the original assertion.[10]

For these and other reasons, falsificationism, even in its more sophisticated forms where it appears not as a criterion for distinguishing scientific statements but for characterising the recommended scientific method, cannot be accepted as an adequate demarcation criterion.

Observation statements and theories

But there are general reasons for supposing that no account of the acceptance and rejection of scientific laws or theories in terms of confirming or counter-instances could ever be adequate. This is because the very notion of an observation or factual statement which is logically independent of competing theories is not an acceptable one.[11] The rejection of the idea of theory-independent observation statements has a long history in conventionalist philosophies of science, but I shall rely largely on two of the most influential recent statements of the anti-positivist position on this question – those of T. S. Kuhn and N. R. Hanson. Both of these writers challenge the positivist conceptions of 'observation' and 'experience' by means of an analogy with the perception of 'gestalts'. Ambiguous figures such as the famous duck-rabbit (Figure 2) are used as prototypes or analogues which help to elucidate the nature of all perception – and of scientific observation in particular. Some observers looking at Figure 2 will see it as the head of a duck (facing left, two appendages forming the beak), whereas others will see it as the head of a rabbit (facing right, the appendages being seen as ears). The same person may see the same figure now as a duck, now as a rabbit. The way details in the drawing are described (ears, beak, etc.) will depend upon how the whole pattern is seen. This is analogous, it is claimed,

Figure 2 The duck-rabbit diagram

to such 'changes of view' as the shift from the phlogiston theory to the oxygen theory of combustion in the latter part of the eighteenth century. Priestley, investigating the 'air' given off by the heating of red oxide of mercury, saw it as 'dephlogisticated air'. Working with quite different theoretical assumptions, Lavoisier saw it as a new species of gas, one of the two principal constituents of air – oxygen. Another chemical example concerns the early history of Dalton's revival of the atomic theory in chemistry. By a complex of theoretical assumptions, arguments by analogy, and experimental determinations the atomic weights of many of the chemical elements were established – especially by the Swedish chemist Berzelius. Some of these atomic weights were determined to a precision of up to four decimal places. Working on the basis of a different version of the atomic theory, involving the assumption that hydrogen is the 'primary substance' so that all atomic weights should be exact multiples of the atomic weight of hydrogen, the British chemist William Prout and his followers reinterpreted Berzelius's atomic weight determinations as approximations to integral values. Whether or not any particular experimental determination of an atomic weight was or was not to be seen as an approximation to an integral value was a question which could only be decided by recourse to theoretical considerations.[12]

Of course it can be argued, in the case of the perceptual gestalt analogue, that some description of, say, the ambiguous figure which is independent of both the duck and the rabbit 'interpretations' can be given. It can, for instance, be described as a pattern of lines on paper. But this does not help the empiricist, for two reasons. One is that in making the description independent of the competing 'interpretations' of the figure, we have also made it irrelevant to any decision between them. Secondly, although this new description is independent of the other two, it nevertheless involves some element of 'interpretation', in the sense that it could be challenged by someone who saw the figure as something quite different – as a curved slit in the paper against a dark background, for instance. Again, the argument leads in the direction of a search for perceptual ultimates, or 'indubitables'. Even here, though, with such apparently unchallengeable observation reports as 'I have a visual sensation of redness' some element of conceptualisation is involved. What counts as 'red' when one uses litmus paper as a test for acidity will be quite different from what is allowed to count as 'red' in spectroscopy. The positivist assumption that predicates closely connected with the senses – such as colour and sound – have an unproblematic and simple referring relation to 'given' perceptibles is quite misleading, as this example shows. Quite generally it can be said that nothing can count as a scientific observation or experience unless it can be described. All description involves conceptual patterning, however elementary, and all conceptual patterning is susceptible of revision.

But, it may be argued, the distinction between observational and theoretical concepts as it appears in the more sophisticated versions of the H–D account is not dependent on any such absolute notion of theory-free observation. All that is required is that, whatever concepts are involved in the observation language in terms of which the theory is to be tested, those concepts do not presuppose the adequacy of the concepts of that particular theory. In this way the notion of 'observation statement' may be relativised to take account of the above objections.[13] To return to the example of the kinetic theory of gases, it is conceded that the temperature, pressure and volume of a gas are not elementary 'givens'. 'Pressure', 'temperature' and 'volume' are constructed concepts with a long history behind them. The claim in this case is simply that the use of these concepts, and of techniques for measuring what they refer to, does not presuppose the adequacy of the kinetic theory, and so can count as an independent test of it. But this only pushes the problem one step further back for the empiricist. If it is conceded that there are theoretical assumptions in what count as observation statements *vis-à-vis* the kinetic theory, then those theoretical assumptions themselves must be testable, presumably in terms of what count as observation statements *vis-à-vis* these particular theoretical assumptions. The empiricist must either accede to an infinite regress here, in which case testability disappears into an ever-receding theoretical distance, or the relativised observation/theory distinction ultimately turns out to rely on the original absolute distinction, which is no longer acceptable.

Relativism

The recognition that no scientific observation or description is theory-independent, that all factual statements in science are 'theory-laden', that what counts as a fact is itself a function of some theory, however elementary, can and has led to a thoroughgoing relativism. Perhaps, if there can be no such thing as a crucial experiment or observation to decide between competing theoretical interpretations of the world, we should give up the claim that science can ever provide objective knowledge? Perhaps, if scientists belonging to different traditions simply see the world differently, with no way of deciding observationally between their 'ways of seeing', then to all intents and purposes they live in different worlds. The world really is whatever you think it is, or perceive it to be. The implications of this drift of thought, that there can be no such thing (or that we could never know if there were such a thing) as objective knowledge or progress in science, are so contrary to current popular estimations of scientific knowledge that most of those tempted by this sort of relativism attempt, often quite inconsistently, to find ways of avoiding it.[14] As should become clear, this tendency to relativism or agnosticism among those who reject the empiricist notion of theory-neutral observation derives not so much from their rejection of empiricism as from their reluctance to reject all of it. That science cannot be objective only follows from the rejection of theory-independent observation if it is first conceded to the empiricist that there is no way of conferring objectivity upon theoretical knowledge other than through observational or experimental testing.

Where do scientific theories come from?

For the final development of this point it will be necessary to consider a further difficulty in the H–D model of scientific theories. This concerns the problem of how to account for the 'generation' or 'production' of theories. The H–D model professes to give only an analysis of the formal structure of theories once they have 'arrived'. As Hanson points out, this alone severely restricts the value of the

H–D model if it is to guide research practice in on-going sciences. Any theory which can be axiomatised in this way is a completed theory. A completed theory is an obsolete or obsolescent one, and so may be of limited relevance to the problems of current research practice.

Induction?

There are two alternatives, consistent with the H–D model, for characterising the construction of theories. One is that they are built up from ground level, so to speak, by the gradual addition of increasingly higher level laws upon an observational base. This process may be thought of as proceeding according to some 'logic' – though an inductive logic, since the inferences involved, from the particular to the general, are not deductively valid. But such an inductive logic faces difficulties, precisely parallel to those faced by the attempt to apply probability theory to the 'confirmation' of universal laws. Also, as was demonstrated by the 'common-cold' example,[15] the rationality of inductive procedures can only be displayed when they are understood as presupposing a theory. No inductive 'logic' could account for the rational procedures involved in the production of a theory.

Conjecture?

The alternative to inductivism which is open to the H–D supporter is the one which gives the H–D account its name. The theory is presented as an ambitious conjecture; a work of individual human imagination; a mysterious act of genius; above all, an act which cannot be represented as formally rational. The study of how theories come into existence is relegated from logic and epistemology to psychology or biography. Theories appear in the mind of the scientist as he reclines in his bath, or sits beneath an apple tree. Hence the 'hypothetico' component of the name of the H–D account: a hypothesis drops from the sky (or from the apple tree) into the scientist's head. The psychological characteristics of those rare geniuses to whom this happens may be of interest in explaining it, but the philosopher's job begins only when the theory has actually arrived.

The logic of discovery: towards an alternative conception of scientific rationality

The anti-positivist assertion that the creation of new theoretical knowledge is not merely a question of the psychological qualities of the individual subject whose creation it is, and that there is such a thing as a 'logic of discovery' has gained ground in recent philosophy of science. Hanson's attempt to develop a concept of a distinct kind of reasoning – 'retroduction' – which is different from both deduction and induction, and his discussion of Kepler's production of the elliptical orbit hypothesis for planetary motion are of considerable interest in this respect.[16] Kepler's argument clearly is an argument, and a compelling one, yet it cannot be displayed as having either an inductive or a deductive form. Such attempts to provide more sophisticated accounts of scientific rationality than the 'formal logic plus observation and experiment' of the empiricists also yield an apparent way of avoiding relativism for those who reject the notion of theory-independent observation.[17] Other criteria, it may be argued, play a part in the rational decision procedures by which competing theories are accepted or rejected. Such aesthetic criteria as simplicity (however interpreted), political and even theological criteria, not to mention philosophical criteria (such as the plausibility of a proposed mechanism) can all be shown to have played a part in the major theoretical revolutions which have taken place in the sciences, and historical raw material of this sort is the basis of attempts to construct a philosophical theory of scientific rationality. But it is important to recognise that such theories, although they regard the creation of new knowledge and non-experimental decision procedures as proper objects of philosophical theorising, not to be left to 'mere' psychology, do not really break away from the 'individual genius' conception which they criticise. Hanson, for instance, criticises the H–D account thus:

> Disciples of the H–D account often discuss the dawning of an hypothesis as being of psychological interest only, or else claim it to be the province solely of genius and not of logic. They are wrong. If *establishing* an hypothesis through its predictions has a logic, so has the *conceiving* of an hypothesis. To form the idea of acceleration or of universal gravitation *does require genius: nothing less than a Galileo or a Newton.* But that cannot mean that the reflexions leading to these ideas are unreasonable or a-reasonable.[18]

The birth of new theories is still conceived of as the creative activity – albeit rational – of individual geniuses.

The relativity of rationality

Even such attempts to construct an alternative account of scientific rationality to that of the empiricists face serious problems. Such accounts cannot avoid the pitfall of relativism unless they can uncover rational principles which are, like the observation statements of the positivist, theory-independent and universally applicable. Yet the historical research of Kuhn and others suggests that rational criteria of acceptability for scientific theories and explanations such as conceptions of what counts as a 'proof' or demonstration, what mechanisms are or are not plausible, conceptions of simplicity and elegance, etc. are relative to particular theories. In Kuhnian terminology, there are no super-paradigmatic standards. Any defence of a particular paradigm must possess a certain circularity, in that whoever rejects the paradigm is also committed to a rejection of the standards by which it is defended. It was such considerations which led Kuhn to reject the idea of a logic of discovery and retreat into a 'social psychology of research'.[19] Whereas individual scientists are the mysterious creators of theories,[20] it is the relevant scientific community which 'chooses' or 'gives its assent' now to one paradigm, now to another.

The production of knowledge

An alternative way of conceptualising the emergence of new knowledge, which rejects the role assigned to individual or social 'subjects' in the major traditions of thought I have discussed so far is present in some Marxist works. A recent example, which I shall discuss in much more detail in a later chapter,[21] is the work of the French Marxist philosopher Louis Althusser. According to Althusser, knowledge is to be thought of as the outcome of a process of production structurally analogous to economic production. In this conception the role of the 'subject' is limited and prescribed by its place in the structure formed by the other elements or factors in the productive process – the 'raw materials', 'means' and 'relations' of production of knowledge. The following passage from *Reading Capital* is quite typical:

> ('Thought') is constituted by a structure which combines . . . the type of object (raw material) on which it labours, the theoretical means of production available (its theory, its method and its technique, experimental or otherwise) and the historical relations (both theoretical, ideological and social) in which it produces. This definite system of conditions of theoretical practice is what assigns any given thinking subject (individual) its place and function in the production of knowledges. This system of theoretical production – a material as well as a 'spiritual' system whose practice is founded on and articulated to the existing economic, political and ideological practices which directly or indirectly provide it with the

> essentials of its 'raw materials' – has a determinate objective reality. This determinate reality is what defines the roles and functions of the 'thought' of particular individuals, who can only 'think' the 'problems' already actually or potentially posed; hence it is also what *sets to work* their 'thought power' as the structure of an economic mode of production sets to work the labour power of its immediate producers, but according to its own peculiar mode.[22]

As we shall see, this alternative way of conceptualising scientific knowledge and its growth or 'production' is not without its own internal difficulties, but it does have distinct advantages over its rivals.

5 Positivism and ideology in the work of Emile Durkheim

In chapter 1 I argued that, historically speaking, the debate in philosophy as to the status of the social sciences (and the very possibility of a 'science' of society) has centred around the mutual opposition of 'positivist' and 'humanist' philosophies. Characteristically, positivism has claimed the territory of human social relations and their history as a proper object for scientific study. In the name of 'unity of science' they have identified the task of capturing this domain as a matter of applying methods of investigation, forms of explanation and standards of proof already established in the physical sciences to this new field. Those I have referred to as 'humanists' have argued against this that the utterly distinctive character of the object of social, historical or cultural understanding (the 'free will' of the human subject, 'intentionality', 'meaning', or whatever) renders the method of the natural sciences quite inappropriate.

In chapter 2 I attempted to situate the philosophical and sociological work of a major nineteenth-century positivist, Auguste Comte, both historically and systematically. In particular, I attempted to show that positivism as a philosophical theory is a variant form of empiricism, and that there are intelligible connections between empiricism as a philosophical theory of knowledge and the specific political and ideological character of the social theory that is produced under its influence. I did not, however, argue that such social theory is an 'application' of positivism or empiricism. Strictly speaking, the incoherence of this theory of knowledge is such that there can be no such achievement as an 'application' of it. For this reason, the connections between epistemology and substantive social ideologies, though intelligible, are not necessary. They are contingent upon substantive assumptions.[1]

Chapters 3 and 4, apparently a diversion into the alien field of philosophy of the physical sciences, were in fact indispensable to the argument of this book. In those chapters, more modern articulations of the positivist account of the natural sciences were subjected to criticism stemming from a number of non-positivist conceptions of the physical sciences, which were also briefly characterised. Whether or not the arguments against the positivist conception of the natural sciences there presented are regarded as decisive, the very existence of more or less viable alternatives to the positivist conception of the physical sciences has important implications. It is now possible to show that the terms of the debate between positivism and humanism exclude certain possible strategies: in the terms of that debate, the impossibility of a science of social relations is equivalent to the impossibility of a *positivist* science of social relations, whereas the project of a scientific social theory, conceived along *non*-positivist lines, is by no means ruled out by a demonstration of the absurdity of the positivist programme for the social sciences. The humanists may still argue, of course, that the distinctive character of the human subject requires a form of understanding quite distinct from that developed in the physical sciences, whether conceived positivistically or non-positivistically, but to do so they must, at least, produce new arguments.

The text which is at the centre of my discussion in this chapter, though it is commonly regarded as an exemplar of positivist methodological thought, is, I shall argue, one of the first major texts (outside the Marxist tradition) to transcend the terms of the positivist/humanist debate. It does so, however, in a partly unconscious and contradictory way, and this no doubt explains the variety of conflicting readings which it has received.[2] The text in question is Durkheim's *The Rules of Sociological Method*, though I shall refer to several other works by Durkheim, both philosophical and substantive in character.

The period of French history during which Durkheim's theoretical position developed resembled the period of Comte's *Cours* in a number of respects. Comte's work was produced in the wake of the political trauma of the French Revolution itself, whilst Durkheim entered the École Normale Supérieure some eight years after the parallel trauma of the Paris Commune and its brutal suppression.[3] For both Comte and Durkheim contemporary forms of political order were unstable and fragile, open to threats from both left and right. I shall argue that underlying Durkheim's work, just as with Comte, was a definite political project. Not surprisingly, the project is similar in the two cases. As well as broad analogies in their positions, there were important historical continuities connecting them. In particular, the dominant intellectual tendency in France was still Comtist in outline, incorporating evolutionary doctrines derived from Spencer and Darwin.[4]

Durkheim, like Comte, conceived of a domain of the social, distinct from other orders of reality, but no less a reality in its own right. Also like Comte, Durkheim advocated the foundation of a scientific knowledge of this domain which would resemble the natural sciences in its approach and forms of explanation. The new science, in theorising the conditions of social order, had a necessary political role in preventing anarchy and social disintegration. Finally, Durkheim's position resembled Comte's in that the conception of the natural sciences it advocated drew upon positivist categories and vocabulary.

However, there were two crucial differences in the intellectual situation of the two theorists. First, the science closest to sociology in the Comtian hierarchy of the sciences (physiology), and the one most relevant to the advancement of sociology, had undergone enormous advances in the intervening years. There is evidence that Durkheim was fairly widely, if not deeply read in both the physiology and evolutionary biology of his time.[5] More importantly, Durkheim draws on biological concepts and distinctions frequently in the course of both his substantive and philosophical writings.

A second difference in Durkheim's intellectual situation was that, whereas the project of a positive science of society remained largely an aspiration in Comte, Durkheim's *Rules* is, among other things, a reflection upon his own substantive research practice, and that of his predecessors.[6] The *Rules* first appeared in book form in 1895, some two years after his major work, *The Division of Labour in Society*, in which Durkheim attempted to theorise the conditions of social order in what he distinguished as two morphological types of society – 'segmental' and 'organised'. This book provoked a number of criticisms of a substantive kind,[7] as well as more fundamental, philosophical critiques. Amongst the latter, the most significant were two connected lines of argument to the effect that, first, Durkheim's notion of a 'conscience collective' was metaphysical in purporting to refer to an entity or essence beyond the reach of experience, and that, second, Durkheim's notion of 'society' as an autonomous order of reality, set over and above the individuals which compose it, was both morally abhorrent and methodologically erroneous. For positivists, with a restricted conception of 'observation' and 'experience', Durkheim's rejection of individualist canons of explanation merely followed from the 'unobservability' of any supra-individual social reality. But there were other, non-positivist grounds for asserting a variety of individualist methodological stances, as we shall see.

For Durkheim, such criticisms amounted to a denial of the existence of the subject-matter of sociology, and therefore of its very possibility as a scientific knowledge. The *Rules* was in part an attempt to render explicit and defend the philosophical foundations of the *Division of Labour*, and simultaneously to demonstrate the possibility of a scientific sociology.[8]

The object of the *Rules*

The arguments and illustrations which make up the *Rules* centre around four related problems. First, Durkheim attempts to establish the status of sociology as an autonomous discipline, distinct from its closest relatives, biology and psychology. For Durkheim, following Comte, this demonstration takes the form of establishing the prior existence of a realm or aspect of reality, distinct and autonomous from the orders of reality of which the other sciences constitute knowledge. Establishing the existence of such an order of reality is, then, a central problem for Durkheim. However, there is a significant concession in the *Rules* that the autonomy of sociology cannot be finally established by such an argument. Durkheim acknowledges the indispensable role of argument by analogy with aspects of other sciences, at least in the early phases of development of a new science:

> Sociology is, then, not an auxiliary of any other science; it is itself a distinct and autonomous science. No doubt, when a science is in the process of being born, one is obliged, in order to construct it, to refer to the only models that exist, namely, the sciences already formed. These contain a treasure of experiences which it would be foolish to ignore. A science can regard itself as definitely established, however, only when it has achieved independence for itself.[9]

I shall argue, however, that neither the inadequacy of Durkheim's argument for the autonomy of sociology nor his persistent recourse to biological analogies is attributable simply to the 'immaturity' of sociology. Indeed, Durkheim was himself to argue for the continuing and indispensable role of analogical thinking at least in the production of sociological knowledge, if not as a form of proof.[10]

A third objective in the *Rules* is the demonstration, against certain of Durkheim's philosophical opponents, of both the possibility and the necessity of a specifically scientific knowledge of the social order, together with, finally, the attempt to construct a conception of the methods and forms of scientific explanation in their application to the new domain.

Social facts and the autonomy of sociology

The concept of a social fact has a crucial role in Durkheim's arguments both for an autonomous discipline of sociology and for the necessity of a scientific knowledge of society. The concept marks two quite distinct contrasts, each bearing upon a different argument, and I shall accordingly discuss the concept of social fact in its bearing on each of these arguments separately.

First, the concept is used to demarcate a particular class of facts (more properly 'phenomena' or 'realities'), having its own homogeneity and distinctive characteristics *vis-à-vis* other classes of facts in the order of nature. The contrast here, then, is between social facts on the one hand, and biological and psychological facts, specifically, on the other. Psychological and social facts are, together, distinguished from biological facts in that they consist of 'representations' whereas biological facts do not.[11] Durkheim never adequately defines 'representations', but it is clear that he refers at least to the symbolic, normative, and generally 'mental' or 'spiritual' nature of the subject-matter of both sociology and psychology. This leaves the question of how to distinguish the orders of reality dealt with respectively by these disciplines. In the one case, Durkheim argues, the phenomena, or 'facts' are collective, in the other, individual representations. That the 'facts' dealt with by psychology exist 'in and through individuals' seems obvious enough, but that there exists a class of supra-individual 'social' phenomena seems to Durkheim (as to many of his opponents) to require demonstration. Part of this demonstration involves drawing upon a supposed general 'principle' of the effects of association or combination in nature. Just as the combination of chemical elements produces a new compound, with properties deriving not from its elements alone but also from their combination, and just as chemical compounds may combine so as to form a living being, again with a new order of properties derived from the association, so the combination of individuals to form a society produces a new type of existence with properties not found in the individuals but deriving from their association. This philosophical notion of nature as a hierarchy of orders of reality, each order generated from a lower order by the combination of elementary parts, and possessing an internal homogeneity deriving from its distinctive 'emergent' properties is close to what Durkheim himself characterises as 'metaphysics' in Comte, but nevertheless is the (inexplicit) logical foundation of Durkheim's claim to have isolated a distinctive order of 'social facts'. As we shall see, this metaphysical foundation for the doctrine of social facts is obscured by the confusion between the two roles of the concept of social fact. For the moment, however, it should be noted that the identification of a distinct order of social phenomena as a product of 'organisation' has several implications. First, the proposed science of sociology has its *raison d'être*: a distinct field of reality waits to be known. Second, the relevance of analogies with the methods of investigation and forms of explanation proper to biology (especially physiology) is established: the phenomena of both fields are effects of 'organisation'. Third, and notwithstanding the last point, the science of sociology will have its own disciplinary autonomy, a consequence of the autonomous laws and distinctive properties of the order of phenomena which it studies. Fourth, a corollary of this, the methodological individualist doctrine, that all (ultimate) explanation in the human sciences must be in terms of the characteristics (actions, intentions, wills, etc.) of individuals, must be rejected.

In most of the above, Durkheim merely reiterates Comtian positivism. But there are differences. For Comte, the facts of sociology are the lowest in order of 'dependence', so that, although a distinct class of phenomena, their autonomy (and therefore that of sociology) is strictly limited. For Durkheim, the autonomy of sociology is absolute. There is no reason why the elaboration of the laws of the 'conscience collective' should await the development of individual psychology. Another difference is that whereas Comte distinguishes only an order of phenomena at the level of the individual, and another at the level of the 'species', Durkheim seeks to establish intermediate orders of realities. The implication of Comte's way of distinguishing the realm of the social is to make sociology a science of humanity, or the human species. For Durkheim, there are at least two intermediate levels of reality: particular societies, and types or 'species' of societies. This, in turn, commits Durkheim to a fundamentally different conception of history from Comte: history cannot be conceived in a 'historicist' way as a process of 'self-realisation' of humanity, and so, in so far as Durkheim is a social evolutionist, he is so in a sense very different from that in which Comte and Spencer are.

So far I have spoken loosely of Durkheim's conception of social facts as referring to an autonomous realm of 'facts', 'phenomena' or 'realities'. This leaves my interpretation ambiguous as between social reality as an assemblage of phenomena, in the empiricist sense of 'objects of experience' and a conception of social reality as consisting of (or at least including) an underlying reality which is manifested or reveals itself in forms accessible to experience. There is no doubt that Durkheim is in considerable difficulty on this question. Though he refers to himself as a 'scientific rationalist', he nevertheless clearly accepts empiricist criteria of validity – theories are to be tested against the perceptible *facts* of social life. Critiques of Durkheim from empiricist/positivist quarters invariably accused him of 'hypostatizing' society, and criticised concepts such as 'social solidarity', 'collective consciousness', and 'collective representation' as referring to illicit occult entities. Durkheim's response to these criticisms was the defensive one of proffering a phenomenalist ('more or less systematized aggregate of phenomena')[12] interpretation of these concepts.

Nevertheless, elsewhere Durkheim goes so far as to specify realism as a general characteristic of scientific explanation: 'Science goes from without, from the external and immediately sensible manifestations, to the interior characteristics of which these manifestations betray the existence.'[13] In the *Rules* itself, Durkheim speaks of the identification of classes of phenomena by their 'common external characteristics', thus presupposing their possession of 'internal' characteristics, inaccessible to perception. But, more importantly, Durkheim's substantive works frequently make use of perceptible and measurable phenomena as indicators of deeper and less accessible realities. In the *Division of Labour*, for instance, Durkheim concedes that social solidarity is an 'intangible phenomenon which does not lend itself to observation', but this does not mean that it cannot be scientifically studied:

> But we can know causes scientifically only by the effects that they produce, and in order to determine their nature, science chooses from these effects only the most objective and most easily measurable. Science studies heat through the variations in volume which changes in temperature produce in bodies, electricity through its physico-chemical effects, force through movement. Why should social solidarity be an exception?[14]

The conception of cause at work in this passage, and others like it, is realist in character, and involves an appeal to what I referred to in chapters 3 and 4 as 'generative causality'. Despite his various disclaimers, Durkheim does adopt realist forms of explanation, and even recognises this in places when he reflects on his own research practice. Mechanical solidarity is not, then, an observable phenomenon which can be correlated with, and therefore shown to be 'causally' connected with, repressive law. Rather, it is an underlying reality which 'generates' repressive law, along with other perceptible phenomena as an effect. To this extent, Durkheim's conception of scientific knowledge breaks from positivism.

But how seriously can we take Durkheim's analogy between the relation heat/phenomena of expansion and contraction, on the one hand, and social solidarity/legal phenomena on the other? First, though it is true to say that expansion and contraction can be observed, it is not true to say that they were simply 'given' in experience. The concepts were constructed and have a long history in science. Similarly, the relationship between temperature and expansion/contraction has to be established for each substance, and in fact the relationship is such that only for some substances, between definite limits of temperature, does it form a basis for temperature-measurement. Further, what is 'measured' or 'detected' by a thermometer is not 'heat' in the same sense of the term as preceded the theoretical work upon which the measurement is based, but 'temperature', newly defined, and with precise relations to the (also newly defined) term 'heat'. Finally, the production of a genuinely 'realist', 'generative mechanism', type of explanation of temperature phenomena necessitated some specification of the physical nature of heat, and the mechanism by which it generates temperature (and other) phenomena. (Both the 'fluid' theory of heat, and the kinetic theory discussed above in chapter 4, satisfy this criterion.)

But Durkheim's concept of social solidarity is not related in this way to observable phenomena. Durkheim does not construct his distinction repressive/restitutive law by theoretical argument, but takes it as given, as imposed by observation.[15] There is no attempt to specify the nature of social solidarity, nor to either specify or establish the mechanism (plausible or otherwise) by which it produces its phenomena. A clue to the true character of the relation in Durkheim is given when he speaks of law 'reproducing' and as 'symbolising' different types of social solidarity. Metaphysical philosophies, from Classical Greek times, through the rationalist metaphysicians of the seventeenth and eighteenth centuries, to nineteenth-century idealism, have claimed on behalf of their often profoundly counter-intuitive conceptions of the general nature of the universe that they disclose its *essential* nature, as opposed to its appearances, or 'phenomenal forms', which constitute the basis of our common-sense judgments. The philosophical essence/phenomena distinction, of course, took many forms, but characteristically the phenomena were held to 'express' or 'manifest' the essence in such a way that, once the 'code' was understood, essence could be 'read off' from the phenomena.[16] The anti-metaphysical strategy of empiricism has typically been to deny the knowability of essences, and restrict genuine (scientific) knowledge to 'phenomena'.

Often, recognition of the restrictive character of this empiricist position has led to the assertion of the necessity of a realist type of explanation in the *linguistic form* of the essence/appearance distinction,[17] but an analysis of the type we have just conducted should be sufficient to establish the difference. Theoretical and empirical reasoning in relation to a specific object of knowledge is necessary for the production of knowledge of generative mechanisms. The philosophical relation essence/appearance is already given, *a priori*, and is merely 'applied' in particular cases, to 'given' contents.

This consideration leads to a general criticism of the role of the concept of 'social fact' in Durkheim's argument for the autonomy of sociology. This rests, as I argued above, on Durkheim's prior claim to have identified and distinguished a class of facts of which sociology was to constitute the knowledge. I tried to show that the identification of this class of facts had its foundation in a philosophical theory of 'orders' of reality with emergent properties. But Durkheim (correctly) rejects this type of philosophical foundation for scientific knowledge, and presents his 'definition' of social facts as based on 'common external characteristics' – i.e. on observation. I shall argue that these 'external characteristics' relate, in the main, to establishing, not the distinctiveness of the class of social facts, but their very status as facts, as realities, and the necessity of a scientific knowledge of them. However, in Durkheim's argument as presented, there is an appeal to an empiricist conception of knowledge and perception. 'Facts', supposedly, can be identified and classified on the basis of 'experience' and 'observation' alone, without prior theory or interpretation. Classification is, however, a theory-dependent exercise. It requires observation and comparison, of course, but it also requires a knowledge of its field of operation, criteria of identity, difference and relevance for characteristics of the 'objects' classified. In particular, the identification of the 'object of knowledge' or 'subject-matter' of a science can only occur in the course of the production of knowledge of it: it is, indeed, one aspect of that knowledge. The limits and scope of applicability of concepts cannot be given in advance of the system of concepts itself, they are rather an aspect of the specification of the concepts. In short, Durkheim's whole attempt to establish a 'space' for the autonomous discipline of sociology is vitiated by its defective, empiricist conception of the relation between a science and its subject-matter. This is not, of course, to argue that Durkheim errs by deriving his definition of the social from 'pure observation'. Rather, he errs in presenting his argument in this form, and submerging the *real* source of his conception of social facts, which is in a general philosophy of nature. This, in turn, is of a piece with the philosophical essence/appearance distinction which he represents as a scientific generative-cause/phenomenon distinction and, finally, with the 'given' (i.e. not theoretically produced) conceptions of 'social solidarity', 'collective representation' to which he applies it.

Underlying these latter, 'given' concepts are the everyday, pre-scientific notions of 'social order' and 'consensus' which are constitutive of the political project which Durkheim's work theorises. I have had occasion to mention before in my discussion of Comte the connections between empiricist conceptions of knowledge and the persistence into supposedly scientific discourse of ideological, pre-scientific categories.[18]

Social facts and the necessity of science

The so-called 'definition' of social facts, to which most of the first chapter of the *Rules* is given over, consists principally in the presentation of illustrative material, drawn from social life, and the attempt to demonstrate that in each case the phenomena selected satisfy certain criteria. These criteria turn out to be quite general criteria for the status of 'reality' or 'existence', which in turn is conceptually connected for Durkheim with being a fit object for scientific knowledge, and no other type of knowledge. In other words, the satisfaction of these criteria by social phenomena establishes what they have in common with facts of all classes – i.e. their status as independent realities. This function of the concept of social fact, then, is to show not that they are a distinctive class of facts, but that they are facts.

The appearance that Durkheim achieves both tasks by the application of these criteria derives from the ambiguous status of the notion of the individual subject in the *Rules*. Of the many functions of this term, two are most relevant to the present argument. First, Durkheim thinks of individual consciousness as constituting the order of reality to which individual psychology addresses itself. This is the sense in which he uses the term when, for instance, he says (on page 3) that psychological phenomena 'exist only in the individual consciousness and through it'. But he also uses the notion of individual consciousness in the sense of 'knowing subject' when establishing the very concept of 'facticity' or 'thinghood': 'What precisely is a "thing"? A thing differs from an idea in the same way as that which we know from without differs from that which we know from within'.[19] There are, then, two distinctions at work in the *Rules* between that which is 'internal' to the individual consciousness and that which is 'external' or 'independent'. In the epistemological distinction, the 'ideas' of the knowing subject are contrasted with the 'things' which lie outside the mind, and are to be known. Alongside this is the distinction between those phenomena ('representations') which belong to the field of individual psychology, and those 'external facts' which result from the association of individuals and constitute the field of sociology. Durkheim's discussion of the contrast between 'subjective' (introspectionist) methods and 'objective' (behaviourist) methods in psychology illustrates the 'interference' between these two distinctions very well:

> Indeed, psychological facts are naturally given as conscious states of the individual, from whom they do not seem to be even separable. Internal by definition, it seems that they can be treated as external only by doing violence to their nature. Not only is an effort of abstraction necessary, but in addition a whole series of procedures and artifices in order to hold them continuously within this point of view.[20]

Principally, I shall argue, it is Durkheim's use of the device of the 'knowing subject' to establish the independent reality of 'social facts' which gives the impression that he uses the method of perceiving 'common external characteristics' to establish the distinctive character of the class of social facts. As we have seen, this is established as part of a general philosophical theory of Nature which runs quite counter to Durkheim's explicit epistemology.

Durkheim gives his 'definition' of social fact, in its less misleading form as a set of criteria for recognising social facts on page 10:

> A social fact is to be recognised by the power of external coercion which it exercises or is capable of exercising over individuals, and the presence of this power may be recognised in its turn either by the existence of some specific sanction or by resistance offered against every individual effort that tends to violate it.

Social facts are to be recognised by their externality to the individual subject, and by their coercive power – their resistance to individual wills. These criteria are equivalent to Durkheim's criteria of 'thinghood' in general, as are the implications that he draws from them. But much of the interest of chapter 1 of the *Rules* consists in Durkheim's illustrations of the way in which social phenomena of various sorts satisfy these criteria. First, the criterion of externality. Each individual executes moral and legal duties, and exercises rights which are defined in law and custom, independently of the individual. Moreover, non-conformity on the part of the individual does not affect the persistence of the practices concerned. Legal and moral rules 'can exist even without being actually applied', that is, presumably, can persist even if no individual conforms to them.[21] Moral rules constituting my culture existed prior to my birth, and were not created by me. It follows from these aspects of the externality of customs, laws, moral rules and so on, that the individual may be subject to laws and rules of which he is ignorant. Sometimes it will be possible to rectify this state of ignorance by checking an authoritative text (for example, in the case of a codified system of laws), but this will not always be the case. A whole category of social facts, what Durkheim calls 'currents of opinion', for instance, are not in this way 'crystallised', and can only be 'detected' or 'isolated' by a statistical analysis of the rates of suicides, births, marriages, etc. which they 'impel'.[22]

An implication of the externality of social facts, then, is that they are, like other classes of fact, not spontaneously self-understood. They are opaque to common-sense thought. In other words, the would-be sociologist stands in the same relation to social facts as that in which the physicist or chemist stands to physical or chemical facts. This is made clear in the introduction to the second edition of the *Rules*.

> Things include all objects of knowledge that cannot be conceived by purely mental activity, those that require for their conception data from outside the mind, from observations and experiments, those which are built up from the more external and immediately accessible characteristics to the less visible and more profound. To treat the facts of a certain order as things is not, then, to place them in a certain category of reality but to assume a certain mental attitude towards them on the principle that when approaching their study we are absolutely ignorant of their nature, and that their characteristic properties, like the unknown causes on which they depend, cannot be discovered by even the most careful introspection.[23]

> Our principle, then, implies no metaphysical conception, no speculation about the fundamental nature of beings. What it demands is that the sociologist put himself in the same state of mind as the physicist, chemist, or physiologist when he probes into a still unexplored region of the scientific domain. When he penetrates the social world, he must be aware that he is penetrating the unknown; he must feel himself in the presence of facts whose laws are as unsuspected as were those of life before the era of biology.[24]

The externality of social facts, then, implies their opacity, their inaccessibility to spontaneous understanding. This, in turn, implies that investigation of a specifically scientific kind is necessary if knowledge of the social order is to be achieved.

The second criterion of social 'facticity' is the 'coercive power' which social facts have over individuals. Sometimes Durkheim says that social facts are 'independent' of the individual will, that they 'constrain' us or 'impose' on us. Sometimes he says that it is 'impossible to free ourselves of them'. We are not normally aware of this coercive power of social facts, but we are made aware of it if, for instance, we break a legal or moral rule. Society responds with a repressive sanction. We are also constrained to use the appropriate language or currency of our particular country, not necessarily because society will impose a sanction upon us if we do not, but because our attempts to communicate or effect an economic exchange will simply fail. A third type of case is where the individual feels no inclination to violate a rule, but obeys out of custom or habit. Society still may be said to exert a coercive power in that the 'internalisation' of the social rule in question has been brought about by an 'unremitting pressure' from the social milieu, mediated by parents and teachers.[25] Socialisation, in other words, is a coercive process by which habitually compliant and law-abiding social individuals are produced.

The humanist critique of Durkheim

Durkheim's characterisation of social facts as external to individuals, as exerting a coercive power over them, and as not spontaneously intelligible, or transparent to them, has provoked continuing opposition from the tradition of thought which insists on the distinctiveness of the human world, and the consequent impossibility of a 'natural science' of human social relations. According to such critics Durkheim's 'reification' of the social world amounts to submission to a conservative scientistic ideology.[26] Although human agents are the creators of their social world, the world they create achieves its own independence. Men 'forget' that their world is their own product, and it becomes an alien power over them, which they cannot understand.[27] A variant form of this humanist ideology is to be found in the conception of alienation.[28] Under capitalism, the product of labour, and the very activity of labour acquires an existence independent of the worker and, in the form of capital, becomes an alien power set over and against the worker, which he cannot understand.

So far, it seems, there is a remarkable parallel between the humanist ideology and Durkheim's conception of the 'facticity' of the social world. But for the humanist the externality, coercive power and unintelligibility of the social world are its transitory 'phenomenal forms'; they do not constitute its 'essence'. Reified social forms characterise only certain epochs or types of society, and it is the job of social theory to demonstrate both this truth, and the road to a reassertion of the supremacy of the human subject over the social world, and the restoration of intelligible social relationships. Durkheim, by contrast, in establishing the facticity of the social as an epistemological conclusion, seems to be arguing for the universal and necessary character of reified social forms. This is at once a denial of history and the advocacy of resignation in the face of a coercive status quo.

A full discussion of objections of this type must await further discussion of Durkheim's own conception of the difference between science and ideology, but for the moment, it can at least be shown that some aspects of what Durkheim calls 'coercion' are a necessary presupposition of any form of human social life. Although it is true that, for instance, different linguistic communities[29] operate with different systems of syntax and semantics, it is clear that communication within any particular linguistic community will require conformity with the prevailing system in that community. Similarly, though societies differ in the normative rules by which they are governed, and indeed, may be characterised by conflicting systems of normative rules, a society in which the allocation of production-tasks and the distribution of means of consumption were subject to no normative regulation whatsoever is a theoretical impossibility ('from each according to ability, to each according to need' is a slogan describing a particular type of normative regulation).

Nevertheless, the humanist contention that there is in Durkheim's epistemology the intrusion of a conservative political ideology can be upheld. Durkheim's classification together as instances of 'coercion' of all cases of exercise of repressive sanctions and all cases of normative regulation of conduct as universal features of social existence, and his attempt to represent this as an observational truth, has clear implications of a politically conservative kind. These derive both from the classification together of cases of political oppression and cases of normative regulation which are conditions of any sort of social life, and from Durkheim's taking the vocabulary (coercion, freedom, constraint, etc.) of political ideology (where these terms have a function in distinguishing, defending, criticising, etc. different forms of political order) and giving it an epistemological task. Nevertheless the epistemological point that Durkheim makes, albeit in an inconsistent and defective way, is important and defensible. It is that social life is not spontaneously intelligible to those who live it, and that it can only be known through scientific investigation.

Common sense and science

The core of Durkheim's theory of scientific knowledge, and his distinction between science and ideology, much of which is presupposed in his discussion of social facts, is given in chapter 2 of the *Rules*. Prior to the foundation of any branch of scientific knowledge and, indeed, persisting in practical life after its foundation, the phenomena with which it deals will be 'represented in the mind not only by rather definite perceptions but also by some kind of crudely formed concepts'. This assertion depends on the general proposition that '(m)an cannot live in an environment without forming some ideas about it according to which he regulates his behaviour'.[30] Some form of conceptual ordering of the natural and social order is indispensable to material and social survival. The ideas (common-sense ideas, 'pre-notions') which are produced in the course of those practices by which immediate needs are satisfied are judged acceptable and are retained if they yield practical results. They tell us of the danger, usefulness, edibility, etc. of things. They classify objects in terms of their relationship to immediate practical needs. An example would be a gardener's classification of plants as flowers/vegetables/weeds. Such concepts, related as they are to practical interests, are loaded with emotional and value-connotations. 'Products of everyday experience, their primary function is to put our actions in harmony with our environment; they are created by experience and for it.'[31]

However, despite the 'practical adequacy' of pre-notions in supporting material and social practices, they may still be *theoretically false*: 'several centuries have elapsed since Copernicus dissipated the illusions of the senses concerning the movements of heavenly bodies; and yet we still habitually regulate our time according to these illusions'.[32] In attempting to gain scientific knowledge, the temptation is to substitute these 'practically adequate' ideas for reality, and to elaborate these ideas instead of investigating reality. This is what Durkheim calls the 'ideological method'. He attributes it to, for instance, political economy, and points out that its use does not at all exclude appeal to 'confirmatory facts'. Its error is to proceed from ideas to fact, rather than from facts to ideas.[33] As we shall see,[34] Durkheim's critique of the ideological method fails to make the crucial distinction between taking pre-notions as objects of knowledge in the construction of scientific concepts and taking them as raw materials, to be transformed through critical analysis.

However, for Durkheim, pre-notions constitute a veil between us and reality. A condition, then, for rebuilding our concepts on sure foundations is the rejection of all preconceptions, in the manner of Descartes's method of systematic doubt. Durkheim is here committed to a thesis of radical discontinuity between scientific and pre-scientific notions. This is not simply a discontinuity in time (the latter set of notions being of earlier origin than the scientific) since they co-exist after the foundation of a science. Rather, the discontinuity is conceptual (the two systems of notions are organised around different problems, and mark different, cross-cutting distinctions) and epistemological (the one system makes claim to 'theoretical truth', the other only to 'practical adequacy').[35]

But how are scientific concepts to be formed, once all preconceptions have been rejected? Durkheim holds to the empiricist thesis that all concepts – scientific or ideological – have their basis in sense-experience. Their differences consist in their different elaborations from this basis:

> (Science) needs concepts that adequately express things as they actually are, and not as everyday life finds it useful to conceive them. Now those concepts formulated without the discipline of science do not fulfil this condition. Science, then, has to create new concepts; it must dismiss all lay notions and the terms expressing them, and return to sense perception, the primary and necessary substance underlying all concepts. From

> sensation all general ideas flow, whether they be true or false, scientific or impressionistic. The point of departure of science, or speculative knowledge, cannot be different from that of lay, or practical, knowledge. It is only beyond this point, namely, in the manner of elaboration of these common data, that divergences begin.[36]

The method of science, then, is to return to nature, devoid of preconceptions, and to classify phenomena on the basis of their immediately perceived external characteristics. This is, of course, the procedure which Durkheim claims to have followed in the definition of social facts. Again, Durkheim takes refuge in a defective empiricist conception of concept-construction. No classification is 'imposed' by a given set of 'perceptions'. Even the most plausible candidates for elementary sensory properties of this sort – for example, colours – do not impose themselves on the perceiving subject. The conceptual discrimination of colours involved in spectroscopy, obeying traffic lights and landscape painting are all quite different and yet colour-perceptions may be reported and acted upon in each. Durkheim's own example of his definition of crime in terms of the 'common external characteristic' of punishment is susceptible of the same objection. Are social practices 'given' to observers without preconceptions as 'punishments'? Consider, for instance, initiation ceremonies, in which 'victims' may be deliberately injured. How would an observer without preconceptions distinguish such cases from punishment?

Still more seriously, there is a contradiction between Durkheim's conception of the replacement of ideological by scientific conceptions and his assertion of the autonomy of sociology. If social facts constitute an autonomous reality, and so must be explained in terms of social facts (rather than being 'reduced' to any other type of facts), then should this not also apply to the social facts of ideological and scientific representations? In particular, Durkheim conceives the rejection of pre-notions as an act of will carried out by an individual subject. Similarly, a scientific approach demands a certain 'attitude of mind' (that of the physicist or chemist).[37] But what of the 'coercive power' of ideological pre-notions over the individual subject? Surely this, if not the logical absurdity of a presuppositionless system of classification, should have demonstrated the inadequacy of Durkheim's conception of the science/ideology distinction. Not only this, but it follows from Durkheim's own position that the attempt to carry out his methodological injunctions would render the theorist not less, but more open to the intervention of unconscious, and therefore uncontrolled, ideological categories into his or her investigations.

A further source of internal difficulty in Durkheim's theory of science and ideology concerns his thesis that pre-notions may have a practical adequacy in that 'they put our actions in harmony with our environment' and may yet be theoretically false. The only way in which this could be so would be if the forms in which our environment presents itself to us in everyday life were fundamentally misleading as to its true character. This is to say that the 'data' of experience and perception are an inadequate basis for genuine knowledge,[38] and yet it is precisely those misleading phenomenal forms, present to us in perception, which Durkheim advocates as the basis for scientific knowledge.

We have seen, then, that Durkheim transcends positivist theories of knowledge in certain respects. In particular he advocates a realist model of explanation (though he does not adequately distinguish it from an 'essentialist' one), together with a sketch of the conceptual and epistemological differences between scientific and ideological thought which goes beyond the simple empiricist contrast between truth and falsity (ideological notions do not have the same cognitive status as scientific ones, but they may have a type of adequacy – practical adequacy). But on the key questions of the process by which sciences are founded, and the criteria by which the cognitive status of scientific concepts is to be established, Durkheim lapses into a peculiarly banal empiricism, remaining trapped within a conception of knowledge as a relation between an abstractly specified 'knowing subject' and an external order of facts.

Knowledge and practical interests

Although Durkheim is extremely vague on just how ideological notions and scientific notions differ in their mode of elaboration from a common basis in sensation, he does give some hints about the source of the cognitive defects of ideological notions. This source is in their closeness to practical interests, and the injunction to reject preconceptions can be seen as a way of freeing science from the grip of practical interests.[39] Of course, Durkheim thought of science as meeting practical requirements too, but its capacity to do so was conditional upon the absence of the dictates of those practical needs in directing the formation of the concepts of science. Science and ideology will, then, be characterised by a different relation to practical life. Ideologies will be internally, conceptually connected with practical needs and interests, whereas science will be connected only by an 'external' application in other practices. The application of this criterion to Durkheim's own work produces some interesting results. Durkheim conceives of the practical application of sociology on an analogy with scientific medicine. Just as medicine identifies and analyses the cause of pathological states of individual organisms and suggests remedies, so sociology (or one of its branches, 'social pathology') will identify and analyse the causes of pathological states of 'social organisms'. To do this, it is first necessary to find a criterion for distinguishing the 'normal' and the 'pathological' among social facts. Durkheim's 'value-neutral' way of doing this is to determine the statistical frequency of the class of phenomena concerned throughout the type, or 'species' of society in which it occurs. If it is general throughout the species, then it is 'normal'.

But Durkheim had already identified, in the *Division of Labour*, the capital/labour conflict and crises of over-production which seemed to characterise 'organised' societies as 'abnormal' (i.e. pathological) forms of the division of labour. In that text Durkheim had diagnosed the causes of such pathological states, and recommended cures – the most important of which was to be a reconstruction of occupational organisations (along the lines of the medieval guilds) in which capitalists and workers would co-operate. Out of this would arise norms – and even, eventually, laws – for the regulation of business based on a mutual recognition of dependence. In short, Durkheim's thought serves to theoretically found a reformist political practice, with preconceived parameters which, in its main outlines, is identical with Comte's project of 'social engineering'. This can be seen more clearly if we compare Marx's analyses of these phenomena with those of Durkheim. For Marx, crises and the capital/labour conflict were universal amongst societies of the type in which they occur ('capitalist' for Marx, 'organised' for Durkheim), since they are consequences of 'contradictions' constitutive of societies of that type. For Marx, transition to a new, classless and non-contradictory type of social order (i.e. one in which the generative causes of the phenomena were absent) was a necessary condition for the abolition of the phenomena.

Now, Durkheim recognised the generality of these phenomena throughout the social type and so would seem to be faced with a dilemma:[40] either concede that the phenomena are, after all, normal, or admit the possibility that the social type is inherently diseased. If the former is accepted then the whole basis for a reformist strategy as 'cure' falls away, whilst the latter is rejected by Durkheim as a contradiction in terms. 'One cannot, without contradiction, even conceive of a species which would be incurably diseased in itself and by virtue of its fundamental constitution.'[41] Durkheim escapes from the dilemma with the *ad hoc* device that the generality of a phenomenon throughout a species may not imply normality if that type is still in the process of transition from an earlier type.[42] Not only is the *ad hoc* device suspicious in itself, but its use to preserve the biological analogy which is at stake runs counter to Durkheim's own constraints on the use of analogical reasoning in science.[43] It would be hard to find a clearer case of prior practical (in this case political) interests and problems determining the structure of a theoretical corpus. By his own criterion Durkheim's use of the normal/pathological distinction is ideological.[44]

6 Kant and the Neo-Kantians

Introduction

So far, I have tried to show how empiricist and positivist theories of knowledge are defective as accounts of scientific knowledge, both when they are applied to the natural and to the social sciences. In the cases of both Comte and Durkheim I have attempted to show that the employment of a defective, empiricist theory of knowledge was connected with serious defects in their respective substantive social theorising. However, Durkheim's work is of especial interest in that his theory of knowledge is not simply 'empiricist' or 'positivist' but is rather a combination of realism and empiricism. Durkheim was a realist in two senses: first, in the claim that a real world (the object to be grasped in scientific knowledge) exists prior to and independent of the theoretical knowledge of it, and second, in the claim that the 'phenomenal forms' in which this reality presents itself to experience may be misleading as to the true character of the reality which 'underlies' and is the causal source of the 'phenomenal forms'. This realist conception of knowledge implies a radical discontinuity between those notions by which social agents grasp and negotiate the 'phenomenal forms' of social reality, and those concepts which constitute scientific knowledge of the social world. But Durkheim's retention of an empiricist conception of the relationship between scientific concepts and 'sensation' prevents his production of any adequate conception either of how scientific knowledges are founded, or of their superior 'cognitive status', compared with ideological notions. I also tried to argue that Durkheim's tendency to substitute a philosophical relation of 'phenomena' to their 'essence' for genuine knowledge of generative causal mechanisms in his substantive social theorising is also connected with his empiricism in the theory of knowledge.[1]

In the present chapter I shall turn to an investigation of the work of some representative thinkers in the principal anti-positivist tradition within the social sciences – the tradition I have labelled 'humanist'.[2] The philosophical sources of humanist approaches in the social sciences at first glance appear to be very heterogeneous – phenomenological, ethnomethodological, existentialist, Hegelian, Neo-Kantian, Wittgensteinian, and even, under some interpretations, Marxian. But it turns out that most of these philosophical traditions are related, through either historical origin, or conceptual affinities or both, to the work of the eighteenth-century German philosopher, Immanuel Kant. No short account could possibly do justice to the enormous philosophical achievements of Kant, but equally no comprehensible account could be given of later anti-positivist currents in the social sciences without some attempt to at least sketch the outlines of Kant's system of ideas, and its place in the history of philosophy.

Kant's philosophy

Early in chapter 2 I made a brief reference to 'rationalism' as the main alternative in the seventeenth century to empiricist theories of knowledge. For rationalism, knowledge-claims are valid to the extent that they conform to the deductive standards of proof already established in mathematics. The capacity to apply universally valid rational principles was supposed by Descartes, as by other rationalists, to be 'equal in all men'. Such rational principles were supposed to be not abstracted from experience, but, on the contrary, innately known. A centre of controversy between rationalism and empiricism concerned the possibility of innate, *a priori* knowledge which is nevertheless synthetic (that is to say, informative about the world, not merely 'true by definition'). Kant's main philosophical achievement can be understood as a reconciliation into a single theory of knowledge of elements of both rationalist and empiricist epistemologies.

As I have tried to show in my discussion of the varieties of empiricism and positivism, the doctrines that the source of knowledge and the last arbiter as to its validity is sense-experience tend to generate radical scepticism as to the possibility of knowledge of a world external to the individual consciousness – the subject of 'sense-experience'. This characteristic of empiricism, though rendering it effective as a sceptical weapon against all forms of mysticism, theology and metaphysics, is not helpful if it is intended simultaneously to give an account and defence of scientific knowledge. Notoriously, for instance, it has been argued that the concept of 'causal necessity', carrying the implication that future possible and impossible courses of events can be predicted, cannot be abstracted from our sense-experience. All that can legitimately be inferred from experience is a notion of causality as mere 'constant conjunction', established causal generalisations carrying no implications for as yet unexperienced phenomena.

Kant's defence of the objectivity of scientific knowledge, including the concept of causal necessity, was presented in his major work, the *Critique of Pure Reason*.[3] For Kant, the knowledge expressed in an objective judgment of science or common sense involves both thought and perception. Judgments of a subjective kind, which merely report experiences, but make no claim as to objectivity, nevertheless require, Kant argues, a conceptual ordering to be imposed on them. The mind does not simply and passively 'record' sense-impressions. Space and time are the (*a priori*) forms in which perceptual experience is ordered. Beyond this, perceptual judgments acquire objectivity – i.e. acquire the status of judgments about the existence and nature of some external reality – only on condition that perceptions are organised by further *a priori* concepts or 'categories' of the understanding. Kant derives these categories in a rather dubious way from the classification of the logical forms of propositions, and claims that his list of twelve 'categories of the understanding' is complete. The details of this argument need not concern us, but the general drift of Kant's defence of scientific knowledge can be grasped through his treatment of the category of causality. Kant concedes the sceptical point that the concept of causal necessity cannot be abstracted from experience, but rejects the conclusion that it therefore has no rational foundation. Rather, the legitimacy of objective causal judgments is to be assumed, and the condition of their possibility to be sought. In this case, the condition of possibility of objective causal judgments is that the 'manifold' of our perceptual experience is organised by the application of an *a priori* concept of causality – i.e. one not abstracted or derived in any other way from experience. As regards the whole system of judgments making up our scientific knowledge of nature (Kant regarded Newtonian physics as embodying an absolute knowledge of nature), a condition of its objectivity is that the *a priori* categories are applied in it according to certain 'synthetic *a priori*' principles, which give the rules for the application of the categories. In the case of the category of causality the relevant synthetic *a priori* principle is that 'all alterations occur in accordance with the law of the connexion of cause and effect'.[4] So far, then, it seems that in accepting the need for recognising principles which are both *a priori* (independent of experience) and yet synthetic (not merely true by definition) Kant is on the side of the rationalists. But there is also a nod in the direction of the empiricists – the synthetic *a priori* principles are only legitimately employed within the bounds of possible sense-experience.

That the categories and principles may be legitimately employed only within the bounds of possible sense-experience – within the field of 'phenomena' – can only be thought of as a limitation on their scope if one supposes the existence of un-experienceable realities. Such un-experienceable realities are, it turns out, implied by Kant's theory of judgment. The ultimate (or transcendental) presupposition of the combination of a subjective perceptual judgment with *a priori* categories of the understanding to yield a single objective judgment is the unity of the judging and perceiving subject. This unity is a 'transcendental' unity (it transcends possible experience) since it is an ultimate condition of experience, and therefore different in kind from anything to be found within experience. Also, the field of moral experience yields evidence for a reality beyond, and underlying, the phenomenal world. This is the world of 'noumena', or things-in-themselves, as Kant called them.

For Kant, the distinctive character of moral experience is connected with the idea of duty – the idea that the individual is subject to universal duties, which call on his/her obedience even in opposition to the desires, impulses or inclinations of the moment. A condition of possibility of the objectivity of such experience is not only that such universal duties do exist, but that the individual will can be determined by them in opposition to the determinations of desires, impulses and the like. This, then, is Kant's way of posing the central problem of combining the mechanistic conception of a causally ordered, 'deterministic' nature with belief in the free will, and hence moral responsibility of human agents. Kant's 'solution' to the problem is to argue that the human subject participates in both the noumenal and the phenomenal world. As part of the phenomenal world the human individual is an object of possible experience (through external sense in the case of other selves, through introspection in the case of oneself), and also part of the causal order of nature. To this phenomenal aspect of ourselves belong our desires and impulses. But as part of the noumenal world, the self is not an object of possible experience (by definition) and is thus outside the scope of the synthetic *a priori* categories and principles of natural science, including the category of cause. There is, then, conceptual room for a 'noumenal' subject, possessed of a free (i.e. not causally determined) will, capable of subjecting itself to universal moral duties. Kant also thinks that the ideas of 'immortality' and of 'God' are, like the idea of freedom, necessary conditions for the objectivity of moral experience.

But Kant is careful to draw attention to the special character of these concepts, or 'ideas' by which reference seems to be made to the noumenal world, beyond possible experience. The ideas of 'God', 'freedom' and 'immortality' are neither abstracted from experience nor are they applicable within it, as in the case of the categories of the understanding. To distinguish these ideas from the 'forms' of perception (space, time) and the categories of the understanding (cause, substance and attribute, etc.) Kant calls them 'ideas of pure reason'. Because they are neither derived from nor applicable to experience, there are very severe limitations on their use, and Kant argues that our thinking goes astray into 'absolute' or 'speculative' metaphysics if the 'ideas' are misused. When the ideas of pure reason are spuriously applied to objects of experience, or equally, when categories of the understanding are applied to the noumenal realm, speculative metaphysics results and our thinking falls into hopeless confusion and contradiction.

But the ideas of pure reason do have legitimate uses. They can give rise to 'regulative maxims' by which we try to systematise, and make more coherent our theorising in the natural sciences – this is their theoretical use. More importantly, though, they have a practical use: as conditions of the objectivity of moral experience, such ideas as 'freedom' are indispensable to practical morality. For Kant, the importance of these ideas for moral life is quite unaffected by his firm insistence that we can have no knowledge (in the strict sense of scientific knowledge) of the objects of the ideas. The noumena or things-in-themselves are by definition unperceivable and since, as we have seen, knowledge requires both thought and perception, they are therefore unknowable. They are objects whose existence is thinkable (and in which we may have faith) but whose nature is unknowable.

Neo-Kantian philosophy

Kant's distinction between a phenomenal world, open to perception and to knowledge through scientific methods and concepts, and an unknowable noumenal world of free subjectivity is, of course, open to serious philosophical objections. The principal difficulty is that the resolution of the problem of free will and determinism (as well as the other problems of speculative metaphysics) requires a good deal to be *said* about the nature of the supposedly unknowable things-in-themselves. Even the claim that they exist and that they are 'things' is hard to interpret as anything but a claim to know the unknowable. Accordingly, attempts to modify, or even altogether abandon Kant's noumenal/phenomenal distinction played a vital role in the development of German philosophy following Kant's death. The German idealist tradition, about which I shall say more in chapter 8, tended to abandon Kant's strictures against speculative metaphysics and developed idealistic philosophical systems which, unlike Kant's, were generally antithetical to the natural sciences. In the latter part of the nineteenth century, however, in the wake of a decline in the German idealist tradition and the spread of positivist philosophy, the 'revolt against positivism'[5] in Germany took the form of a return to Kantian philosophy.

The Neo-Kantian movement which established itself in the dispersed academic centres of Germany from the 1860s onwards was initially hostile both to German idealist developments of Kant and to positivism, though the influence of positivism was at work in the tendency to relativise the distinction between noumena and phenomena (i.e. this was treated as no longer a 'qualitative' distinction) or else to reject the notion of a noumenal world altogether. Later, however, and particularly amongst the philosophers and sociologists of the Heidelberg circle (Windleband, Rickert, Simmel, Weber, Lukács, and others) there was a tendency to reinstate the work of Hegel, and with it the respectability of 'noumena' (in one guise or another).

For all of the Neo-Kantians a fundamental division was drawn between the natural sciences, on the one hand, and the spiritual, human or cultural sciences on the other.[6] Their logical and epistemological enquiries into the differences between the two groups of sciences – or two types of knowledge – laid the foundations for the whole humanist tradition in the social sciences. However, there were important differences within the Neo-Kantian movement itself and these centred around the questions, (1) was the difference between the natural sciences and the others primarily one of method, or of subject-matter? and (2) in so far as it was one of subject-matter, how was the difference to be characterised?

In the early work of Dilthey (and of Simmel) the difference between the natural and 'spiritual' sciences was essentially one of subject-matter. Man and the animals are distinct from the rest of nature in their sharing of a reflexive 'life experience' – an inner life. The life experience to which Dilthey referred was not 'noumenal' but was, rather, the object of introspection (of 'inner sense'), and could also be detected in others through its outward expressions. Just as Kant had investigated the conditions of possibility of knowledge of the physical world, so Dilthey set out to investigate the conditions of possibility of knowledge of the mental, or spiritual world. Dilthey's answer to this problem of knowledge of the inner life of others was that our sharing of a 'life experience' enables us to infer from the outward expressions of others their inner states on the basis of an analogy with our own inner states. We are thus able to 're-live' or 'imaginatively identify with' the inner states of others. It is 'imaginative identification' or understanding (*verstehen*) in this sense which distinguishes the type of knowledge proper to the 'spiritual sciences' from that of the natural or physical sciences. But Dilthey, in common with later *verstehende* sociologists such as Max Weber, regards 'understanding' achieved in this way as uncertain, and standing in need of supplementation by explanation of a causal kind.

In his later work, Dilthey came to realise that the psychological foundation he had earlier hoped to give to all of the social sciences was inadequate. Inter-subjective 'understanding' is possible only on condition that the subjects between whom the understanding takes place share a common culture.[7]

> Every single human expression represents something which is common to many and therefore part of the realm of objective mind. Every word or sentence, every gesture or form of politeness, every work of art and every historical deed are only understandable because the person expressing himself and the person who understands him are connected by something they have in common; the individual always experiences, thinks, acts, and also understands, in this common sphere.[8]

This sphere of 'common culture' is equivalent to Hegel's 'absolute spirit' and, as a quite distinct object of knowledge from the mental states of individual subjects, it requires a distinct type of understanding. Any cultural item may be said to have a meaning or significance (which Dilthey connects with 'function') which can only be grasped by relating it to the cultural totality – the 'complex of meanings' – to which it belongs. Clearly the 'meaning' of an action or proposition in this sense is quite distinct from the mental states – intentions, desires, emotional states, etc. – of the actor or speaker. Our capacity to directly apprehend the 'meanings' of cultural items (as distinct from 're-living' another's mental states) involves, then, *verstehen* of a rather different type – sometimes called 'hermeneutic understanding'.

Rickert and the historical method

Heinrich Rickert, one of the leading philosophers of the Heidelberg Neo-Kantian circle, rejected both the psychologism of the early Dilthey and the attempt to classify the sciences on the basis of a prior classification of their subject-matters. He thus escapes the objection to which, as we saw, both Comte and Durkheim were open, that they suppose the possibility of a classification prior to any conceptualisation of the 'things' to be classified:

> Two groups of *objects* that differ from each other, as mind and matter do, with respect to the nature of their actual existence can never serve as a basis for differentiating between one group of empirical sciences and another.[9]

Rickert does not, however, escape the objection (he would not have regarded it as an objection) that his classification of the sciences rests upon a prior taken-for-granted ideology, rather than being a result of the production of scientific knowledge. He differs from the positivists in openly proclaiming this, instead of concealing it beneath the 'givenness' of perceived external characteristics.

For Rickert, then, philosophy is concerned not with material differences between subject-matters but formal, or epistemological differences of methodological *approach*. But since it is also implicit in Rickert's position that there is an 'internal' relationship between method and subject-matter (as distinct from the 'external' relationship between a single method and the whole variety of subject-matters in the positivist conception) his *formal* distinction between the method of the natural sciences and that of history implies the material distinction between 'nature' as the subject-matter of the natural sciences, and 'culture' as the subject-matter of the cultural sciences.

The source of the methodological difference between natural and historical sciences is in a respective difference in our *interest* in their subject-matters:

> Methodology has to observe that the one treats its subject matter, nature, as devoid of value and without meaning and brings it under general concepts, whereas the other represents its subject matter, culture, as meaningful and relevant to values and therefore does not content itself with the generalizing method of the natural sciences.[10]

In so far as the natural sciences are concerned with the world of sensory perception (whether of 'inner' or 'outer sense') in isolation from human values and meanings, then their method will be 'generalising'. Following Kant, Rickert argues that the world of experience presents itself as an 'immeasurable manifold', too diverse and extensive to be 'represented' or 'copied' in our knowledge in all its detail and extent.[11] The construction of scientific concepts, then, consists in a 'reconstruction' of the data of experience by a process of 'simplification', abstraction and selection.

For each scientific study there must be some principle of selection according to which the data 'essential' to scientific knowledge can be selected from the non-essential. In the natural sciences, our interest in individual things and happenings, being divorced from values and meanings, is simply as instances of general concepts. In the construction of scientific concepts, then, aspects of empirically given reality are selected as essential in so far as they represent what is common to a class of individuals: hence the 'generalising' method of these sciences. In so far as they are approachable in this way all objects of sense-perception belong to a unified 'nature', and may be objects of a natural scientific knowledge. A natural science of psychology, of the 'inner life' in so far as it is merely an object of perception or introspection, is thus quite acceptable in Rickert's view. Indeed, the whole of nature, defined (formally) by Kant as the existence of things 'as far as it is determined according to universal laws' is a fit subject for science.[12]

But there is no surrender here to the positivists' 'unified science'. Rickert's abandonment of the whole world of sensory experience and universal laws to the natural sciences is undertaken so as better to defend the more strategically important non-sensory world. Distinct from those sciences which confine themselves 'to the world of sensory perception as the totality of all physical *and psychical* events' are those sciences which 'take into consideration that which has "significance" or "meaning" in the world and which can be grasped neither by "outer" nor by "inner" sensory perception, but which can be "understood" only in a non-sensorial fashion'.[13] Here again, as objects for investigation by a distinctive historical method, are Kant's 'noumena', or things-in-themselves. These objects which have an 'understandable' meaning, but are inaccessible to sense-perception, constitute the sphere of 'culture', and define the limits of legitimate application of the historical method.

'Culture' is defined 'materially' by Rickert as 'the totality of real objects to which attach generally acknowledged values or complexes of meaning constituted by values and which are fostered with regard to these values'.[14] Culture consists of all those items either produced by or fostered by human beings for the sake of valued ends. Since cultural objects owe their constitution as such to their relationship to human values, there arises the possibility of an interest in them quite different from the interest we have in natural phenomena. Our interest in them for their relevance to value requires that we consider them in their 'unique', concrete individuality. In constructing concepts of them, we select as essential what is peculiar to them, what distinguishes them from other objects. Hence the 'individualising' method of history. And within what is peculiar to the individual cultural item or object, historical sciences will be interested in those characteristics which give it its specific relevance to value. A second, and for Rickert rather secondary, distinguishing feature of cultural objects is that they are 'non-sensorial *meanings* or complexes of meaning' which alone are '*directly* understood' and when encountered 'require of science a kind of treatment different in its essential principles . . .'.[15] But like other Neo-Kantians Rickert did not believe that there was any incompatibility between the *verstehende* approach and causal explanation in history. His point was, rather, that 'causes' are only of interest in so far as they have 'culturally significant' (or 'value-relevant') events or items as their 'effects'.

But there are three obvious difficulties in Rickert's position here, two of which are very damaging, the third perhaps not so. The first difficulty is that in so far as Rickert uses the authority of Kant's phenomenal/noumenal distinction to distinguish the objects of the natural sciences from those of the cultural, thus far is he constrained from consistently speaking of the 'causes' of cultural objects. The whole point of Kant's noumenal/phenomenal distinction is lost if causality is admitted into the noumenal realm. The point can be put more generally: if cultural objects really are to be thought of as 'noumena' in the Kantian sense, then they cannot be objects of knowledge at all, even knowledge of a distinctive kind.

The second difficulty is that the causal connections Rickert postulates are supposed to be connections between unique and unrepeatable historical events or 'cultural objects'. However much it may be objected to the positivist account that the 'covering-law' conception is not a sufficient characterisation of causality, at least some element of generality is presupposed in all causal judgments. The claim that *a* caused *b* implies at least that if *a* had not occurred (supposing no other alteration in the conditions under which *b* occurred) then *b* would not have occurred. The only basis for such counter-factual inferences is in the supposition that some relationship of a general kind persists between events of type *a* and of type *b*. Rickert's conception of historical causality, then, must be regarded as incoherent.

The third apparent difficulty is in his notion of the individualising method of concept-construction. It may be argued that concepts, like causes, are logically general. A concept must have the possibility, at least, of applying to a multiplicity of instances, yet Rickert seems to be proposing a science constructed of concepts which characterise unique particulars. Rickert does, however, recognise this problem, and attempts to meet it by distinguishing between 'elementary' concepts, which are indefinable, and are general in their application, on the one hand, and 'complex' concepts which are constructed out of them and are particular in their application, on the other. Apart from the now well-known difficulties involved in this type of classification of concepts,[16] the defence is plausible. In general, the more complex a concept, the more diverse the 'determinations'[17] it includes, the narrower is its field of application (compare, for example, the concepts 'labour', 'domestic labour', 'match-box making'). But it is now generally understood that however complex a concept, that is to say, however detailed and specific a description in general terms, it is always logically possible that there exists more than one individual which satisfies that general description.[18] Ultimately, then, the coherence of Rickert's characterisation of the individualising method in history depends on whether the 'uniqueness' which he claims for historical particulars is 'logical' uniqueness or mere 'matter-of-fact' uniqueness.

Finally, the connection between Rickert's notion of 'culture' and Kant's noumenal world is brought out even more clearly in his treatment of the objectivity of historical science. First, Rickert claims that the construction of historical concepts according to the criterion of relevance to value does not imply that the historian must make value-judgments, or express particular valuations. Though it is true that this distinction can be made, it can nevertheless be argued, against Rickert, that value-commitments of a more general kind are involved even in the judgment that a particular set of characteristics is relevant to some particular cultural value. However, even if we allow Rickert this point, there is still a problem about the selection of values according to which judgments of value-relevance are to be made. Here Rickert argues that in so far as the historian and his/her audience share a common culture, the audience will acknowledge or at least 'understand' the values which guide the historian's selection of materials. The objectivity of history, then, is to be understood as a function of the 'objectivity' of the values according to which its concepts are constructed. Rickert distinguishes 'values' in true Kantian fashion from desire, fancy and caprice, in terms of the 'obligatory', normative and universal character of the former. Either certain values are universal within a culture or, at least, they are 'expected of' those who belong to the culture:

> The fact that cultural *values are universal* in this sense is what keeps concept-formation in the historical sciences from being altogether *arbitrary* and this constitutes the primary basis of its 'objectivity'. What is historically essential must be *important* not only for this or that particular historian, but for *all*.[19]

But so far this notion of the objectivity of values is not strictly Kantian in that it allows of cultural relativity in their validity. Thus the objectivity to which the historian may attain is an objectivity relative to his/her own period and culture. But if history aspires to the system of the natural sciences – if, in other words, it attempts to achieve a coherence beyond the multiplicity of particular empirical historical studies, and even to culminate in a 'universal' history of human development – then it must pre-suppose the validity of certain universal human values, i.e. values which have a claim to recognition transcending particular cultures. It is necessary, of course, only to suppose the existence of such universally valid values – not to know them.

Rickert is clearly ambivalent as between these notions of historical objectivity, but unfortunately for him there is no real choice. His relativistic conception of historical objectivity rests on the assumption of a shared culture relating the historian and his/her audience, but neglects the question of the intelligibility, for the historian, of the values which 'constitute' the complexes of meaning which he studies. Not only must the historian share certain values with his/her audience, but those values must also extend to the object of study. Thus, unless the historian is to be confined to studies of his/her own culture, in his/her own period, transculturally valid values are a presupposition of the objectivity even of particular historical studies. In this way the radically historicist and humanist character of Rickert's Neo-Kantian methodology is displayed. A condition of the objectivity of historical knowledge is the transcultural validity of certain universal human values, in terms of which historical development is to be understood. Such values are a philosophical presupposition of historical science, and therefore are not representable as results of historical investigation. There is thus no way of demonstrating the truth of this presupposition, and without it history loses its claim to objectivity.

7 The methodology of Max Weber, and Peter Winch's 'Corrections'

Introduction

It would be difficult to overestimate the importance of the contribution to sociology made by Max Weber, a contemporary of Rickert, and also a member of the Heidelberg circle. Unlike Rickert, Weber contributed equally to the development of substantive sociological theory and to the debate on methodology, though it is mainly to the methodological writings that I shall refer.

Weber's methodological writings are usually characterised as effecting a reconciliation between positivist and Neo-Kantian positions. This is not particularly misleading so long as it is remembered that Neo-Kantianism was a diverse movement, some tendencies within which had already made substantial philosophical concessions to positivism.[1] Although Weber's position was not, of course, entirely consistent throughout his life, it is possible to say that, in general, he rejected the view attributable to some Neo-Kantians (though not Rickert) that the cultural sciences are exclusively concerned with the uniqueness of their objects of study, and that the category of causality is inapplicable in them. Weber differed from Rickert, however, in clearly understanding that causal explanations presuppose generalisations of a law-like kind. Weber was, on the other hand, committed to the widespread Neo-Kantian insistence on the methodological peculiarities of the cultural sciences. For Weber these peculiarities centred around the two related concepts of 'value-relevance' and 'interpretative understanding': the cultural sciences differ from the natural in the distinctive role of valuations in the formation of concepts in the former, and in the distinctive type of knowledge involved in them. A third area of methodological differences was thought by Weber to be the use of 'idealisations' in the cultural sciences. But here he is quite simply mistaken in his assumption that there is no place for these in the natural sciences.

The definition of sociology

Weber's famous definition of interpretative sociology encapsulates most of these points:

> Sociology (in the sense in which this highly ambiguous word is used here) is a science which attempts the interpretive understanding of social action in order thereby to arrive at a causal explanation of its course and effects.[2]

An exposition of Weber's methodological position can usefully proceed with an analysis of each of the concepts and contrasts involved in the definition.

First the concept of social action. The characterisation of sociology in terms of the understanding and explanation of social action involves two important contrasts. First Weber is distinguishing the paradigmatic objects of sociological knowledge for him – individual social actions, their meanings and causes – from the 'supra-individual' social entities (states, institutions, classes, collective consciousnesses, or whatever) whose existence is supposed in much sociological theorising (for example that of Durkheim) and also everyday thinking about social relations. Weber does not actually deny the existence of such 'entities', but argues that for interpretative sociology they must be 'treated as solely the resultants and modes of organisation of the particular acts of individual persons . . .'.[3] Weber's position here would now be regarded as 'methodological individualist', involving the claim that in so far as collectivities may be said to have characteristics independent of the individuals which make them up, those characteristics are to be explained in terms of individual actors and their actions.[4] But a good deal of Weber's substantive work seems to run counter to this methodological prescription. For instance, Weber's famous definition of class situation as 'market situation', 'the typical chance for a supply of goods, external living conditions, and personal life experiences, in so far as this chance is determined by the amount and kind of power, or lack of such, to dispose of goods or skills for the sake of income in a given economical order',[5] carries the implication that the 'life chances' of an individual will be determined by that individual's location in the given distribution of property and skills, and also in the distribution of requirements for such. As well as this, since market situation in this sense is not the exclusive determinant of life chances, the distribution of power and social honour in society may also be a determinant of the life situation of the individual. The economic, social and legal 'orders' of society which Weber here distinguishes are social facts. It may or may not be that they are merely 'resultants' of the acts of individuals, but there is no doubt that they also play a part in explaining the situation of individuals and therefore their actions.

Must this be regarded as a straightforward case of the failure of Weber's methodology to grasp the character of his own substantive explanatory strategies? There is a way of reconciling them. In relating market- or 'class'-situation to the generation of action ('communal' or 'societal' action) oriented to a recognition of a common class-situation among members of a class, Weber says that such action by no means necessarily follows from the sharing of a common class-situation. Among the relevant conditions is the 'transparency' of the relationship between the causes and consequences of class-situation: '(f) or only then the contrast of life chances can be felt not as an absolutely given fact to be accepted, but as a resultant from either (1) the given distribution of property, or (2) the structure of the concrete economic order'.[6] This suggests the possible interpretation that it is not 'social facts' (for example, 'economic structures') which determine conduct, in this sort of case, but rather the perception by actors of their situation as determined by social facts. If agents orient their behaviour in accordance with the belief that supra-individual collectivities exist, then, so far as the interpretation of their behaviour is concerned it will be as if such collectivities did exist. It follows that the sociologist may legitimately interpret courses of action in terms of concepts such as 'state', 'corporation', 'economic structure', etc. without commitment to the existence of any *entities* designated by the terms. It will be noted that this strategy for preserving methodological individualism closely parallels the instrumentalist interpretation of theoretical terms in the natural sciences,[7] and is also consistent with what Weber says elsewhere, in his methodological work:

> One of the important aspects of the 'existence' of a modern state, precisely as a complex of social interaction of individual persons, consists in the fact that the action of various individuals is oriented to the belief that it exists or should exist.[8]

But not only is such an 'instrumentalist' interpretation of 'collective' terms in sociological explanation subject to the principal arguments against instrumentalism as such (see chapter 4, pp. 67–70), but there are independent arguments against the methodological individualism it is designed to preserve. Steven Lukes has recently argued that the methodological individualist programme is quite vacuous unless it specifies which type of characteristics of individuals and their actions it is claiming as explanatory 'ultimates'.[9] Descriptions of individuals in terms of their anatomical structure, physiological or emotional states and dispositions, etc., are, for instance, implausible candidates. On the other hand, descriptions of individuals and actions such as 'is a student', 'is on the dole', 'is cashing a cheque', whilst more plausible, get their plausibility precisely from the presuppositions they carry about the location of the individual in more or less clearly specified systems of social relationships.

The individualist can, of course, reply to this type of argument by insisting on the further resolution of these presupposed 'social facts' into the individual social actions whose resultants they are. But (*a*) there is no rational justification for preferring this stopping-point as the 'bedrock' for sociological explanation to any other and (*b*) in any case the same problem re-emerges with this further resolution: are we to characterise these actions, in turn, in terms of their presuppositions of social facts, or in terms only of physiological, 'mental', etc. characteristics of the individuals concerned? If the former option is followed, then the individualist is faced with an infinite regress, whilst if the latter course is taken sociology is reduced to a philosophical anthropology (explanation in terms of universal 'human' characteristics – subjectivity, free will, creativity, etc.) or to a physiological psychology (other forms of psychology, e.g. psychoanalysis, do involve presuppositions – however covertly – of a historical social kind, e.g. a certain type of family structure). Neither of these 'reductions', because of their very universality,[10] is able to account for the historical and cultural specificity of the different forms of individuality (this is not, of course, to deny the possibility that, for example, certain physiological facts may limit the range of possible forms of individuality).

A final point here is that certain elements in Weber's research practice do escape this attempt at representing his substantive work as consistent with his 'methodological individualism' and 'instrumentalism'. When Weber suggests, for instance, that the connections between causes and consequences of 'class-situation' may be more or less 'transparent', implicit in what he says is the supposition that the beliefs social actors have about the structural determinants of their life chances (and in accordance with which they orient their conduct) may be more or less accurate. Further, it seems that whether or not structural determinants are in this way evident to social actors will itself be a structural feature. These claims are quite inconsistent with an 'instrumentalist' interpretation of actors' beliefs in social facts. For such an interpretation it must be a matter of irrelevance for sociological analysis whether or not such beliefs are true: the distinction between their being held as beliefs, and their being true beliefs cannot, according to the instrumentalist interpretation, arise. Despite his own methodological prescriptions, then, Weber does adopt 'realist' strategies of explanation. Interestingly, not only do such strategies carry an implicit commitment to the sort of realist epistemology that (as we shall see) Marx attempted to make explicit, but also it is in his 'realist' moments that Weber is closest to Marx in the substantive content of his explanations (for instance, in his conception of the relationships between class-consciousness and the 'transparency' of the economic structure, and in his recognition that the ultimate determinants of market position have to do with the distribution of property and relationships to production).[11]

Action and behaviour

To return to Weber's definition of sociology and of social action. I said that the specification of 'social action' as the object of sociological knowledge was intended to mark two contrasts. One (between individual social action, and the characteristics of supra-individual collectivities or 'social facts') has already been dealt with in some detail. The other (which, incidentally, excludes the possibility of Weber's methodological individualism ending up as a form of physiological-psychological reductionism) is the contrast between 'action' (*Handeln*) and 'behaviour' (*Verhalten*). Weber includes in the concept of action 'all human behaviour when and in so far as the acting individual attaches a subjective meaning to it'.[12] For Weber, even though there may be no physical or bodily movement – for example in cases of refusal to do something which is expected of one, such as vote, or console a friend – an action may nevertheless have been performed, since the failure to move in that situation will have a definite significance or meaning.

But Weber's definition of action in terms of 'meaningful behaviour' only leads to the further problems: what is it for an item of behaviour (or its absence) to have meaning, and how is the meaningful to be distinguished from the non-meaningful? Sometimes Weber seems to argue that for an item to be meaningful is for it to 'be related to some intended purpose':[13] my opening the door is meaningful in its relationship to my intention or purpose of going through it. But Weber's much discussed typology of actions ('traditional', 'affectual', 'value rational' and 'goal-oriented') is such that only actions conforming to one type of action would in the fullest sense count as actions (Weber himself concedes that traditional and affectual action are on the borderline of meaningfulness) on this criterion of meaningfulness. Also Weber is prepared to accept examples of an individual 'doing' something – such as giving something away – without having any particular reason for, or intention in doing it, as actions. Finally, there are some cases – for example, where the action concerned is the utterance of a statement – in which the meaning of the action seems to be quite irreducible to the intentions of the actor (speaker). If I use the expression 'sit down!', intending my hearer to stand up, no matter how hard I 'intend' this will not affect the way my hearer interprets what I say. This is because what I say has an already socially established meaning, and only because of this is it possible for any individual to express intentions by means of the use of language.

None of the foregoing, of course, establishes that meaningfulness is not in some general way connected with intentionality, only that the meaning of an act is not to be identified with the intention with which it is performed. Nevertheless, the general unsatisfactoriness of Weber's rather vague indications on this matter have led others, Peter Winch in particular, to suggest other accounts of the meaningfulness of social actions. Winch quotes an untranslated paper of Weber in which the notion of meaningfulness is analysed in terms of 'commitment to future action'.[14] Even in the absence of my having reasons for doing it, my giving something away (if I am correctly described as so doing) commits me to something in the future – for instance, the renunciation of future rights to dispose of it and recognition of that right in someone else. Winch's claim is that an act can commit the actor to something in the future only if it is governed by some rule, and, finally, the criterion of whether an item of behaviour is rule-governed is whether it makes sense to distinguish with respect to it correct and incorrect ways of doing it. By this last point, it seems that Winch must be understood to include the susceptibility of the behaviour to any sort of critical evaluation or appraisal. For instance, the use of a particular hold at a given instant in a wrestling match may be evaluated according to the rules of the game (it is or is not legitimate); according to rules of performance (it is or is not competently, or 'correctly' carried out); according to the rules of tactics and strategy (it is or is not a means to the object of winning the match); according to stylistic or aesthetic rules (it is or is not graceful, elegant, effortless, etc.), and so on.

By contrast, falling off a bike, starting with fright, reflexes, etc., whilst they are bodily movements (or involve bodily movements) are items of behaviour with respect to which it makes no sense to carry out critical appraisals. They therefore do not count as meaningful behaviour in Winch's sense and so are not, Winch would claim, 'actions' in Weber's sense of the term. They are physical happenings which, like other physical happenings, may be of interest to the physical sciences, may be susceptible of causal explanations in terms of physical laws and so on, but are not proper objects of sociological understanding. Winch's notion of rule-governed behaviour, whilst it has limited textual support as an interpretation of Weber's category 'action', is helpful in that it does seem to provide a criterion for distinguishing action from behaviour in broadly the same way as Weber did, in that it helps to make clear why Weber and others thought that social action required a distinctive type of understanding and also (although Winch doesn't mention this) in that it makes clear at least a part of what Weber and Rickert meant by the 'value-relevance' of the objects of historical and sociological knowledge.

However, Winch's category of meaningful behaviour, and Weber's notion of 'action' both involve obscuring important differences between the senses in which different types of action are meaningful. Winch, in applying Wittgenstein's account of linguistic meaning to social action, implicitly assimilates the meaning of actions to linguistic meaning. This is justified, of course, where the action concerned is itself linguistic. There are also varieties of non-linguistic social actions – gestures, grimaces, signals, etc. – which nevertheless have a definite symbolic content, and are like linguistic utterances in that they are used to 'say something' (which may or may not be translatable into linguistic form). But not all rule-governed actions are like this – my action in opening the door in order to go through it, the cessation of conversation amongst students when a teacher begins to speak, the differences in the treatment of those on the 'professional and executive' register and others in employment exchanges, etc. are all meaningful in some sense, and are all certainly rule governed. The actors concerned are not, however (necessarily) saying anything by their actions, and the actions are not assimilable to cases of linguistic meaning. However, there is some justification for extending the term 'meaning' to apply to these cases (so long as it is recognised that some extension is involved) in that the everyday practices, rituals, sequences of conduct mentioned do presuppose or 'embody' conceptions and beliefs, in some cases about the physical world, in other cases about the social world. In the silence of students during a lecture, for instance, is embodied the recognition of a complex of presuppositions concerning the power and authority relations between teachers and students, distinguished in terms of a hierarchy of professional and academic qualifications, normative expectations and so on. This is so whether or not any of the participants is conscious of it, and despite the possibility that many of the participants may reject the normative commitments involved. Except for the latter point, this is what Winch means when he says that 'social relations are expressions of ideas about reality'. Where Winch goes wrong, as I argued in chapter 1, is in supposing that this is all social relations are. More on this later.

So far it might seem that the action/behaviour distinction is, like the positivist classification of 'orders' of reality, a classification of possible objects of the sciences, prior to the theoretical development of the sciences themselves. But Weber, like Rickert, distinguishes the object of sociology in terms of the interest we have in it, or the frame of reference in terms of which it is to be identified and understood. Take for example the physical movement usually described as 'winking'. This may be an indication that something is a secret, a greeting, an old-fashioned way of making sexual contact, a reaction to a speck of dust in the eye, a nervous tic, etc. The same physical movement in each case may have several different meanings (usually distinguishable by contextual clues) or have no meaning (except in the sense of 'symptom') at all (as in the last two possibilities). As physical movement the 'wink' is susceptible of physiological identification and explanation; as a 'meaningful' action the same movement is susceptible of 'interpretative understanding' by onlookers (who may include sociologists). The action/behaviour distinction is not, then, between two types of entity or happening in the world, but between two frames of reference in terms of which they are to be 'cognitively appropriated' (understood/explained), there being a good deal of overlap in the applicability of the two frames of reference, and a good deal of uncertainty at their boundaries (coughs, mistakes, etc., whilst apparently 'meaningless', may have 'unconscious' or unrecognised meanings). There is not, in Weber, any commitment to the Neo-Kantian relegation of 'meanings' to a separate noumenal world, and so in supposing the possibility of understanding and causal explanation of actions Weber does not face the same difficulties as did, for example, Rickert.[15]

Action and social action

For Weber, action as such is not the object of sociological understanding, but rather a sub-class of actions: social actions. Social action, Weber says, is action 'which takes account of the behaviour of others and is thereby oriented in its course'.[16] Solitary prayer, for Weber, is an example of meaningful action which is not social[17] (though it is odd that he should want to exclude it from sociological analysis). Winch argues against this distinction that all action (meaningful behaviour) is necessarily social.[18] This is because, Winch argues, the rules governing such action must be publicly recognisable. For it to make sense to distinguish between doing something correctly and doing it incorrectly (Winch's criterion of 'rule-governedness' and therefore of meaningfulness), it must also be possible to distinguish between thinking one is doing it correctly and actually doing it correctly. For any rule, in other words, there must be a public way of correcting its application (otherwise it would not count as a 'rule'). All meaning, therefore, presupposes a social setting, or practice within which the actions or expressions which have a meaning play a part. This is so even for solitary prayer: for such acts to take place there must exist a culture in which there are religious concepts and people are taught how to talk, and then, by analogy how to 'talk to God'. All action is, for Winch, in this sense social. There is, of course, no real disagreement between them, since each means something different by 'social action'. To argue that some actions are oriented to the behaviour of others whereas others are not does not involve denying that all action presupposes a social setting of some sort. It might well be argued, however, that Winch's broader notion of social action better represents the scope of sociology's interest.

Interpretative understanding

Weber, along with the Neo-Kantians, argued that to recognise 'action' as meaningful carried with it a commitment to 'understand' it in a way different from the 'understanding' or 'explanation' of any item of the physical world (e.g. a bodily movement). Weber was not so concerned as were some of the Neo-Kantians with the differences between the understanding of 'psychological states' (intentions, desires, etc.) and the understanding of symbolically meaningful expressions (in particular, linguistic or artistic objects), although he did appear to believe that these differences in the objects of *verstehen* might require differences in the methods by which it was achieved.

It should not now be necessary to rescue the concept of *verstehen* from the dead weight of positivist misrepresentation under which it has suffered for so long, save to mention that *verstehen* was not, for Weber, equivalent to a 'method' of imaginative identification, empathy, or whatever for capturing 'meanings'.[19] *Verstehen* is not a method at all but an 'objective', an 'achievement' – it is a distinctive type of knowledge which may be achieved by a variety of methods, or no 'method' at all. When Weber says that 'it is a great help to be able to put one's self imaginatively in the place of the actor and thus sympathetically to participate in his experiences, but this is not an essential condition of meaningful interpretation',[20] he is evaluating 'imaginative identification' as a way of achieving *verstehen*, and so cannot suppose *verstehen* and 'imaginative identification' to be the same thing. In general, when positivist commentators represent *verstehen* as a method of generating or validating 'hypotheses' they assimilate what Weber has to say to their own categories of thought, and then subject this 'revised version' of Weber to their own canons of criticism. However, Weber does distinguish between understanding as achieved by a process of imaginative identification, or empathy, and understanding achieved by a recognition of the rational connection between means and ends, or steps in a proof. The former method is most appropriate for the understanding of 'emotional reactions' such as anger, ambition, jealousy, etc.[21] Weber seems to hold this view because he thinks of the expressions of anger, ambition, jealousy, etc. as expressions of inner states whose existence and nature is problematic for other persons – an imaginative leap into the psyche of the other is necessary if we are to recognise an expression of anger as such and not as an expression of fear, love, etc. Here Winch's arguments (derived from Wittgenstein) offer a helpful corrective. The expressions of fear, love, jealousy, etc. are and must be recognisable (not necessarily easily, though) in terms of socially established rules for the expression and identification of emotions, the latter including such cues as the identification of the total situation as one in which the emotion – anger, jealousy, etc. – would be appropriate. Of course, imaginative identification may be required if one is to be adequate to the needs of a friend or relative who is stricken with grief, anger, love, etc. but Winch's arguments show that it isn't required for the recognition of love, anger, etc. for what they are.[22]

For both Winch and Weber, the concept of *verstehen* refers primarily to the spontaneous and immediate 'recognition' of acts and their meanings in everyday life. The peculiar feature of this understanding is not simply its immediacy, but the way in which actions can be related to one another and to their overall context in terms of logical or conceptual connections. The capacity to recognise acts in this way, in terms of the symbolic universe to which they belong, is a condition for living any sort of social life. It is this point which underlies Winch's dismissal of the notion (which he wrongly attributes to Weber) that some sort of empirical investigation, culminating in statistical generalisation, is necessary to 'confirm' intuitive recognitions of the meanings of actions:[23] if such investigations were required for the interpretation of meaning, then the living of social life (which presupposes adequacy in the interpretation of others) would be rendered impossible.

Winch's treatment of the concept of *verstehen* is also illuminating in that it draws attention to the condition of possibility of the type of understanding involved in participants in forms of social life 'spontaneously' recognising one another's actions. This 'condition of possibility' is precisely that they are participants in a shared 'form of life', or 'culture' (which amount to the same thing for Winch). This is why understanding of 'alien' cultures is problematic for Winch: to the extent that the social relations of a society 'express' ideas which differ from our own, to that extent the society will be unintelligible to us unless we are prepared to undergo – in practice, or vicariously – a secondary socialisation into the form of life we wish to study. Only by grasping the concepts in terms of which members of an 'alien' society think of themselves and their world is it possible to understand their form of life. Winch's target here is the type of 'ethnocentric' anthropology which represents 'primitive' societies in terms of concepts drawn from the social practices of the metropolitan countries, and to the extent that Winch's arguments are successful against this type of anthropological 'imperialism' they have a real polemical value. However, in so far as Winch's conception of 'understanding' carries the implication that any attempt to found a cross-cultural methodology, involving concepts applicable trans-historically and cross-culturally must be misconceived (i.e. it would require actions and practices to be 'understood' in terms of concepts extrinsic to their own cultural universe), it is radically corrosive of the whole project of a scientific knowledge of history and society. This becomes still more clear when it is recognised that this notion of participants' understanding also rules out the possibility that the participants in a form of life should, collectively, misunderstand or misrepresent to themselves its true character. This follows from the restriction that 'understanding' of actions must always involve situating them, classifying them, identifying them, etc. in terms of the criteria at work in the practices of the culture to which they belong. It is, therefore, the participants in any social practice who decide what is to count as 'correct' and 'incorrect', and who are the last arbiters as to *what* act is being performed. This would rule out most sociological and Marxist notions of ideology, as well as the functionalist sociologists' distinction between 'latent' and 'manifest function'.[24]

To some these implications have seemed like a *reductio ad absurdum* of the Winchian position: if it leads to these conclusions, then it must be wrong! Whilst never being unduly worried about the prospect of undermining the scientific pretensions of sociology, Winch, both in *The Idea of a Social Science* and since, has recognised some necessity to modify his position so as to avoid some at least of these extreme implications. One early attempt was to distinguish between 'reflective' and 'unreflective' understanding, the former involving the giving of accounts of social practices which might include 'technical' concepts, not available to the participants.[25] The restriction imposed here was that such concepts should in some sense be based on, or 'presuppose' the concepts of 'unreflective' participants' understanding. But since the logical relations involved here were not elaborated by Winch no clear methodological prescription could be derived – almost anything or almost nothing might be permitted. An attempt to avoid at least the restrictions on cross-cultural understanding appeared in a later article, in which Winch argued that there were, in certain universal human experiences –

birth, sex, death – the raw materials for some sort of cross-cultural understanding.[26] But here relativism is avoided at the cost of either founding social science upon certain biological facts of human existence (a strategy which Winch would, rightly, almost certainly want to avoid) or deriving it from a philosophical anthropology, an *a priori* conception of universal human nature. This, as we saw, was an implication also of Weberian 'methodological individualism' and also of Rickert's conception of value-relevance in the construction of historical concepts.

Although much anthropological work has exaggerated the degree of cultural homogeneity to be met with in so-called 'primitive' societies, there is no doubt that Winch's arguments do derive some of their initial plausibility from their focus upon such societies. In my earlier criticism of Winch (chapter 1, pp. 14-15) I used the example of the relationship between 'employee' and 'employer' to undermine the Winchian thesis that social relationships are merely 'expressions of ideas'. I there argued that each participant (or class of participants) may be expected to conceive of the relationship differently. It is generally true of certain types of societies (including capitalist, but not only capitalist ones) that not just certain categories of relationship are conceived differently by the occupants of different social positions, but further, that there are in these societies mutually incompatible and competing conceptualisations of the whole social order. The deployment of the different descriptions rendered possible by each of these 'cultural universes' ('capitalism'/'private enterprise'; 'fair return on capital'/'exploitation'; 'moderate'/'scab'; 'queer'/'gay' and so on) carry with them similarly incompatible practical and evaluative commitments. These are, after all, the conceptions of the world through which individuals and groups experience their lives, formulate their needs, objectives, wants and desires, and in terms of which their social practice is directed.

Now, there are three possible positions open to Winch in the face of this type of argument. One is to reject my characterisation of certain types of society as culturally heterogeneous. The existence of disagreements as such, of course, could hardly be denied, but it is open to a 'Winchian' to argue that these disagreements do not stem from radically different 'conceptual schemes'; mutually contradictory sets of beliefs can be articulated within a single conceptual framework. Agreement about the techniques and instruments of measurement is a presupposition of the institution of 'measuring', but this by no means implies that there cannot be disputes about the actual dimensions of things.[27] Similarly, a condition of mutual intelligibility is agreement in the deployment of a common stock of concepts, but this by no means excludes the possibility of disagreement in judgments: 'Roche's profits were excessive'/'Roche's profits were quite legitimate' are, apparently, incompatible judgments, but they don't necessarily presuppose incompatible conceptual frameworks. But the examples I gave earlier do involve different and incompatible schemes of concepts, not just different beliefs within a single framework. In the face of a recognition of this, a second line of defence is open to a Winchian: such competing conceptualisations are 'parasitic' upon a deeper, primary fund of concepts which constitutes the 'core' of the culture. Only if this is so is it possible to speak of a single culture or 'form of life' at all. Mutual intelligibility can be established by reference back to areas of culture which are held in common. But the existence of this 'common core' has to be demonstrated and, even if this can be achieved, the very recognition even of partial conceptual contestation in a single society implies that the notion of social relations as 'expressions of ideas' is at best a partial account.

Thirdly, our hypothetical 'Winchian' might simply concede the co-presence in a single society of incompatible conceptualisations of the social relations and practices constituting that society. If this is conceded and combined with the notion of *verstehen* as 'participants' understanding' then it follows that the participants who possess these incompatible conceptualisations will, indeed, be mutually unintelligible. A good deal of work in the sociology of education and the sociology of language, however defectively conceptualised, supports this conclusion.

Two important implications can be drawn from all this. First, if there are conceded to be even partial sets of incompatible conceptualisations of a single system of social relations (e.g. that system which relates 'employer and employee') it follows that one or both of the sets of participants' concepts must be rejected if we are to conceptualise the unity of the system of social relationships. A corollary of this is that the concepts 'culture' (= symbolic universe) and 'society' or 'social formation' (= form of life?) are not equivalent in meaning. Second, even an adequate account of participants' understanding would have to make reference to the way in which social actors individually and collectively 'negotiate' interactions in which incompatible conceptualisations are involved. Sometimes, of course, these interactions will be best described as conflicts in which each side exercises power to attain its objectives (as in the case of strikes, lock-outs, legal/military repression, and so on) but there are also procedures which, though taking account of power-relations, also involve the articulation of conceptualisations, and the search for the presuppositions of existing practices in such a way that dialogue between competing conceptual systems may be constructed (these procedures are at work formally in trade union negotiations but also occur informally on the shop floor, in the market-place, in the relations between the sexes 'at home' and at work, and so on). These procedures are given more explicit formulation and may even be systematised in intellectual disciplines such as literary criticism, philosophical analysis, history and sociology.

It is this aspect of 'interpretative understanding', the implications of which are unrecognised by Winch, that constitutes the greater sophistication of Weber's treatment of the concept. In his essay on the 'Logic of the Cultural Sciences' Weber distinguishes the interpretation of the 'textual linguistic meaning' of a cultural (e.g. literary) product and its 'value-interpretation'.[28] Weber seems to regard the former as relatively unproblematical (unlike Winch) and says little about it except that it is, logically speaking, a presupposition of the latter type of interpretation. Goethe's correspondence with Frau von Stein or Marx's *Capital* may be evaluated according to ethical, literary/aesthetic, logical or 'intellectual' criteria. In each case, the wealth of empirical detail will not simply be reproduced, but a selection will be made on the basis of 'significance' in terms of each of these criteria. Since these criteria are, in a broad sense, evaluative, such an interpretation will be one which 'suggests' (presupposes) 'various possible relationships of the object to values'.[29] Value-interpretation, then, whilst not expressing a definite evaluation of the object will involve a selective conceptualisation of the object in the light of its relationship to some value (moral, aesthetic or intellectual/cognitive). The key role of value-interpretation in historical research is in 'constructing' the historical individuals which are then to be explained causally.

> It functions . . . as a source of guidance and direction, in so far as it 'interprets' the content of an object – e.g. Faust, Orestes, Christianity of a particular epoch – with respect to its possible relations to values. In doing the latter it presents 'tasks' for the causal work of history and thus is its *presupposition*.[30]

Further, the claim of the social sciences to a 'value-free' understanding and explanation of social phenomena depends, in Weber's formulation of the problem on (*a*) the possibility of such value-interpretations *not* involving value-judgments and (*b*) the possibility of a causal explanation of the historical individuals so 'constructed' in which values play no further part. However, even if both of these points are conceded, Weber still faces the same problem as Rickert with respect to the objectivity of historical interpretations. The values with respect to which the historian selects his material as 'relevant' will be the values of his culture. As these change, so conceptions of what is 'relevant' and so appropriate for historical explanation will change.[31] Weber recognises this, and seems prepared to accept the implications of such a relativism of historical 'significance' or importance (if not of historical truth). In criticising Weber on this question, Runciman argues that Weber fails to distinguish value-relevance, as a criterion for selecting historical material, from theoretical presuppositions.[32] But, of course, there is not necessarily any problem for Weber here. As I argued above, competing conceptualisations of a single social reality will carry with them commitments of an evaluative kind. Not only this, but Weber includes within 'value-relevance' relevance to scientific and generally intellectual values. Thus Marx's *Capital* may be the object of an interpretation relevant to the value of the logical validity of its arguments.

However, it can legitimately be objected that Weber only poses the question of 'scientific' criteria of interpretation where the cultural object to be interpreted is itself a scientific work. The general value-framework in terms of which a cultural object is to be interpreted (i.e. in terms of which its concept is to be constructed) is, for Weber, a function of both the value-framework in terms of which the cultural object was itself constructed (e.g. Winch's 'participants' understanding') and the value-choices of the historian/sociologist, these value-choices themselves being relative to the culture of the historian or sociologist concerned. There are, of course, familiar difficulties which arise when these value-frameworks differ, and Weber is in roughly the same sort of trouble as Rickert in the attempt to construct a concept of historical objectivity.

It is not possible, within Weber's conceptual position, to pose the possibility of an objective and scientific employment of the various techniques and criteria for 'interpreting' cultural objects which he discusses.[33] In speaking of the possibility of 'objective' interpretations I am not, of course, proposing, in a positivist way, a method of interpretation of cultural objects, symbolic systems, literary texts and the like which is devoid of all presuppositions. This would clearly run counter to my earlier critiques of positivist accounts of concept-construction. The suggestion is, rather, that a practice of interpretation of cultural objects might be 'objective' in the sense that its 'presupposition' is a scientific theory.

This suggestion, which avoids the internal difficulties of both the relativism/philosophical anthropology 'couple'[34] and positivist epistemology, requires that a distinction be drawn between two types of conceptual structure. First are the conceptual frameworks, carrying normative and evaluative practical commitments, in terms of which social actors (including, in Weberian methodology, historians and sociologists) understand themselves, their actions and their relationships. In so far as these are articulated theoretical systems I shall refer to them as 'theoretical ideologies'. In so far as they exist principally in the everyday social practices of actors and groups of actors I shall call them 'practical ideologies'.[35] The term 'form of social consciousness' will do service to refer to the unity of a particular ideology whether in its theoretical or practical form. According to Weber's methodology, what I have called 'theoretical ideologies' are the source of criteria of interpretation and concept-construction in sociology and history.

Consider the possibility of a second type of conceptual structure: a set of systematically logically related concepts and propositions which is logically discontinuous with the conceptual frameworks in terms of which actors and groups understand themselves and their relationships, and whose system of concepts neither presupposes nor implies evaluative and normative commitments of a practical kind. This may be regarded as a 'first approximation' to a concept of scientific theory, by contrast to theoretical ideologies as defined above. More needs to be said by way of elaboration and defence of this concept, but the general solution it offers to the problem of 'interpretative understanding' and its validity should be apparent.

Weber and other Neo-Kantians consider the interpretative understanding of propositions, actions, and cultural objects generally (including what I have called 'theoretical ideologies') as always presupposing some standpoint within some symbolic universe (what I have called 'form of social consciousness'). This presupposed form of social consciousness may be identical with that of the object of interpretative understanding (especially in the case of Peter Winch), or it may (problematically) be a different form of social consciousness (the historian or sociologist's own culture). As we have seen, this produces the dilemma of relativism, or a 'philosophical anthropology' as the only basis for any defence of historical objectivity. The proposed alternative to this is that objective criteria and techniques of interpretation may form part of a scientific theory (in the sense outlined above) which contains within it a specification of the general causal connections between theoretical ideologies, forms of social consciousness, and their extra-theoretical conditions of existence. Such a science of social formations would involve the production of criteria for the construction of concepts and interpretations not dependent upon any relevance to values, nor upon any particular ideological standpoint, but upon logical techniques for analysing the structure of conceptual systems, and the above-mentioned theoretical knowledge of causal connections.

This distinction between theoretical ideologies and scientific theories is, of course, not without its own notorious difficulties. I shall discuss these further in my next two chapters, but for the moment it should be sufficient to emphasise the central conclusion of the present section of this book: that the alternative strategies in accounting for 'sociological understanding' lead to conclusions impossible to reconcile with any claims to intellectual seriousness on the part of the social studies. But before going on to discuss, in the context of the Marxist tradition, a variety of attempts to make a distinction between science and ideology it is necessary to complete the present critical discussion of 'humanist' strategies in the social sciences with a discussion of the place and function of causal explanation in such strategies.

Direct understanding and explanatory understanding

Weber, like Rickert, held that causal explanation and interpretative understanding are not incompatible: interpretation is involved in the construction of concepts of historical particulars, which are then to be explained causally. Unlike Rickert, however, Weber is aware that particular attributions of causality presuppose knowledge of a general kind:

> The simplest historical judgment represents not only a categorially formed intellectual construct but it also does not acquire a valid content until we bring to the 'given' reality the whole body of our 'nomological' empirical knowledge.[36]

History is for Weber, as for Rickert, a 'particularising' discipline in that the interest which underlies the selection and construction of historical particulars always involves the application of a knowledge of generalities, which are the concern of the auxiliary, generalising discipline of sociology.

Since, on Weber's individualist premises, the object of sociological knowledge is social action, then the question of the nature and possibility of causal explanation in sociology resolves itself into the question of the causal explanation of action. Accordingly, in part 1 of *Wirtschaft und Gesellschaft*, Weber distinguishes between 'direct observational understanding' (*aktuelles Verstehen*) and 'explanatory understanding' (*erklärendes Verstehen*).[37] The 'recognition' of an act or proposition as of a certain type, *verstehen* in the sense so far discussed, constitutes 'direct observational understanding'. It is in this sense that we understand the proposition 2 × 2 = 4. Explanatory understanding is achieved when we

> understand in terms of *motive* the meaning an actor attaches to the proposition twice two equals four, when he states it or writes it down, in that we understand what makes him do this at precisely this moment and in these circumstances. Understanding in this sense is attained if we know that he is engaged in balancing a ledger or in making a scientific demonstration.[38]

Explanatory understanding, then, is explanation of action in terms of motives (reasons, intentions, etc.) and this (at least in the case of rational action) consists in 'placing the act in an intelligible and more inclusive context of meaning'. Weber later defines a motive as 'a complex of subjective meaning which seems to the actor himself or to the observer an adequate ground for the conduct in question'.[39] Further Weber distinguishes two respects in which such motivational explanations may be adequate or inadequate: 'Adequacy at the level of meaning' is achieved when the supposed motive and its relation to the action to be explained are intelligible or 'typical' according to 'our habitual modes of thought and feeling'. But an explanation which is adequate at the level of meaning is so far only a plausible hypothesis. For the explanation to be causally adequate it must be established that 'according to established generalisations from experience, there is a probability that it will always actually occur in the same way'.[40] But a statistical generalisation connecting events is not, by itself, adequate as an explanation, adequacy at the level of meaning is also required.

The concept of cause which Weber draws on here is very obviously that of the positivist tradition: the 'covering law plus initial-condition' model. Once again, Peter Winch provides a forceful criticism of Weber's position.[41] Winch's own account of explanation in terms of motive is very like Weber's own. For both, to explain an act in terms of the motive of its actor is to situate it in the broader context of established standards and modes of conduct (complexes of meaning). But for Winch this is merely to provide a fuller and richer interpretation of the meaning of the act. It has nothing in common with a causal explanation, nor could it ever be supplemented or corrected by a statistical investigation of behavioural regularities. For Winch, the very notion of a causal explanation is quite out of place in the sphere of human action. However, Winch's general critique of the possibility of causal explanation of action does not distinguish at all clearly between the following five possibilities.

1 That actions may be explained causally, but not in terms of motives, reasons, etc. (rather, e.g., in terms of their physiological determinants).
2 That explanations of actions in terms of motives, reasons, etc. are causal in the positivist sense of causality.
3 That explanations of actions in terms of motives, reasons, etc. are causal in the 'generative mechanism' or 'realist' sense of cause which I outlined in chapters 3 and 4 above.
4 That explanations of actions in terms of motives, reasons, etc. may be causal in some further, as yet undefined sense.
5 That there may be causal explanations in the social sciences which take social phenomena other than action as their explananda.[42]

I shall argue that, whilst some of the arguments advanced by Winch and others are effective against theses 1–3, they are ineffective against 4 and 5.

Thesis 1 is dispensed with straightforwardly: bodily movements may be explained physiologically, not actions. The requirement that an action be explained sociologically is a requirement that a wink be explained differently from a nervous tic. Even if it were discovered that there were physiological concomitants of different 'meanings', this could only be established on the basis of prior generalisations at the level of actions and meanings.

Against thesis 2 is ranged a variety of arguments, some of which are not always clearly distinguished from one another. First, it may be argued that motives, etc. are not causes because a cause must be an event, temporally preceding its effect, and motives are not 'events' which 'precede' actions. Certainly, on Weber's definition of motive itself, motives are not events. But not only are there, in the physical sciences, many types of causal explanation, but also many types of candidate for the status of cause: dispositions, states, processes, constituents, structures, forces and powers may all figure as causal determinants of events, or other states, processes, etc. Only if it were shown that motives were to be analysed in none of these ways might this argument be effective, and even then it would not be conclusive. The argument is effective, however, against the vulgar positivist reduction of causal relations to relations between 'events', but it is equally effective against this reduction whether it concerns the physical sciences or the explanation of human action.

Second, it may be argued that a background of one or more general laws is required for the attribution of causes. In the case of action-explanations it is not plausible to argue that there is a general law (including statistical laws) connecting 'motive' (e.g. balancing a ledger) and action (writing down '$2 \times 2 = 4$'), and so it follows that motive-explanations cannot be causal. Donald Davidson argues that, although causal attributions do involve the implication of some general law, very few causal attributions (even of a physical nature) could be validly made if it were required that the relevant causal law were known and could be specified.[43] In claiming that a particular motive, reason, etc. caused an action, we do imply that some causal law connects motive and action under some description or other but it is not necessary that this be known or specifiable. But this is unsatisfactory since, among other things, what constitutes actions and motives as such is their description. To explain the action sequence 'working off a fit of anger' under the description 'digging the garden' is not necessarily to explain the former action sequence at all. Nevertheless, there are generalisations which are presupposed in the attributions of motives and reasons as explanations: these are generalisations concerning the cultural expectations, standards and norms of the context in which the action takes place, as well as character traits, values, beliefs, etc. of the actors involved. There will also be assumptions of a particular kind about the situation in which the act was performed. Peter Winch argues, however, that these generalisations describe regularities of a kind fundamentally different from those described in the causal laws of the natural sciences.[44] The regularities involved in social life are 'rules', not 'laws', and this is a crucial disanalogy between the two realms. It is, for instance, characteristic of rules that when they are applied in new circumstances, the outcome of their application depends on decisions as to 'how to go on' and is thus indeterminate. It follows from this that an observer may correctly identify the rule according to which a course of action is being performed, and yet make predictions about its outcome which fail. The contrast with natural laws is that failure of prediction implies a mistaken identification of either initial conditions or the causal law in operation.[45] Without going along with Winch in his apparent acceptance of a naive falsificationist account of the logic of prediction in the physical sciences, it is clear that there is at least *some* sort of disanalogy here. The question is: is this disanalogy sufficient to establish that motives, reasons, etc. are not causes? Since any serious philosophical analysis of explanatory structures in the physical sciences must reveal a considerable variety of types of generalisation as presupposed in causal explanations (see chapters 3 and 4), and since it is also clear that the (neo-positivist) account of natural laws by which Winch makes his contrast is defective, it must remain an open question whether generalisations which describe normative regularities are adequate as backing for particular causal attributions. There is certainly a distinction which plays an important role in common-sense accounting for action between 'reasons' and 'rationalisations'.[46] It is presupposed in this distinction that at least sometimes when reasons are advanced as explaining an action the claim is that the presence of the reason is what makes the difference between the act's being performed and its not being performed. This element in concepts of cause as 'what makes the difference' between something's happening and its not happening, the notion of 'agency' (in a non-intentional sense of the term), seems to be a constant, despite other logical differences in the use of causal explanations. In so far as explanations in terms of reasons, motives, etc. involve the claim that the relevant action would not have occurred had not the motive, reason, etc. been present (assuming no other difference), then it may be argued that they are explanations of a causal kind, whether or not the generalisations which back the counter-factual claim describe normative or any other type of regularity. It will be appreciated, of course, that this criticism of Winch's arguments against the causal status of motive-explanations succeeds only in defending thesis 4 above and leaves quite untouched Winch's case against thesis 2.

The third general argument against the causal status of action-explanations in terms of reasons, motives, etc. is connected with the humanist thesis of the 'value-relevance' of cultural phenomena. Reasons and motives come up for evaluation as good or bad (motives), adequate or inadequate (reasons), honourable or dishonourable (intentions) and so on. By contrast, it makes no sense to ask of the cause of Dutch Elm disease whether it is honourable/dishonourable, valid/invalid, etc.

Now, as Keat and Urry have effectively argued,[47] it does not at all follow from the appropriateness of evaluating reasons, motives, etc. according to various rational, ethical or aesthetic standards that they may not also be causes. Further, the very social practices of evaluating reasons, motives, etc. according to these various standards would entirely lose their point if it were not the case that the motives and reasons so evaluated had some causal relevance in the generation of action. A consequence of rejecting the causal status of reason- and motive-explanations, then, would be to relegate all of those practices which might be included under the category of 'ideological struggle' to the status of 'epiphenomena' which merely 'reflect' causal processes occurring externally to themselves, but in themselves have no causal influence. However, it must also be recognised that this feature of motives and reasons – that they come in for 'evaluations' both in respect of their status as causes of actions and in respect of their rationality, moral worth, etc. – is a further disanalogy in what we might call the 'logical grammar' of causality in the explanation of social action, compared with other conceptions of causality. Again my argument is to be construed as a defence of thesis 4 above, and not of thesis 2.

Finally, there is a cluster of objections to the idea that reasons, motives and intentions are causes which are frequently confused, but are really distinct, though related. These objections are all connected with the positivist notion that, if *a* is to be represented as the 'cause' of *b* then *a* must at least be distinguishable from *b*. That this condition for adequate causal attribution is missing in the case of reason- or motive-explanations of action is argued in a variety of ways. Sometimes it is said that the connection between motive (reason) and action is conceptual, not empirical, as it should be if the connection is a causal one. Sometimes it is claimed that motive and action are not independently describable, or, sometimes, that they are not independently identifiable.

Let us suppose that a trade unionist votes for a strike because she believes that she and others have a legitimate grievance. If this belief, the argument goes, is the cause (or part of the cause) of her voting, then there should be am 'empirical', matter-of-fact relationship between her having the belief and her voting. But how do we know that she believes that she and others have a legitimate grievance? Among other things, by watching her voting behaviour at union meetings. If she does not vote for a strike, and there is no other explanation of this (fear of redundancy, conscientious objection to industrial action, etc.) then *prima facie* this action is grounds for withdrawing the description of her as believing she has a legitimate grievance. In other words, voting for a strike is among the criteria on the basis of which the appropriateness of the description 'believes she has a legitimate grievance' is decided: there is a conceptual, not an empirical, connection between action and belief. The belief cannot therefore be (part of) the cause of the action.

Against this it has been argued, correctly, that the conceptual structure by which the natural world, too, is described and explained may also build in causal presuppositions into descriptions. A 'clone', for example, is an organism grown from a culture of somatic cells from another organism, by-passing the ordinary reproductive processes. Describing an organism as a 'clone', then, involves an assumption about its causal origins. If it is discovered that the organism was produced by ordinary reproductive processes, the description would have to be withdrawn: there is a conceptual relation between a 'clone' and having certain causal origins. Other descriptive terms having built-in causal presuppositions include 'thunder', 'wound', 'crater', and so on. So, it would seem, explanations of actions in terms of reasons and motives are entirely symmetrical with causal explanations of natural phenomena in this respect.

But the argument is not to be concluded so readily. The conceptual relation between 'cause' and 'effect' in the physical-science examples is retained only if cause and effect are described in certain ways: 'thunder' may be redescribed as 'loud rumbling noises', or 'clones' as 'organisms', whereupon their causes (atmospherical disturbances and cultures of somatic cells, respectively) cease to be conceptually connected with them. The requirement that cause/effect relationships be matter-of-fact, or 'empirical' may, then, be expressed as a requirement, not that cause and effect be non-conceptually connected under every description, but rather that there should be available some logically independent descriptions for them. If motive- and reason-explanations are subjected to this test, then the outcome is different. To return to the trade unionist example, it is relatively easy to find a description of the act of voting for a strike which renders it logically independent of the purported 'cause' – belief in the legitimacy of the grievance; such a description would be 'raised her arm (at such and such a time, etc.)'. But under the new description there is no longer any explanatory connection between the belief and the 'action' (indeed, under this new description the action has now become a mere physical movement). A new asymmetry between causal explanations in the physical sciences (as represented by the positivist tradition) and action-explanations: in the former, logically independent descriptions can always be found for cause and effect, whereas in the latter motives, reasons, etc. only explain actions to the extent that there is some sort of logical or conceptual connection between the reason (motive, etc.) and the relevant action-description. Here again is our old friend 'adequacy at the level of meaning': reasons, motives, and intentions are not even plausible candidates for the status of explanations unless their relationship to the actions they 'explain' is 'intelligible' or 'typical' according to our 'habitual modes of thought and feeling': to explain an act in terms of reasons and motives is at least in part to render it intelligible in the light of the norms and standards of its cultural context. This is not, and cannot be, a condition of adequate explanation for any physical happening. But of itself this is insufficient to establish that action-explanations are not also causal in some modified sense of that term.

However, what this argument does achieve is to give further rational support to the position sometimes adopted by Weber, and also by Winch, that explanation in the social studies must be restricted in the concepts employed to those available to participants in the 'culture' or 'form of life' which forms the context of the actions to be explained. Weber's methodological individualism and his Neo-Kantian opposition to any type of biological (or 'natural-psychological') reductionism logically commit him to a strategy of action-explanations in terms of motives, reasons and intentions. It follows that this type of restriction on concept-construction must be adopted in any sociology which claims to be an implementation of the Weberian methodology. Similarly for the paradigms of explanation which Winch is committed to. So is there, after all, something in these conceptual restrictions despite their subversive implications for any aspiring scientific sociology?

First, it may be argued that the explanatory strategies adopted in Freudian, and the various post-Freudian traditions of psychoanalysis do centrally involve the production of action-explanations in terms of motive, intention, etc. which deploy concepts not available to the actors involved, yet which succeed in being explanatory. Without entering into the debate about the scientific status of psychoanalysis, it is fairly easy to show that, at the levels of the explanation of particular actions or syndromes, psychoanalytic explanations do not involve the use of concepts very far removed from those immediately available to actors. Unconscious motives, repressed desires and the like must relate to actions and 'symptoms' in a way which is intelligible at the 'level of meaning', albeit in a somewhat extended sense. Such explanations fall well within the criterion Peter Winch lays down for the acceptability of technical concepts, even in its most restrictive interpretation.[48]

But whatever the status of action-explanations, and however restricted concept-construction must be in the production of this type of explanation, there are no adequate grounds for supposing that the social sciences should be or even can be restricted to this one type of explanation. To refer again to my example of the trade unionist's action of voting for a strike, when the act has been explained in terms of the network of beliefs, aspirations and standards which form its immediate ideological context, there remain many further questions to be asked. What maintains the existence of this complex of beliefs, standards and practices (which we might call 'trade union consciousness', so long as it is recognised that this phrase refers not to some disembodied system of 'ideas', but primarily to a set of practices and relationships), how did it originate and how has it changed under different circumstances? How are these beliefs and practices distributed in a population, and against what contradictory beliefs and practices are they in tension and conflict as real social forces? In so far as these conflicts are an aspect of conflict between classes and strata in society, what is it that generates and maintains class-conflict and the very existence of social classes? How, in the sense of 'by what mechanisms' (in the family, educational system, firms and trade unions themselves) are individual human beings transformed into social subjects with their own particular ideological dispositions, distributed into the various classes and strata, and incorporated into the various social practices, rituals and outlooks that are characteristics of those classes? None of these questions can even be asked within a rigorous methodological individualist framework. Almost all of them are questions whose answers would be causal explanations, but by no means of a uniform type. Finally, and crucially for the present argument,[49] there is absolutely no rationale given either by Weber or by Winch for restricting the theoretical framework in terms of which these questions are posed and answered to the conceptual structure which constitutes the 'symbolic universe' of the actors involved. Moreover, the very existence within a single social system of a multiplicity of such 'symbolic universes' makes such an explanatory restriction impossible to apply consistently.

But, if we may be certain that the Weber/Winch restriction of sociological explanation to 'action-explanation' has no adequate rational basis, there still remains the problem of whether action-explanations themselves may be causal. If reasons and motives are only explanatory of actions in so far as they are described in such a way that their descriptions are conceptually connected, then it seems that they (i.e. the reasons and motives) are not identifiable or describable independently of the actions they are supposed to explain. On the positivist account of causality this is sufficient to rule them out as candidates for causal explanation. But is it sufficient on the realist, 'generative mechanism' account of causality which I outlined in chapters 3 and 4? According to the kinetic theory of gases, various relationships between volume, temperature, and pressure of gases are explicable as caused by states of motion, collisions, etc. of imperceptible particles. Not only is there no way of 'identifying' states of motion of molecules independently of their various macroscopic effects, but the concepts by which they are described get their sense through a series of logical relationships with the concepts by which the various macro-properties (temperature, pressure, etc.) are specified.

This analysis suggests that the relation between, for example, motives and the actions they explain is analogous to that between a theoretical entity (molecule) and the observable happenings it explains. There certainly is, in the way the concept 'motive' is used, the echo of a mechanistic conception of inner psychic 'forces' which 'generate' conduct. This aspect is quite explicitly theorised in psychoanalytic theories. On the other hand, there are the various disanalogies between motive- and reason-explanations and both the positivist *and* generative-mechanism concepts of cause that I have discussed above. These are, most notably, the relationship of reasons and motives to critical evaluation of various types, and the distinctive character of generalisation and its relation to prediction which figure in action-explanations. The most plausible inference to be drawn from this survey is that such explanations are, indeed, causal, but that they are causal in a sense different from, though intelligible in comparison with, both the positivist and realist conceptions of causality (thesis 4). Further, none of this rules out the possibility of causal explanations of ideological systems, their distribution, conditions of existence and transformations, the reproduction of individuals as social agents, their distribution into the social classes, and so on (thesis 5).

Finally, it requires to be mentioned that, his methodological strictures in *Wirtschaft und Gesellschaft* notwithstanding, Weber does discuss the formation of ideal–typical concepts and causal explanation of historical particulars which are not individual actions in certain of his methodological writings. Certainly a good deal of his substantive work contains discussions of and attempts to explain supra-individual historical particulars without any obvious attempt to reduce these to individual action-descriptions. In the introduction to *The Protestant Ethic and the Spirit of Capitalism* Weber constructs an ideal–typical concept of one historical particular: modern Occidental capitalism.[50] Because of the profound contemporary value-relevance of this historical particular, importance attaches to the explanation of its origins. Weber's thesis is that among the causes of the origin and development of modern capitalism, along with purely economic, scientific, technical, legal and administrative conditions, is the presence of a certain type of religious ethic. As is well known, Weber advances this thesis as a refutation of a 'one-sided materialistic' interpretation of history, without wishing to embrace an equally one-sided spiritual interpretation. Implicit in this text, then, is a recognition of the acceptability of what I have argued for under thesis 5 above. Unfortunately Weber's positive contributions to the theoretical account of historical causality are limited to the merely gestural notions of 'multi-causality' and 'elective affinity'. The Marxian foundation/superstructure distinction, with its related causal concepts of 'determination in the last instance' and 'relative autonomy' is notoriously bewildering and problematic, but at least it begins to pose the question of historical causality in a theoretical way.

It has been the thesis of this chapter and the previous chapter that the various Neo-Kantian and 'humanist' philosophical accounts of the methods and forms of explanation peculiar to the social or 'cultural' studies are radically defective. At certain points in the discussion arguments have been directed at untenable doctrines or internal contradictions in particular texts in the 'humanist' tradition. At other points the arguments have been of a more general character, designed to conclusively fault 'humanism' as a general philosophical/methodological strategy. In particular, although a variety of asymmetries between certain types of explanation to be found in the different sciences (most notably concerning the 'interpretation' of symbolic items and systems and the distinctive character of the causality involved in action-explanations) have been rightly identified by writers in the 'humanist tradition' no rational foundation has been established for any fundamental division between the natural sciences and the 'cultural' or 'human' studies. The materialist insistence that the methods and forms of explanation adopted by the sciences must be adequate to the distinctive character of their objects involves rejection of the positivist external imposition of a universal scientific method without, at the same time, surrendering to the 'humanist' rejection of *any* notion of the unity of science.

8 Karl Marx and Frederick Engels: philosophy of history and theory of knowledge

Introduction

So far my argument has taken the form, first, of a critical rejection of positivist and empiricist theories of knowledge as either adequately representing the nature of scientific knowledge, or providing adequate practical norms or standards for the production of new scientific knowledge. My argument was conducted with reference not only to a conception of empiricism in general, but also to certain representative empiricist philosophies of both the natural and the social sciences. Second, I have attempted to show that the principal, Neo-Kantian, humanist tradition of thought fails to establish its thesis of a fundamental divide between the natural sciences and the 'human', 'cultural' or 'historical' studies.

This thesis fails on two counts. First, the contrast it draws relies excessively on an uncritical reception of positivist interpretations of the natural sciences. The impossibility of a 'positivist' social science by no means implies a radical discontinuity between the sciences of man and nature if, as I have tried to show, a positivist natural science is also impossible. Second, the positive arguments of Neo-Kantian humanists that 'our' interest in 'human' and 'cultural' objects, or the nature of these objects themselves (their 'meaning', 'intentionality', 'spontaneity', or whatever) require an altogether unique type of knowledge and method of study are not sufficient to establish this conclusion. They establish no more than that the various historical and social sciences require a method and forms of explanation adequate to the specificity of their object. This is no more and no less than could be said of any science.

Finally, any claim to objectivity of historical knowledge is rendered, in the humanist account of its nature, entirely suspect. Either 'understanding' cannot transcend the limits of its culture, in which case historical knowledge is merely 'relative', or 'understanding' presupposes some universal human 'essence' which is the basis of cross-cultural intelligibility. The first alternative faces grave intellectual difficulties, not least the well-known paradox that if the statement of relativism is true, then its truth is only relative. But even if the relativist were prepared to espouse this conclusion, the rest of us would require more powerful positive arguments for giving up the search for objective knowledge than the relativists have so far given. The second alternative, that of founding historical knowledge, and the justification of its claim to objectivity, on a 'philosophical anthropology' is equally suspect. To resurrect philosophy as a source of knowledge equivalent to the sciences is, albeit within a narrower sphere, to resurrect the aspirations of the speculative metaphysics whose pretensions were so effectively demolished by Kant. And, just as with those speculative systems themselves, philosophical conceptions of human nature abound, and contradict one another, without any prospect of authoritative criteria of validity to establish which, in the end, provide the 'objective' knowledge which each claims.

Is there, then, an alternative to positivism and humanism in the philosophy of the social sciences? The cautious answer to this is that there is, 'in the work of' Marx and certain post-Marxist writers, such an alternative. I say that such an alternative is present 'in the work of' Marx in order to avoid two confusions. One is that I might, but should not be, understood as offering an interpretation of Marx which is 'historically accurate' in the sense of 'complete', 'balanced' or 'true to the texts'. I aim only to extract from Marx what is relevant to the present argument – i.e. a distinctive philosophical position, counterposed to both positivism and humanism – whilst recognising that there is a great deal in Marx which is humanist, and not a little that is positivist. The second source of confusion is that I shall often refer to works of a substantive kind as sources for Marx's philosophical positions. This is partly because Marx wrote few extended epistemological tracts (and none to compare in scale with those of Durkheim or Weber) and partly because what Marx did write in the way of explicit epistemological statement requires interpretation in the light of his substantive work no less than does that of Durkheim and Weber.

The 'reading' of Marx's philosophical achievement as anti-positivist and anti-humanist which I shall offer (like much else in this book), owes a great deal to the work of the French Marxist philosopher Louis Althusser, but it also departs from Althusser's work on a number of fundamental questions.[1] I shall not, here, take issue directly with other readings of Marx. It is well known that attempts have been made to represent the Marxist theory of history as 'scientific' in the positivist sense of the word. This has had its effects on the interpretation of the content of Marx's historical doctrines and also upon political practice guided by that interpretation. The 'Machist' tendency in Russian Social Democracy, against which Lenin polemicised in *Materialism and Empirio-Criticism*, is an early example of this.[2] Similarly, humanist philosophical readings of Marx, whether Neo-Kantian, Hegelian or Existentialist, abound, and at times have predominated both within the 'Marxist' camp and amongst its antagonists. I shall not devote to these often sophisticated and persuasive interpretations the attention they deserve, partly for reasons of space and partly because many of the arguments I have already used against 'positivism' and 'humanism' apply to them equally in their Marxist and non-Marxist forms.

Nevertheless, no reading of Marx, however anti-humanist, could justify the exclusion of all reference to the relationship between Marxism and Hegel. This, unfortunately, is the least 'summarisable' of all intellectual/historical relationships.[3] What follows in the next two sections has no pretensions to balance or to definitiveness, it is merely my route to the central argument of the chapter.

Kant and Hegel[4]

I mentioned, in chapter 6, how the Neo-Kantian movement of the latter part of the nineteenth century in Germany had been preceded by another philosophical movement also having its principal source in Kantian philosophy. This philosophical movement, of the end of the eighteenth and early nineteenth centuries, was the German Idealist movement. Its best known representatives were Fitche, Schelling and Hegel.

To say that German Idealism, and the philosophy of Hegel in particular, has its 'source' in Kant's philosophy may be misleading, since Hegel refers far more often with approval to certain of the Classical Greek philosophers and, indeed, frequently defines his own positions against those of Kant. Nevertheless some of the most fundamental concepts and distinctions of Hegelian philosophy can best be understood as elaborations upon and transformations of Kantian ones. Both the unity and the opposition between Hegel and Kant are well illustrated in this passage from the preface to Hegel's *Science of Logic* (1812):

> The exoteric doctrine of Kantian Philosophy that Understanding cannot go beyond Experience, because if so the faculty of cognition would be a merely theoretical intelligence which could by itself produce nothing but idle fancies of the brain – this doctrine has given a scientific justification to the renunciation of Speculative Thought. . . . *Philosophy* and crude *Common Sense* playing thus into each other's hands for the

> downfall of Metaphysics, there was presented the strange spectacle of a cultured people having no Metaphysic – as it were a temple, in all other respects richly ornamented, but lacking its Holy of Holies.[5]

Hegel, then, is the advocate of a reinstatement of the very speculative metaphysics which the Kantian critical philosophy seemed finally to have put paid to. Moreover, it is no mere 'reinstatement' that Hegel is after: the old metaphysics was, if anything, not speculative enough! What is needed is a completion of the speculative enterprise which Descartes, Leibniz and even Spinoza only pursued inconsistently and with faint heart. Not only should speculative metaphysics be reinstated and 'completed', but without it, philosophy and culture itself have the heart torn from them; the metaphysical enterprise has a religious, sacred character.

But this rejection, and even inversion, of Kantian philosophy – the denigration of science and common sense in favour of metaphysical speculation – is expressed in terms of Kant's own distinction between 'reason' and 'understanding'. Indeed, it is possible to represent Hegel's central objection to Kant as the complaint that he does not apply his own distinction rigorously enough. In the understanding, objective judgments concerning the world of appearance (the phenomenal world) are made by the application of the categories of the understanding (cause, substance and attribute, necessity and possibility, etc.) to sense-perceptions. As Hegel recognises in the above quotation, the operations of the understanding, in applying the categories, are limited to the sphere of possible experience – to the phenomenal world. The ideas of pure reason, by contrast, cannot be used to produce objective cognitive judgments at all. They have a limited, 'heuristic' use in science, but above all have a 'practical' use in providing a foundation in faith for moral conduct and responsibility. The ideas of pure reason – freedom, God, immortality – are thus indispensable to the religious and moral life, to human beings as individual subjects; but the attempt to use the ideas of pure reason to express theoretical knowledge of things as they are in themselves (of the noumenal world) necessarily leads to 'antinomy' and contradiction. Similarly with the attempt to apply the categories of the understanding beyond the bounds of possible experience. This necessarily contradictory character of metaphysical thought – of the speculative exercise of 'reason' – is the basis of Kant's critique of metaphysics.

For Kant the logical principles of identity, non-contradiction and excluded middle, principles which he adopted relatively uncritically from traditional logic, were formal conditions for the coherence of any thought. Contradictions must be excluded from thought not because the world itself is non-contradictory (whatever that might mean!) but because to assert something and then deny it is to fail to assert anything. For Hegel, by contrast, these logical laws, along with the categories, have their legitimate sphere of application only within the understanding, within the common-sense and scientific description and explanation of the phenomenal world. Kant's application of the principle of non-contradiction in the critique of speculative metaphysics is just as unjustified as the metaphysicians' use of the category of causality in the sphere of things-in-themselves. Nevertheless, according to Hegel, Kant was correct in recognising the necessity of contradiction in the metaphysical function of reason. Kant failed, however, to comprehend the significance of this: that the contradictions of metaphysical thinking must be united in a higher, transcendent unity: the absolute idea, or spirit.

For Hegel, the speculative knowledge of the absolute idea, the highest function of reason, is the highest form of knowledge. In so far as thought remains restricted to the scientific and common-sense 'understanding' of phenomenal reality it is not only cut off from knowledge of the ultimate, spiritual reality which lies beyond the phenomena, but thought also fails to grasp the phenomena themselves. As the phenomena are mere appearances of the true reality, they have their essence, so to speak, 'outside' themselves: they cannot be fully comprehended except through a knowledge of that of which they are the 'appearances'.

We are now in a position to understand in what sense Hegel thought it necessary to 'complete' the task of metaphysics, and also in what sense the metaphysical enterprise is religious. The only type of 'unity' which can transcend and 'unite' contradictions is a unity of a 'spiritual' or 'ideal' kind. In a certain sense, what metaphysical reason comes to know is itself. All philosophy worth the name is thus idealist – it postulates the only ultimate reality as spiritual or ideal in nature. This is clearly expressed by Hegel in volume 1 of the *Science of Logic:*

> The proposition that the finite is of ideal nature constitutes Idealism. In philosophy idealism consists of nothing else than the recognition that the finite has no veritable being. Essentially every philosophy is an idealism, or at least has idealism for its principle, and the question then is only how far it is actually carried through. This is as true of philosophy as of religion; for religion equally with philosophy refuses to recognise in finitude a veritable being, or something ultimate and absolute, or non-posited, uncreated, and eternal.[6]

The pre-critical metaphysicians (Descartes, Leibniz, Spinoza and others) were correct in refusing to reduce the infinite to the finite realm of science, common sense and appearance; in insisting on the reality of spiritual being, beyond the illusion and 'appearance' of the perceptual world. But whilst as true philosophers they are idealist in their 'principles', they are nevertheless materialist in the details. In seeing the 'infinite' as irreconcilably opposed to the finite, material, perceived world, they fail to 'actually carry through' their idealism to its completion. Infinite, spiritual being is asked to co-exist with its opposite, the finite and material. This has two consequences, both, in Hegel's view, very damaging: one is that the carefully separated and purified 'infinite', since it must be limited and bounded by its opposite, the finite, cannot be truly an infinite at all. The second consequence is that the infinite is conceived only in an abstract, negative way as the 'other', beyond and outside the here-and-now material world.

Hence the need to 'complete' metaphysics. This requires that reason liberates speculative thought from the traditional logical 'laws' – in particular, the principle of non-contradiction. The contradiction between the finite and the infinite can be reconciled by reason in the higher (infinite) unity of finite and infinite: the infinite, so to speak 'absorbs' and 'includes' the finite within itself, and so becomes truly infinite. As a result of this 'dialectical' reasoning, then, the ultimate ideality, spirituality of the finite, material world is revealed, and conversely, the presence of the infinite in the finite, material world is also demonstrated. The separation of the spiritual domain, its exclusion into the 'beyond' is overcome. Finally, the religious character of metaphysics is now clear: religion represents in a mythical form what this dialectical exercise of reason demonstrates in a philosophical, theoretical form.

By now it should be clear how radically subversive of the pretensions of science (and common sense) is Hegel's philosophy. The realm of the finite, perceptible, material world, which is the object of the 'understanding' with its categories, and traditional logical principles, has no true independent being. Hegel makes use of the Classical Greek sceptics to show the inherently contradictory character of the world of science and common sense: when, for us, the sun is rising, for others it is setting – the sun both is and is not setting; the idea of motion implies that a thing must be in and not in position *A* at one and the same time, and so on. The contradictory character of the world of science and common sense can be expressed by saying that its essence, its reality lies outside it, beyond it: in its negation. To truly comprehend what a thing is, it is necessary to understand what it is not. The abandonment of the principle of non-contradiction in favour of the dialectical law of the unity of contradictions in some higher totality is the only way of transcending the limits imposed by scientific and common-sense thought. Here, again, is the 'humanist' conception of a philosophical source of knowledge, not in this case equivalent to the knowledge of the sciences, but of true knowledge, by contrast to the contradictory and limited 'understanding' of the sciences.

Hegel's own 'completion' of the work of metaphysics with his dialectical logic and conception of the absolute idea is conceived by him as an outcome of the whole process of historical development of religion and philosophy. The dialectical motions described in his logic are to be thought of as a historical process, played out in intellectual history, whereby the absolute idea is finally 'realised'. But this formulation is defective. Since reality itself is, ultimately, the absolute idea, this historical process is the activity of the absolute idea itself, manifested in the works of the great philosophers, and culminating in the work of Hegel himself. We should say, then, that the absolute idea 'realises' itself in these philosophical works. But in what sense 'realises'? First, and most obviously, 'realises' in the sense of becoming aware of its own nature. Whereas in earlier phases of the development of thought human beings have thought of themselves as distinct from each other, and have distinguished also between themselves and the natural world, now absolute spirit, working through the medium of finite minds, comes to a full recognition of the ultimate spiritual unity of these things as 'modes' or 'aspects' of itself. Further, since this self-realisation involves also the recognition that economic, political, etc. history is ultimately only an aspect of the self-realisation of the spirit, history itself (not just the history of philosophy) may be thought of as the process of self-realisation of the absolute spirit. Finally, this process of self-realisation is to be understood not just as a process by which the absolute spirit achieves self-knowledge, but also a process whereby the absolute spirit makes itself real – manifests itself in the world.

History, then, including human history, of course, but also the history of the natural world, is for Hegel the process of self-realisation (in several senses) of the absolute spirit.[7] The absolute spirit is the result, or outcome of this process of history and, paradoxically, the original, self-consistent and self-creative source or 'ground' of history. Accordingly, the process itself, whereby the absolute spirit appears as 'conditioned' by its own previous history, is relegated to the status of mere appearance.

A final word needs to be said about this 'process' of history. The contradiction between the finite and its true 'being' or 'essence' the infinite cannot be overcome by a single dialectical transcendence into the absolute idea. Each contradiction finds its synthesis in some higher conceptual unity. But this unity is itself faced with its own contradiction, which in turn requires transcendence into a still higher synthesis. It is only, therefore, at the culmination of a great hierarchy of contradictions and syntheses that the final, all-inclusive unity of the absolute spirit is achieved. Any developmental process, therefore, up to and including the historical process as such, proceeds by way of a series of mediating stages. To take a lowly example, the metamorphosis of the butterfly involves a series of stages: egg, larva, pupa, adult. In terms of Hegel's dialectical logic the adult stage can be thought of as the 'self-realisation', or 'essence' of the insect. As an egg, the insect exists merely as the negation, or denial of this ultimate 'essence' (which can also be thought of as a 'potentiality'). The larval stage represents the 'negation of this negation', the 'supersession' of one stage by the next, higher, developmental stage. But the larval stage too is, although a higher stage, still a negation of the ultimate potentiality of the 'self-realised' insect. Successive stages of 'negation' and 'negation of negation' therefore intervene, as steps in the overall self-realisation of the 'essential' insect. History, too, is a succession of stages, in which the contradiction between one negation of the absolute spirit and its negation is the motive force for a series of transformations resulting in the self-realisation of the absolute spirit.

Hegel, Feuerbach and Marx

It is well known that Marx and Engels were at first identified with the circle of 'left-wing' critics and interpreters of Hegel known as the 'Left Hegelians'. Conscious of the limitations of this philosophical milieu, Marx and Engels were immediately attracted to the Left Hegelian Ludwig Feuerbach's 'materialist inversion' of Hegel's philosophy. It is also well known that soon after this they distanced themselves not only from the Left Hegelians in general, but also from Feuerbach. Nevertheless, Marxist and non-Marxist interpreters alike have predominantly conceptualised the relationship between Marxism and Hegel in terms of the metaphor of 'inversion', of a setting 'right-side up' of Hegel's inverted philosophy.[8] In questioning the adequacy of this notion of Marxism as the 'inversion' of Hegel it will be necessary to pose the question of the relationship between Marxism and Hegel in two distinct fields of enquiry. Whereas for Hegel the process of history and the process of knowledge are ultimately identical, any materialist theory must suppose the distinctness of these processes. It will therefore be necessary to consider separately the relationship between Marxism and Hegel's philosophy of history and the relationship between the Marxist and Hegelian theories of knowledge. Finally, no account, however brief, of the relationship between Hegel and Marx can avoid the question of the continuity of Marx's theoretical work – to what extent Marx's work can be seen to form a coherent and consistent 'corpus' and, conversely, to what extent it is necessary to recognise the 'earlier' and 'later' works as divided from one another in their basic concepts, forms of argument and intellectual concerns. If there is a sense in which (certain of) the earlier works are Hegelian, how far is it necessary to represent the 'mature' works as also 'Hegelian'?

Philosophy and the theory of history

First, then, the relationship between Marxism and Hegel's philosophy of history. To put it very crudely, Feuerbach's 'inversion' of the Hegelian dialectic and speculative philosophy had taken the form of a transposition of subject and predicate, of 'being' and 'consciousness'. Whereas, for Hegel, real, material existence had been reduced to the status of a mere aspect or 'predicate' of the self-subsistent 'absolute idea', Feuerbach asserted that ideas and consciousness were, rather, a mere 'predicate' of real, material existents. Thought is a product, immediately, of the human brain, and, historically, of the development of Nature, of which it remains a part. This inversion can also be represented as an inversion of the appearance/reality distinction as it exists in Hegel's philosophy of history. Whereas spirit or 'consciousness', in Hegel, is the true source and underlying reality of the historical process, it nevertheless appears as its product – as the outcome of the historical process. In Feuerbach thought/consciousness really is the outcome of the historical development of nature, but appears (in religion and speculative philosophy) to be its origin and ultimate 'truth'.

Feuerbach's critique of Hegelian speculative philosophy involved the claim that thought requires some real object – not just the object which does the thinking, but the object about which it thinks (which may, for Feuerbach, be identical). The object of thought cannot be a 'deduction' from thought's own internal contents:

> it is precisely logic which knows from its own resources only about itself, only about thinking. Therefore that which is other than logic cannot be deduced from logic. . . . If . . . there were no Nature, unspoiled virgin Logic would never have succeeded in bringing one forth from itself alone.[9]

The source of our knowledge of the existence of external nature is in sensory experience, and without such experience our thinking would lack any real content. However, Feuerbach doesn't here submit to any form of empiricism, nor to the kind of mechanical reductionism that characterised eighteenth-century French materialism. Thought is indispensable, along with sense-experience, for genuine knowledge.[10] Also man is active in the knowledge process, not a passive receptor of 'sense-impressions'. Feuerbach's conception of knowledge is also reminiscent of that of Bacon in that 'experience' is understood in a wide sense, so as to include practical activity; knowledge is, for Feuerbach, continuous with other practical activities, needs, and interests of human beings.

The 'idea', 'consciousness', then, cannot be the source and 'reality' of historical development. But how does Feuerbach explain what he has shown to be the illusion of speculative philosophy? The speculative philosophy, he argues, is merely religion in an abstract and conceptual form. He is therefore able to apply to it the form of explanation which he devised for the comprehension of religion – of Christianity in particular.[11] Religion is a form of dream, or fantasy, in which human desires for the satisfaction of real needs take on a fantastic form. In this fantastic form 'men' attribute to a superhuman or supernatural being, prior to and independent of themselves, their own essential qualities and powers. Religion (and, hence, speculative philosophy) is thus a form of human self-alienation. So long as 'men' lack the power to realise their human essence in practice, they overcome the contradiction between their present conditions of existence and their essential human qualities in imagination, by creating Gods in their own image. Here, then, is yet another 'inversion' of Hegel. Whereas the positing of finite, material existence constituted the self-alienation of absolute spirit in Hegel's philosophy, for Feuerbach the postulation of the absolute spirit is an instance of man's self-alienation.

Implicit, then, in Feuerbach's 'inversion' of Hegel, is a conception of history in which 'man', rather than the absolute idea, transcends successive self-alienations in the course of his 'self-realisation'. To know what the self-realisation of human essence would be, it is necessary only to investigate the qualities which 'man' attributes to God: these are his own essential, divine qualities and powers. They are three in number – will, reason and love. These essential characteristics are ends in themselves, and constitute the aim of human development; and as essential characteristics they are what unites all human beings into a single species. 'Man' is a 'species-being' not only in the sense that all human beings have certain characteristics in common, but also in that their existence as a species is the object of a common conscious practice. Human beings are related to one another above all through love. The realisation of the human essence – of 'man's' 'species-being', then, will involve the achievement of a definite state of society, and of that society's relationship to nature. In short, the realisation of 'man's' species-being is a task that need no longer take fantastic or imaginary forms, but which is to be accomplished in practice – in technology and in the political establishment of a democratic and republican state.

Despite Feuerbach's assertion of the independent existence of matter, and his frequent reference to the necessity of philosophy's roots in practice, experience and in science (to the need for philosophy's replacement by 'anthropology' – the science of 'man') it is clear that history – now, admittedly, the history of 'man', and not the idea – still obeys the laws of the Hegelian dialectic. Hegel has been set on his feet, but it is still Hegel, whether upside down or right-side up. The only history which 'moves' by assertion, contradiction, negation and negation of negation is a conceptual history: a history subject to the laws of thought, and not to its own independent rhythms, structures and causality. The 'essence' of 'man' which is realised can only be a philosophically established concept of 'man'. In short, we are back, as Feuerbach himself proclaimed, to a form of humanism. The content of the Feuerbachian concept of 'man' is not derived from the 'senses', nor from any science, but from the philosophical inversion of Hegel. No matter how much richer and more philosophically defensible this conception of human essence is than the individualist philosophical conception of the eighteenth century it remains a philosophical concept, and as such it stands in contradiction to Feuerbach's own intellectual programme.

In case this rather schematic discussion of Feuerbach seems to be a digression, I should come to the point of it. The point of it is that there exists at least one text by Marx which takes the form of a realisation of Feuerbach's programme: this is the *Economic and Philosophic Manuscripts* of 1844. In these *Manuscripts* Marx investigates the writings of the French and English Socialists, and also the principal political economists. The extraordinary achievement of the *Manuscripts* is to 'comprehend' these diverse intellectual sources through the Feuerbachian 'system' of concepts in such a way that political economy and socialism themselves appear as 'moments' in a Feuerbachian self-realisation of the species-being. In the justly famous passages on 'estranged labour', Marx argues that the private property whose laws are described, but not 'comprehended' in political economy is merely a manifestation of human self-alienation. In production, the product of the worker is set over and against him as an alien object, and he is separated even from his own productive activity. The self-alienation of the economic activity expressed in theoretical form by the political economists is the analogue of the religious self-alienation exposed by Feuerbach:

> Just as in religion the spontaneous activity of the human imagination, of the human brain and the human heart, operates on the individual independently of him – that is, operates as an alien, divine or diabolical activity – so is the worker's activity not his spontaneous activity. It belongs to another; it is the loss of his self.[12]

This alienated labour, which also involves a separation between man and man, and also of man from himself, can only be understood as 'alienated' by contrast to what it is an 'alienation' from, or 'denial' of: the human essence, or species-life. The very concept of 'alienation' is logically inseparable from some form of philosophical humanism, and from the (historicist) conception of history as the process of self-realisation of this human essence. The content which Marx gives to the notion of human essence – the species-life – richer than the content given to it by Feuerbach. The relationship between 'man' and nature, central to Feuerbach, is expressed by Marx in the notion of nature as 'man's' 'inorganic body'. 'Man' as a species is engaged in collectively, freely, and creatively 'humanising' nature. This 'humanisation' involves material, productive transformation of nature, but also intellectual and artistic 'production':

> The whole character of a species – its species-character – is contained in the character of its life activity; and free, conscious activity is man's species-character. . . . The object of labour is, therefore, the objectification of man's species-life: for he duplicates himself not only, as in consciousness, intellectually, but also actively, in reality, and therefore he sees himself in a world that he has created. In tearing away from man the object of his production, therefore, estranged labour tears from him his *species-life*, his real objectivity as a member of the species.[13]

Marx's notion of the human 'essence' is also richer than Feuerbach's in that it is filled out with the content of the political doctrine of communism:

> *Communism* as the *positive* transcendence of *private property* as *human self-estrangement*, and therefore as the real *appropriation* of the *human* essence by and for man; communism therefore as the complete return of man to himself as a *social* (i.e. human) being – a return accomplished consciously and embracing the entire wealth of previous development. This communism, as fully developed naturalism, equals humanism, and as fully developed humanism equals naturalism: it is the *genuine* resolution of the conflict between man and nature and between man and man – the true resolution of the strife between existence and essence, between objectification and self-confirmation, between freedom and necessity, between the individual and the species. Communism is the riddle of history solved, and it knows itself to be this solution.[14]

The fundamental theoretical unity of Hegel, Feuerbach and the Marx of the 1844 *Manuscripts* is at its most transparent in this passage. As

Marx himself recognises, both in his preface to the *Manuscripts*, and in the final fragment ('Critique of the Hegelian Dialectic and Philosophy as a Whole'), the *Manuscripts* are an extension and 'fulfilment' of the method implicit in Feuerbach's inversion of Hegel.[15] Since the verdict on Feuerbach was 'idealist in materialist clothing', so the same verdict must be declared on the Marx of 1844. This is not, of course, to say that the *Manuscripts* are intellectually worthless, or of purely historical interest. Elements of the critiques of Hegel and of the political economists appear in a new form in the later work, and are a lasting contribution. But much more than this, the *Manuscripts* are an ethical-philosophical denunciation of capitalist production and the society based on it of quite exceptional depth and beauty of expression. Moreover, they are a denunciation which has lost none of its vigour and persuasive power in the 130 years that separate us from their composition. Such documents of ideological struggle have a place and importance in the struggles of today no less great than in the Europe of the nineteenth century, but the reader who looks to the *Manuscripts* for a scientific theory of capitalist production, its laws of development, conditions of existence and so on will look in vain.

The claim, then, that Marx's later work is a continuous deepening and extension of the programme set out in the *Manuscripts* of 1844 and other earlier works implies that there is nowhere in Marx's work the elements or foundations of the scientific theory of history – historical materialism – which 'orthodox' Marxism, following Marx and Engels themselves, has claimed to find there. If Feuerbach's 'inversion' of Hegel is merely Hegel back on his feet, if Marx of 1844 is merely Feuerbach on Hegel's feet, exploring new territory; and if the later Marx is merely the Marx of 1844 but older, then all remain within the confines of Hegel's idealist dialectic and speculative philosophy of history. The pretensions to science are mere rhetoric.

But Marx himself, only months after composing the *Manuscripts* reappears, in the *German Ideology* and the *Theses on Feuerbach*, as a critic of Feuerbach. Much later, in the 1859 preface to his *Contribution to the Critique of Political Economy*, Marx is able to refer to the *German Ideology* as the text in which he and Engels achieved self-clarification in the attempt to settle 'accounts with our former philosophical conscience'.[16] Also in that preface Marx lays stress on the importance of the empirical studies of economic questions to which he was driven for his own intellectual development. He also mentions his critical re-examination of Hegel's philosophy of law, which enquiry led him to 'the conclusion that neither legal relations nor political forms could be comprehended whether by themselves or on the basis of a so-called general development of the human mind, but that on the contrary they originate in the material conditions of life, the totality of which Hegel, following the example of the English and French thinkers of the eighteenth century, embraces with the term "Civil Society" '.[17] In other words, the inversion of Hegel? But immediately after this, Marx adds the clause '. . . that the anatomy of this civil society, however, has to be sought in political economy'. What are the consequences of searching for the 'anatomy' of civil society in political economy? If the search is a Feuerbachian one, then the consequence is the discovery of 'alienated labour' as the source and consequence of the private property whose laws are the object of political economy. But this extension of Feuerbach to a new field of enquiry, from Feuerbach's preoccupation with religion and speculative philosophy to the sphere of economic relations, if it is to be achieved rigorously, demands more than an extension of the same method. Whereas religious self-alienation is the creation of a superhuman fantasy-object, economic self-alienation is the creation of a 'superhuman' material and social reality. Alienated labour is at the root of an alienated form of economic life. In so far as religious and philosophical self-alienation takes the form of fantasy, of dream, and hence of 'error', it might seem that liberation from it might be achieved by dissolution of the fantasy, by the critical exposure of the 'error'. But an alienated form of economic life cannot, in this way, be understood as an 'error' to be dissipated by criticism. Only the abolition of estranged labour itself, together with its manifestation in private property – in short, the emancipation of the workers and the establishment of a communist order – can transcend alienation as Marx now understands it. The problem is not one of criticism and understanding, but of revolutionary practice.

The new significance which Marx's attempt at a rigorous extension of Feuerbach forces him to give to the concept of 'practice' becomes the means by which he effects his critique of Feuerbach, and a condition for his own intellectual transition. The recurring theme of the *Theses on Feuerbach* is the latter's failure to 'grasp the significance of "revolutionary", of "practical-critical", activity'.[18] Further, this new conception of alienation and its transcendence as involving 'contradictions', antagonisms internal to material, social life itself, which require revolutionary practice for their resolution has implications for the analysis of Feuerbach's own chosen territory, the critique of religious self-alienation.

> Feuerbach starts out from the fact of religious self-alienation, of the duplication of the world into a religious world and a secular one. His work consists in resolving the religious world into its secular basis. But that the secular basis detaches itself

> from itself and establishes itself as an independent realm in the clouds can only be explained by the cleavages and self-contradictions within this secular basis. The latter must, therefore, in itself be both understood in its contradiction and revolutionised in practice.[19]

But if what 'moves' history is now revolutionary practice, transforming an internally contradictory reality, this practice must be the practice of particular individuals, groups and classes, under definite organisational forms, and with specific strategy and tactics. And if this is what moves history, then it cannot be the contradiction between men as they exist and the essence or nature of 'man' as some abstract goal of history which is the motor force of historical change. This conclusion (unlike much else in that text) is expressed with great clarity in the *German Ideology*.

> The individuals, who are no longer subject to the division of labour, have been conceived by the philosophers as an ideal, under the name 'man'. They have conceived the whole process which we have outlined as the evolutionary process of 'man', so that at every historical stage 'man' was substituted *for the individuals and shown as the motive force of history*. The whole process was thus conceived as a process of the self-estrangement of 'Man'. . . . Through this inversion . . . it was possible to transform the whole of history into an evolutionary process of consciousness.[20]

In short, the philosophical humanism of Feuerbach and of the Marx of 1844 is here exposed by Marx as a form of idealism. The significance of this recognition is given added emphasis by three short, paradoxical sentences of the sixth thesis on Feuerbach. 'Feuerbach resolves the religious essence into the *human* essence. But the human essence is no abstraction inherent in each single individual. *In its reality it is the ensemble of the social relations*.'[21] But the 'ensemble of social relations' is precisely what is transformed in history. If the human essence is identical with the ensemble of social relations then it must be transformed in history. How then can it be the universal aim and motive force of history? It can't: the 'human essence' disappears into a new conception of history as 'ensembles of social relations' and their transformations. Without the concept of human essence its correlative concept of self-alienation, and the whole Hegelian historical dialectic lose their theoretical place.

However, this decisive theoretical shift away from philosophical humanism, whose symptoms I have tried to identify in these works of 1844–5, does not result in the sudden abandonment by Marx and Engels of all elements of their 'former philosophical conscience', nor does it result in the emergence, fully formed, of a scientific theory of history. A number of questions, then, need to be posed:

1 Why do elements of the earlier 'philosophical anthropology' remain despite the theoretical critique they have already received by 1845?
2 What are the basic concepts of the new conception of history which emerges in the course of the critique of this philosophical anthropology?
3 What, if any, role remains for philosophy?
4 In so far as scientific status is attributed to the new non-philosophical knowledge of history, on the basis of what conception of the nature of scientific knowledge is this attribution made?

Of course, no full answer can be given here to any of these questions, but each requires at least some attention. First, let us presuppose, for the moment, the justice of the claim that there is in the later work of Marx and Engels, and those who have continued this work, the elements of a scientific theory of history. It does not at all follow from this that every text written by Marx and Engels after 1845, from private letters, marginal notes, historical analyses and political manifestoes to theoretical critiques of other thinkers and extended expositions of their own doctrines, must be regarded as all reducible to a single function: contributions to the science of history. To do this would be to ignore the involvement of Marx and Engels in political activity and in ideological struggle, it would be to fail to recognise what Marx and Engels, as educators and as polemicists rarely failed to recognise: that different audiences, with different needs and interests, require different responses from those who would communicate with them. The necessity for ideological struggle did not end with the 1844 *Manuscripts*, and so neither did the need for ideological texts, such as those manuscripts (one can conduct an ideological struggle with oneself!). But 'humanist' and Hegelian forms of expression occur even in texts such as *Capital*, and these cannot be explained away in this manner. First, *Capital* itself is not internally homogeneous. It contains a good deal by way of illustrative historical material and asides on particular political economists, as well as occasional passages of ethical denunciation reminiscent of the 1844 *Manuscripts*, but there are, as we shall see, passages of central importance to Marx's argument which are expressed in the Hegelian terminology.[22] There are, consistent with the approach I have adopted so far, two ways of interpreting these: (*a*) as areas of theoretical weakness in Marx 'patched up' so to speak, by the intervention of philosophical concepts, and (*b*) as merely an old terminology which does service for a new concept not yet fully articulated, or given its proper terminological recognition.[23]

Historical materialism

Our second question, as to the basic concepts of Marx's supposed scientific theory of history, is one which is in a sense ancillary to the main topic of this chapter, Marx's philosophy. Nevertheless, it is of some help in trying to get clear about Marx's philosophical theory of scientific knowledge if we have some prior understanding of the theoretical system whose claim to scientific status was to be defended in terms of that philosophical theory (of course, this relation of elucidation is reciprocal). Unfortunately for the later history of Marxism, there exist few attempts by either Marx or Engels to give a systematic exposition of their theory of history. The nearest thing to this is the 1859 preface to which I have already referred, but it is defective in a number of respects, not least its extreme brevity and imprecision. Marx's most extended theoretical work is his *Capital*. Only the first volume of this, however, was actually prepared by Marx for publication, and its scope is restricted to the analysis of capitalist economic production. Any attempt at systematic elaboration of a theoretical system, then, must 'unearth' concepts and relations between concepts from a host of writings, many of them inconsistent, in which those concepts are put to work, but relatively rarely explicitly defined. Nicos Poulantzas has provided a threefold classification of the concepts specific to historical materialism which, despite its preliminary nature, provides some helpful clarification.[24] First, historical materialism is a theory of history on condition that certain of its concepts are trans-historical – that is to say, they have some valid applicability in all historical forms of society.[25] Such concepts include these of mode of production, raw materials, instruments, and relations of production, property relations and relations of 'real appropriation', labour and social formation, (possibly) the concepts of a theory of transition between social formations, and the concepts of the different structural levels within a mode of production and social formation (the political, the ideological and the economic). Poulantzas calls the theoretical structure formed by these concepts the 'general theory' of historical materialism.

Second, there are the 'particular' theories whose concepts provide the theoretical analysis of each of the 'modes of production' (primitive communist, ancient, Asiatic, feudal, capitalist, socialist) identified in the general theory. The concepts of some of these 'modes of production' have hardly more than gestural status in Marx's work,[26] whilst the capitalist mode of production receives enormous theoretical attention. The 'particular theory' of the capitalist mode of production includes as constituent concepts the concept of commodity, the distinction between use and exchange value, the distinction between labour and labour-power, the concepts of money and of capital itself, the distinctions between variable and constant capital, and between value and surplus value, the concepts of profit, interest and capitalist ground-rent, and also the concepts of the non-economic (ideological and political) structures characteristic of the capitalist mode of production – trade unions, political parties, a definite range of forms of state, a specific form of family and so on. Finally, there are what Poulantzas calls 'regional theories' – theories of the particular structural 'levels' or 'regions' within each mode of production. An example, concepts pertaining to the economic level of the capitalist mode of production, would be the set of concepts from 'the concept of commodity' to 'capitalist ground-rent' above.[27]

Finally, three other theoretical levels should be added, to complete Poulantzas's classification. First, intermediate in degrees of abstraction between Poulantzas's 'general theory' and 'particular theory' are certain concepts which are applicable to more than one type of mode of production or social formation, but which are not absolutely universal in their applicability. These include the concepts of class and class-struggle, the concept of the state (which is defined, in Marxism, in terms of social class) and, in some versions of Marxism, the concept of ideology. It may also be argued that there does not exist, and cannot exist, any general theory of transition from social formations of one type to those of another (general theory of revolutions), but even if this argument is valid it does not rule out the possibility of a theory of transitions of one type (e.g. a theory of the transition from capitalism to socialism, or from feudalism to capitalism). If such theories do exist their concepts also belong to this intermediate level of abstraction. Second, there is the most concrete level – the giving of what Lenin called 'concrete analyses of the current situation'. This is the level at which the theoretical apparatus of historical materialism is put to work in the explanation of particular historical events and processes. That concepts of all these levels of abstraction are at work in the analyses that Marx gives in his *18th Brumaire*, and *Class Struggles in France*, and that Lenin, Trotsky and others gave of the revolutionary process in Russia and elsewhere is hardly disputable. But nowhere in the corpus of Marxist literature is there any sustained attempt to give theoretical expression to the logical conditions, rules and constraints involved in the employment of these concepts in concrete analysis. This may be compared with the precise and quantified knowledge which exists, for example, in the application of the kinetic theory of gases to particular cases, concerning the degree of difference between the theoretically established behaviour of the 'ideal gas' and the behaviour of particular gases in particular temperature-ranges, etc. It is in this area, in my view, that much important philosophical work in Marxism remains to be done.

Finally, there is a third level of abstraction which is not easy to fit into Poulantzas's classification. This level consists of concepts of a very abstract kind which, though they take different forms in different sciences, do occur in all sciences. These are concepts such as 'structure', 'cause', 'mechanism', 'existence' and a few more. It has been argued by Althusser, and other 'anti-humanist' interpreters of Marx, that Marx's concept of the social totality, the 'social formation', is the concept of a complex, or 'over-determined', 'structure in dominance'.[28] That is to say, it is a system of relations within which several sub-systems are combined. Within the system as a whole certain elements predominate in determining the relations within and between the component systems, though each sub-system retains its own 'relative autonomy'. 'Contradictions' may exist within and between structures. This is Althusser's way of interpreting the 'orthodox' Marxist claims that with respect to the 'superstructures' (ideology, politics) the economic structure is 'determinant in the last instance' in any social formation, and that, nevertheless, each of the structures has its own 'effectivity' and relative autonomy. Clearly this whole account of the structure of a social formation involves a notion of causality which is quite inconsistent with the positivist account of causes in terms of antecedent conditions and general laws connecting phenomena. It has much more in common with the 'generative mechanism' conception of causality which I elaborated in chapters 3 and 4. Just as the theoretical explanation of relations between such variables as pressure, volume and temperature of gases in terms of a generative mechanism (states of motion of molecules) in the kinetic theory involves the presupposition of a class (or classes) of theoretical entities, so it is in the case of this Marxian type of structural explanation. The concept of structure of the capitalist mode of production, for instance, in terms of which Marx explains certain general features of the dominant ideology under capitalism,[29] has a status in Marxist theory analogous to the concept of the internal structure of an 'ideal gas' in the kinetic theory:[30] both refer not to real but to 'abstract' entities, constructed by abstraction from theoretically irrelevant characteristics of particular cases (particular gas-samples, particular social formations).[31] The general form of explanatory mechanism, in both cases, can then be applied (in combination with other elements of theoretical and concrete knowledge) to the structural explanation of particular real cases, by a process of approximation (cf. the enormously complex structural explanations of particular political events and processes which Marx gives in writings such as *Class Struggles in France* and the *18th Brumaire*). The point to be made here, though, is that just as there is in the case of the kinetic theory of gases a distinction to be made between abstract theoretical entities (the point-masses and Newtonian motions of the molecules constituting the 'ideal gas') and real theoretical entities (the real molecules, which may be multi-atomic, have a finite diameter and so on), so there is in Marx's theory a distinction between the abstract theoretical entity (the capitalist mode of production whose structure is analysed in *Capital*) and real theoretical entities (for example, the capitalist mode of production in the Russia of 1917, in complex combination with other modes of production, and subject to an international distribution of capital, etc. all of which 'determinations' give it its distinctive characteristics as a specific instantiation of the abstract concept).[32] Not all concepts of historical materialism, of course, refer either to real or to abstract theoretical entities. Some concepts, the concept of 'production in general' for instance, have a function in the overall articulation of the theory but are merely abstractions which make no reference to any actually existing entity, structure, practice, etc. nor to any hypothesised 'ideal' entity.[33]

Dialectical materialism

There are yet other concepts which might be held by some commentators to belong to this, the most abstract level of concepts constituting Marx's theory of history. These are the concepts and principles of the 'dialectic'. In Engels's classic statements[34] of the materialist dialectic, these concepts and the laws stated in terms of them constitute a separate discipline – dialectical materialist philosophy – and so are not, strictly speaking, concepts belonging to the theory of history at all. But the peculiar nature of this – supposedly 'scientific' – philosophy is such that it gives us the laws of motion, of development, of things in general. The 'laws' of the dialectic – the 'negation of negation', the unity and 'interpenetration of opposites', the 'transformation of quantity into quality' – are laws not just of one domain but of all nature. Since, on the materialist view, nature includes human history and human thought, the concepts and laws of the dialectic must apply, as the principles of development and change, in nature, history and thought. Dialectical materialism, so understood, involves the conception of the relationship between philosophy and the sciences which I discussed in chapter 1, under the heading the 'master-scientist', or 'metaphysical' conception. But Engels opposes it to metaphysics, arguing that metaphysical thinking, like common-sense thinking, is static, and governed by formal logical laws such as the laws of identity and non-contradiction: 'For him [the metaphysician] a thing either exists or does not exist; a thing cannot at the same time be itself and something else. Positive and negative absolutely exclude one another; cause and effect stand in a rigid antithesis one to the other.'[35] Dialectical thought, by contrast, recognises that all things are constantly in motion, coming into being and ceasing to exist, that no distinctions are fixed, that contradictions are universal, and so on. It does not seem to bother Engels that these 'discoveries' were the result of the method of speculative philosophy, and are only externally applied by him to the results of the natural sciences. Nor does it seem to matter to Engels that the dialectic of the finite, material world whose contradictoriness Hegel demonstrates in the passages from which Engels derives his dialectic forms part of an argument the conclusion of which is that the finite, material world has no independent existence.[36] As the Italian Marxist philosopher, Lucio Colletti, has demonstrated, the 'laws of the dialectic' extracted by Engels, Lenin and Plekhanov from Hegel's *Science of Logic* cannot logically be separated from their conclusion: an idealist philosophy of nature.[37] It is after all, relatively easy to understand how two propositions ('This is the final crisis of capitalism'/'This is not the final crisis of capitalism') may contradict one another, but somewhat less easy to understand what may be meant by saying that opposite electrical charges, opposite physical forces, chemical association and dissociation, and so on 'contradict' one another;[38] less easy to understand, that is, unless one interprets nature itself as the 'postulate' of thought in contradiction with itself. In rejecting the formal logical 'laws' of identity and non-contradiction as metaphysical, Engels is siding with Hegel's completion of the idealism implicit in seventeenth- and eighteenth-century metaphysics not just against 'pre-critical' metaphysics and 'common sense' but also against science itself.[39]

By contrast with Colletti, Louis Althusser has been much more equivocal on the status of 'dialectical materialism' as a universal philosophical science of the development of all things. Whilst criticising Engels's conception of the dialectic he has nevertheless retained until relatively recently a fundamentally similar notion in his own work.[40] But whatever his position on the status of Engels's 'master-science', Althusser has also argued that the 'structure' of the dialectic must be transformed if it is to be adequate to grasp the relations between the elements of a social formation and its 'movement'. Althusser follows Mao Tse-tung in emphasising the complexity of the social totality, and of its processes of change.[41] History does not 'move' as a result of the 'simple' opposition of contradictions and their supersession.[42]

A particular social formation at a particular time will be 'inhabited' by a multiplicity of contradictions, in complex reciprocal relations of dominance and subordination, each determining to some degree the character of the whole, and 'reflecting' in itself, in turn, the character of the whole; (contradictions are, in this sense, 'overdetermined').[43] It is thus possible to distinguish a principal from the secondary contradictions and, in each contradiction, because of its 'uneven development', between a principal and a secondary aspect ('term'). Althusser's own additions, as well as 'over-determination' include 'fusion', 'rupture', 'displacement' and others.[44]

In the thoughts of Mao and Althusser, then, the dialectic has found a new respect for the material reality (social formations and their histories) to which it is applied, and has accordingly 'changed its structures'. But there is as yet no clearly defined function, still less set of criteria of validity, for this range of concepts, resting as they do on a range of barely stated metaphors drawn from psycho-analysis, linguistics and logic. The investigation of these texts by Mao and Althusser yields one conclusion at least: where all this talk of 'the dialectic' makes any sense at all (which is by no means everywhere), it is an inadequate and often dogmatic attempt to give theoretical expression to the concept of historical causality which is present in the historical writings of Marx, Engels, Lenin and Mao himself.

In one sense, Colletti's critique of the dialectic is more thorough-going than Althusser's. He reinstates, as a hallmark of materialism, the Kantian distinction between 'contradiction' and 'real opposition'. There are no contradictions in reality, only in thought.[45] Counter-acting forces, tendencies, processes, etc. in nature are properly called 'real oppositions', a concept in no sense reducible to that of contradiction. Forces and processes in nature that are opposed to each other are separate and independent; they have no dialectical 'unity' or 'identity' with one another. Marxism can go ahead as a scientific theory of history, without the burden of a 'logic' opposed in principle to the logic of the other sciences (or rational discourses in general, for that matter). But in a recent article[46] Colletti has argued that in Marx's analysis of capitalism there is, indeed, to be found the work of the positive scientist, who deals with the same reality as the other political economists, explains it, like they do, as a law-governed reality, and obeys the logical 'law' of non-contra-diction in doing so. But there is also to be found Marx the philo-sopher for whom the 'reality' of capitalism is an inverted, fetishised, alienated form of appearance of social relations. The philosopher Marx is able to identify dialectical contradictions – 'separations' between opposites (use-value/value) whose 'essence' is to be united. This is no restoration of dialectical materialism: dialectical contra-diction is not a universal feature of reality; on the contrary it is specific to capitalism, which is an 'inverted' reality. However, the reality of capitalism, as Colletti concedes, is an 'inverted' reality only from the perspective of a philosophical theory, and it is science not philosophy that is 'the only means of gaining knowledge of the world'.[47] The conclusion of Colletti's argument, then, is: in so far as

Marxism is scientific (and, that it can only be scientific when it treats of alienated, fetished social forms seems to be implicit in Colletti's argument) it obeys the 'law' of non-contradiction, and its oppositions are 'real oppositions' with nothing to do with any 'dialectical unity'. In so far as the dialectic has any place in the Marxist theory of history the theory is philosophical, and gives us no knowledge, in the proper sense.

This conclusion, it seems to me, besides offering very limited prospects for any proposed 'science' of history, simply fails to grapple with the characteristics of historical causality which have given rise to a hundred years of dialectical 'mumbo-jumbo'. Forces in opposition in society – whether classes or structures – are grasped with the same elementary concept of 'real opposition' as will do for opposed forces in nature. Marx, as Colletti himself recognises, takes the difference between production as production of values, and production as production of use-values (utilities), as the source and genesis of the central 'contradictions' of capitalism: that between forces and social relations of production, and also the 'antagonism' between the classes (workers and capitalists) formed on the basis of these contradictory structures. Here, too, is the basis for the explanation of the genesis of crises in terms of complex combinations of these contradictions with others in a single social formation. Now, Colletti is right in arguing that the classes, tendencies, processes and structures in opposition here are properly to be regarded as distinct from each other and as related as real antagonists, and not as 'contradictories'. But equally, there is a point in the dialectical materialists' identification of these opposites as 'identical' or as forming a unity, and this point can be expressed without any 'ascent' into philosophy. First, the theoretical concepts in terms of which the opposing classes and tendencies are specified and distinguished are in each case defined at least partly in terms of one another (the working class in terms of the capitalist class, and vice versa. This is part of what Mao means when he says: 'Without the bourgeoisie there would be no proletariat; without the proletariat, there would be no bourgeoisie').[48] Second, what makes this necessary is the theoretical postulate that the opposing classes, tendencies, processes, etc. share a common causal condition of existence: the structure of the capitalist mode of production. The mechanism which generates the classes also generates their antagonism. The existence of the opposed classes and their antagonism is conditioned by the existence of a totality of which they are (distinct) aspects. The concept of causality at work here, again, has much in common with the 'generative-mechanism' concept of causality, but is distinctive in that the 'mechanism' generates antagonistic processes and tendencies. There are, however, partial parallels in the physiology of development (for example in the production of hormones with countervailing effects) and in the physiology of the nervous system (sympathetic and parasympathetic systems). The exploration of analogies between the types of causality involved in these cases could yield results of methodological relevance to historical methodology, so long as Durkheim's warnings are taken to heart.[49]

Philosophy and the 'science of history'

So far in this chapter I have argued for an interpretation of Marx and Engels (and also have tried to defend the position so interpreted) which I stated somewhat dogmatically in chapter 1. According to this view, the production of a genuine knowledge of history (or any other field of enquiry), that is to say, the production of a science,. deprives the speculative philosophies which have previously occupied that domain of their 'medium of existence'. Thus, the 'end of philosophy' which is proclaimed in certain of the works of Marx and Engels is the end of speculative philosophy masquerading as knowledge. The 'end of philosophy' thesis does not, as I argued in chapter 1, imply an end to philosophy in all its forms and types. If the new 'science' of history is to attain the status of a science, then it requires the standards and criteria of science to be applied in its construction. Implicit in the standards that Marx and Engels apply to their theory construction and critiques of other works,[50] and explicit in their defences of the scientific status of historical materialism, is a theory of knowledge and of science. As we have seen, in so far as 'dialectical materialism' has any right to be taken seriously at all, it reduces to the attempt to construct a concept of historical causality. Such an attempt has at least a 'family resemblance' to more 'orthodox' work in the philosophy of science. But there exists a number of texts by Marx and Engels which are explicitly devoted to the philosophical analysis of the nature of knowledge and explanation, and methodological problems of a very general kind.

I shall distinguish, within the Marxian theory of knowledge, two distinct, but conceptually connected aspects: the theory of ideology, and the theory of science.

The theory of ideology

Much of Marx and Engels's discussion of ideology is metaphorical in character; ideologies are 'fantasies', 'illusions', 'reflections', 'inverted images', 'echoes' of material life. Many, but not all of these metaphors contain two theses about ideology. One thesis concerns its status as a 'reality', the other its status as knowledge – its cognitive status. I shall deal separately with these two aspects of ideology since, although related, they are distinct, and were regarded as such by Marx and Engels.[51] First, then, the status of ideology as a 'reality'. The overwhelming weight of the metaphors I have quoted, and others like them, is to suggest that for Marx there are one-way causal links only between 'material life' and ideology. That ideology is an 'insubstantial epiphenomenon', a reflection which depicts but does not affect the course of real historical life. It is significant, however, that such formulations are most common in the texts which are most in the grip of the strict inversion of Hegel (especially the *German Ideology*): 'materialism' consists in asserting that 'thoughts' are the phenomenon, material life their essence, as against the idealists' assertion of the converse. The later formulations, 'determination in the last instance' and 'relative autonomy of the superstructures' are clearly attempts to correct these lapses into economic reductionism.

However, the relationship between ideology and class struggle which Marx and Engels describe in the *German Ideology* itself is quite inconsistent with the 'epiphenomenon' conception of ideology. First, they distinguish a stage at which ideas are 'directly interwoven' with and are the 'direct efflux' of material life from a stage, consequent upon the division of labour, at which consciousness can 'really flatter itself that it is something other than consciousness of existing practice'.[52] At this latter stage, society is class-divided, a part of the ruling class making the 'perfecting of the illusion of the class about itself the chief source of their livelihood'. Both the ruling and the subordinate classes produce ideologies in which their particular interests are represented as identical with the general interest of society, whilst the ideology of the ruling class either disguises or legitimises its domination. Now, two points are clear from this. First, if ideas are, in this sense, weapons in the struggle for political power between social classes, then they cannot be mere epiphenomena. They must have a real existence, in the sense of having some contributory effects on the maintenance or overthrow of a social order. It is in this sense that Marxism contains a 'materialist' conception of ideology: not that ideology is an immaterial effect of material practice, but that it has a material reality of its own. Second, although Marx and Engels separate the status of ideology as 'directly interwoven' with material life, and its status as an 'illusion' created by ideological specialists of the ruling class as characteristic of different historical stages, it does not follow that ideology does not continue to be 'directly interwoven' with material life in the later stages. The distinction Marx and Engels draw here may, in fact, be identified with the distinction I drew in chapter 7 between practical and theoretical ideologies: interwoven with the material practices of a social class is its 'practical ideology' (its ideology in a practical state).

This practical ideology, articulated in a theoretical form is the work of the ideologists of that class, is a weapon in class struggle, and is what I have called a 'theoretical ideology'.

Further, Marx and Engels's discussion of ideology recognises what, I have argued, interpretative sociology cannot coherently theorise: that is, the co-existence in a single social formation of a multiplicity of mutually inconsistent 'symbolic universes' or 'complexes of meaning' (ideologies, or forms of social consciousness). But for Marx and Engels, too, there is a central difficulty. Of these contending forms of social consciousness, one predominates over the others – this is the ideology of the ruling class. The ideas of the ruling class are the dominant ideas because of the ability of the ruling class to 'regulate the production and distribution of the ideas of their age'.[53] This explanation of the domination of the ideas of the ruling class in the sense that partially, at least, they invade the consciousness of the subordinate classes, postulates that this domination derives from the control by the ruling class over the means for the production and distribution of ideas.[54] The theory has several serious weaknesses. First, it readily reduces itself into a form of conspiracy theory, and does not recognise the involvement of the ruling class itself in its own illusions. Second, since the working class does not control the means of production and distribution of ideas, it is hard to see how the ideas of the subordinate classes come to be produced at all; the 'dominant ideology' turns out to be the only ideology. Third, the ideological formation both of individuals and of classes is, on this view, reduced to their passive reception, as 'blank sheets', of ideologies produced by specialists and distributed through specialised apparatuses (the churches, schools and, in our time, the media of mass communications). No recognition is given, in this conception of ideology, to the active involvement of social actors and classes in their own ideological formation, nor to the limits this places on the range of ideological interpretations of social reality which the ideologists of the ruling class present. These interpretations must be adequate to the recognition and negotiation of social life for actors of both ruling and subordinate classes. They must, in other words, have some degree of cognitive effectiveness, they cannot be mere illusions.[55]

A quite different account of the source of ideology in social life and its relation to class domination exists in Marx and Engels's work in tension with this one. The classical sources for this conception are the discussions of the 'fetishism of commodities' and the 'wage-form' in *Capital*, volume 1.[56] In the first case, where independent producers produce for the market, the division of the total useful labour of the society between the different producers is only manifested in the exchange of the commodities they produce, in the market. The social relations between individual producers take on the appearance of relations between things. But this appearance is no mere appearance:

> To the [producers], therefore, the relations connecting the labour of one individual with that of the rest appear, not as direct social relations between individuals at work, *but as what they really are*, material relations between persons and social relations between things.[57]

In the comparable case of the wage-form, the exchange between labourer and capitalist takes on the appearance of the buying and selling of a commodity, labour. But, as Marx shows, 'labour' cannot be regarded scientifically as a commodity. What is really being exchanged is a special property of the labourer which is distinguished from other commodities by the fact that its consumption creates a value greater than its own. This property is labour-power. The discovery of this hidden reality enables us to distinguish within the working day a part during which the labourer works for himself (that part during which he creates a value equivalent to that of his labour-power) and a part during which he produces value for the capitalist (surplus value). In short, what the wage-form 'disguises', and the concept of labour-power 'reveals', is the essential relation of the exploitation of the labourer by the capitalist.

In both these examples Marx distinguishes between phenomenal forms of social reality, and 'essential' or 'real' relations underlying them. The phenomenal forms act as a kind of 'disguise' or 'veil', so that forms of consciousness based upon phenomenal forms necessarily misconceive the real relations:

> This phenomenal form, which makes the actual relation invisible, and, indeed, shows the direct opposite of that relation, forms the basis of all the juridical notions of *both labourer and capitalist*, of all the mystifications of the capitalist mode of production, of all its illusions as to liberty, of all the apologetic shifts of the vulgar economists.[58]

On this conception, then, ideology has its source in the forms of appearance of social life itself. The extent of the defectiveness of ideology, as knowledge, is a consequence of the extent to which these forms of appearance mask or disguise the real relations whose appearances they are.

This conception of ideology, too, has its weaknesses. First, the basic conceptions of social actors of both the major classes of the capitalist mode of production (in this example) have their source in the appearance of that social/economic form itself. Ideologies, then, are not the characteristics of social classes, but of modes of production. The problem of the mechanism by which the dominant class maintains the domination of its ideas is solved 'at a stroke', at the cost of rendering the 'dominant' ideology the only ideology in each mode of production. Second, the distinction 'essential relations/phenomenal forms' is an example of Marx's 'coquetry' with Hegel's terminology, and its precise theoretical meaning and function in Marx's text remains undefined. Third, this conception of ideology has deleterious consequences for any theory of 'science' constructed on its basis. The strikingly similar conception of 'pre-notions' in Durkheim led there to the positing of an empiricist act of rejection of presuppositions in favour of direct perceptual contact with reality, as a means of acquiring knowledge.[59] In Marx, the problem is sometimes presented as one of 'stripping away' the mystical veil, of uncovering the disguise, to reveal naked reality underneath. This way of posing the problem fails to theorise the labour of production of new concepts which science involves, as Marx himself recognises elsewhere. At other times, it seems that only history will give us genuine knowledge, in providing us with forms of social reality which are 'transparent', and in which the disparity between essence and appearance does not arise.[60] This, too, is quite inconsistent with Marx's own project in *Capital* (i.e. the attempt to produce a scientific knowledge of capital from 'within' capitalism).

The theory of science

I have space to comment briefly on only two of Marx's explicit texts on scientific methodology. The first is a section of the *German Ideology* in which Marx and Engels discuss historical methodology, and the second is a passage from the introduction to the *Grundrisse*, in which Marx discusses the method of political economy.[61] The theory of scientific knowledge given in the *German Ideology* is defective in several respects, and is by no means an expression of the 'final' position of Marx and Engels, but it is nevertheless a theory of more sophistication than is generally assumed.[62] It may be conveniently summarised in the form of six theses, in addition to the thesis I have already discussed (that speculative philosophies are the predecessors of sciences and lose their 'medium of existence' when sciences are founded). The six theses are:

1 The positive science of history is the 'representation (*Darstellung*) of the practical activity, of the practical process of development of men'.[63]

2 This representation, or depiction, consists in the observation and arrangement of historical material, under the guidance of certain

'premises', which are themselves to be 'made evident' by the study of the material life of each historical epoch.[64]

3 Premises, in this sense, are the 'axioms' or 'first principles' of the theoretical system of history. They are asserted as necessary truths (e.g. 'men *must* be in a position to live in order to "make history" ')[65] which are substantive, yet which do not stand in need of empirical evidence. They do, however, need to be made evident by actual study of each epoch, and are asserted in conjunction with historical 'illustrations'.

4 Marx and Engels also use the term 'premises' to refer to 'starting-points' in the real world from which the concrete study of history must proceed. These 'premises' are basic facts of social life: 'the real individuals, their activity and the material conditions under which they live . . .'.[66] These premises – the 'given', the 'raw data' – of scientific historical investigation can be 'verified in a purely empirical way', and are 'empirically perceptible'.[67]

5 The materialist method differs from that of the empiricists for whom history is a 'collection of dead facts'.[68]

6 (*a*) The materialist method is to be contrasted with philosophy in that it is not speculative, starting instead with observable and verifiable facts.
(*b*) Another contrast with philosophy is that its premises 'govern' empirical investigation without thereby providing a 'recipe or schema . . . for neatly trimming the epochs of history'.[69]

I have space for a brief commentary only on these theses. First, theses 4 and 6(*a*) have appeared to some as sufficient to brand Marx's whole theory of knowledge here as empiricist. Marx himself (see thesis 5) would not have agreed. For Marx, sense-perception was not a 'theory-neutral' arbiter of competing propositions and theories. The Marx of the 1844 *Manuscripts* had only recently written that the 'forming of the five senses is a labour of the entire history of the world down to the present' and, in a magnificent formulation, the 'senses have therefore become directly in their practice *theoreticians*'.[70] Second, theses 3 and 4 imply Marx's recognition of two of the levels of abstraction in the theory of history which I distinguished above (the level of 'general theory' and that of 'concrete historical analysis').[71] The point of theses 4 and 6(*a*) is to be understood as the denial that *a priori* reasoning or speculation can yield knowledge at the level of concrete analysis.

The status of the 'premises' which are the subject of thesis 3 and which belong to the 'general theory' of history is less clear. They do not require empirical verification, and so may be regarded as *a priori* (though synthetic). However, they do not constitute a rigid schema developed independently of historical study and into which historical facts must be crammed (thesis 6(*b*)). These basic categories and propositions of the theory of history must have their applicability to each historical period demonstrated, though this demonstration will be a theoretical exercise differing from empirical verification of factual statements. The relationship between these basic categories and concrete analysis is that they guide it, rather than being rigidly applied in it.[72]

The second of Marx's methodological texts is the 1857 introduction to the *Grundrisse*. This text is a paradoxical one, and the importance attached to it must be assessed in the knowledge that Marx deliberately suppressed its publication. Early in the introduction Marx sheds more light on the status of the categories of 'general theory' (his 'premises' of the *German Ideology*).

> There are categories which are common to all stages of production and are established by reasoning as general categories; the so-called general conditions of all and any production, however, are nothing but abstract conceptions which do not define any of the actual historical stages of production.[73]

Marx is here asserting that such general concepts have no referential function. He is also saying, nevertheless, that 'production in general is an abstraction, but a sensible abstraction'.[74] The *a priori* character of the 'premises' of historical materialism is again brought out – they are established by reasoning. Also, 'production without them is inconceivable'.[75] Again, though, Marx argues that even such abstract categories as these must have their validity established in each epoch by actual studies. This process is not a process of empirical verification; rather, general concepts are 'brought to light' by 'comparison', each concept being itself a 'multifarious compound comprising divergent categories'.[76] The point of Marx's denial of any referential function to concepts such as 'production in general' is that it is through giving it a referring function that the political economists smuggle in characteristics of bourgeois production as universal characteristics of production.

In the third part of the introduction ('The Method of Political Economy')[77] Marx comes closer to an explicit definition of the scientific method. He begins by distinguishing two sorts of concepts – concrete, complex concepts (e.g. 'population'), and abstract, simple concepts (e.g. 'value', 'money'). Concepts of these two levels of abstraction are linked by the processes of 'analysis' and 'synthesis'.[78] However, these processes are not symmetrical. Marx says that the method of political economy at its inception was to take complex concepts as its point of departure, and to move by analysis to simple concepts. Only later were economic systems devised which moved by synthesis from abstract to concrete. What is distinctive about these forms of 'analysis' and 'synthesis' is that, according to Marx, the concrete, complex concepts with which the process starts have a different epistemological status from those with which it ends. The process begins with 'imaginary' complex concepts and ends with scientific ones, the final phase, the synthesis of concrete concepts from simple, abstract ones being characterised by Marx as 'the correct scientific method'.

The whole process is carried out 'by way of reasoning' (thought), ending up with the 'reproduction of the concrete situation'. Marx emphasises the distinction between, on the one hand, the conceptual totalities yielded by synthesis and, on the other, the concrete situation, the reality which they 'reproduce'. This distinction between the real world and its transformations, and the conceptions of it, with their transformations is one of the main points of the text. But Marx's own frequent use of the term 'category' to refer both to concepts and to the realities the concepts denote does not help him in making the point clearly.

The real world remains 'outside and independent of' the intellect, so long as a purely theoretical attitude is adopted, and must be regarded as a precondition of all comprehension. But as well as being a precondition of comprehension, the real world is the point of origin of perception and imagination. Perceptions and images, in turn, are the raw materials which are transformed into concepts in the process of production of those concepts which constitute the knowledge of the real world. Marx also speaks of this transformation as the 'assimilation' of images and perceptions.

A difficulty of interpretation arises here, since Marx speaks of scientific concepts not only as the products of transformations carried out by the intellect, but also as the products of 'historical conditions'. This could easily be taken as a historicist thesis that scientific concepts are merely expressions of the historical epoch in which they appear. However, an interpretation much more in line with the rest of the text is that the process of intellectual transformation which yields scientific concepts as its product itself has historical conditions. Certain theoretical transformations can be carried out under some historical conditions, not under others. Marx gives at least two reasons for this. The first is that the reality denoted by the concept in question, though present in all periods, is only at its fullest development in certain of them. The second is that the reality denoted by the concept may have a number of different forms of existence (e.g. labour, surplus value). A more advanced society will offer a better vantage point for comparing the different forms, and so constructing the concept of their common features.

However, though such concepts have a validity for all epochs (cf. the earlier remarks concerning production) they retain their full validity only under the conditions in which they are produced. This feature of varying 'degrees of validity' of concepts is a striking difference between history (and, perhaps, geology and biology) and the natural sciences. It is a thesis of the utmost importance in Marx's epistemology, underlying his central criticism of classical political economy that it takes 'categories' of bourgeois society as universal and eternal in their application.

9 Towards a materialist theory of knowledge

Introduction

So far, I have attempted to demonstrate the necessary inadequacy of empiricist and positivist philosophies of science, and of social science in particular. I have also argued that their 'humanist' opponents, in so far as they deny the possibility of a 'positivist' science of society, do not succeed in proving the impossibility of a science of society as such. Similaily, their arguments to the effect that social knowledge is quite distinct in kind from knowledge in the physical sciences do not succeed in establishing their conclusion.

Nevertheless, in the course of the critique of positivist and instrumentalist philosophies of the natural sciences, the elements of an alternative were sketched.[1] In Durkheim's *Rules of Sociological Method* were found certain elementary principles of a materialist theory of knowledge and ideology, marred by their combination with empiricist concepts.[2] In the course of the discussion of the concepts of *verstehen* and explanatory understanding, in chapters 6 and 7, were developed the outlines of non-positivist concepts of causality appropriate to the social sciences, and a number of concepts belonging to the theory of ideology.

In chapter 8, the works of Marx and Engels were searched for a theory of knowledge which avoids the defects of the positivist and humanist theories. Some of the characteristics of the theory of history for which the status of scientific knowledge is claimed were discussed, together with a brief commentary on a small number of texts in which Marx and Engels outline their conception of science, ideology and their difference.

In this final chapter, I propose to use a critical discussion of the work of the contemporary anti-humanist Marxist philosopher, Louis Althusser, to sketch the outlines of a materialist theory of knowledge which is defensible against the type of criticisms I have directed against its principal rivals. This will lead me to some concluding remarks about philosophy and its relationship to the sciences.

Materialism in Marx and Durkheim

First a few words about the term 'materialism'. Materialism in its metaphysical sense is the doctrine that the universe consists of 'matter' only: 'thought', 'consciousness' is reduced to the status of mere 'appearance' or 'epiphenomenon'. Materialism in the theory of history has often been interpreted as the thesis that economic life is the sole determinant of social relations and the historical process. The sense in which I use 'materialism' here corresponds to neither of these uses. A first approximation to my use of the term to refer to theories of knowledge can be expressed as follows. A theory of knowledge is materialist if and only if

1 it recognises the reality of the object of knowledge, independent of the 'knowing subject', the process of production of the knowledge, and the knowledge itself;[3]

2 adequacy to the object of knowledge is the ultimate standard by which the cognitive status of thought is to be assessed;

3 it recognises the existence of 'thought', 'ideas', 'knowledge' as realities in their own right;

4 it theorises these realities as not *sui generis* but as the result of underlying causal mechanisms.

These criteria apply to 'knowledge' in the very broad sense including both sciences and ideological forms of consciousness. What I have so far called 'realism' concerns the satisfaction of criteria 1 and 2, and so is closely connected with the concept of materialism. I shall, in the discussion which follows, use these criteria for materialism in the theory of knowledge also as criteria of adequacy for theories of knowledge. In part, these criteria have been implicit in my criticisms of other theories of knowledge and any theory of knowledge which satisfied these criteria would be both non-positivist and non-humanist. I cannot prove that materialism as I have defined it is the only alternative to positivism and humanism, but that it is an alternative should be sufficient to give it some plausibility as the basis of a theory of knowledge, in the light of the difficulties faced by both positivism and humanism. I should stress that materialism as I have defined it consists only in the recognition of several criteria of adequacy in the construction of a theory of knowledge, and it by no means rules out the possibility that more than one theory of knowledge might satisfy these criteria. As to the rational justification of accepting materialism as a source of criteria of adequacy, this question must await the final section of this chapter.

Durkheim's theory of knowledge goes some way towards satisfying the first three criteria although, as I have argued, his way of satisfying the second criterion is defective in that the measure of adequacy to the object of knowledge is the empiricist myth of theory-neutral sensation. Durkheim's theory of knowledge fails to satisfy criterion 4 in the case of scientific knowledge because this is represented as the consequence of a mysterious 'act of will' on the part of the scientist, and in the case of ideology because 'ideas' are the fundamental reality for Durkheim. Nevertheless, Durkheim's thesis of the 'opacity' of social reality with its corollary of distinctions between the 'phenomenal forms' of that reality and the underlying reality itself, and between the 'pre-notions' which are 'practically adequate' to the phenomenal forms and scientific concepts which grasp the realities, is both non-empiricist and non-humanist. As we saw in the latter part of chapter 8, the theories of Marx and Engels concerning both science and ideology are realist in that they satisfy criteria 1 and 2, though not necessarily in a way that is theoretically defensible. The theory of ideology in *Capital* closely resembles that of Durkheim in its main outlines. Social reality is divided into 'essential relations' and 'phenomenal forms'. Ideological notions are based on phenomenal forms, whilst scientific concepts grasp 'real' or 'essential' relations. But for Marx it is 'abstraction', rather than 'sensation' which enables the phenomenal forms to be penetrated 'in thought'. The proliferation of undeveloped metaphors such as 'reflection', 'image', 'representation' in the texts of Marx and Engels imply their acceptance of criterion 2, if their ways of satisfying it are defective. Certain of their metaphors also suggest that Marx and Engels rejected criterion 3 but, as we saw, their theory of the part played by ideology in class-struggle implied acceptance of criterion 3, whilst the concept of science given in the Introduction to the *Grundrisse* as a process of production of knowledge by transformation of concepts from raw materials also implies their acceptance of criterion 3 in respect of science.

With regard to criterion 4 the situation is more complex. As we saw, there are the elements of two theories of ideology in Marx and Engels. In the first, ideologies are the products of specialist ideologues who constitute a fraction of the dominant class. In so far as this is reduced to a 'conspiracy theory' then so far it fails to satisfy criterion 4, though as we shall see it can be elaborated in such a way as to satisfy the criterion. As to the other concept of ideology as a result of the 'phenomenal form' of a mode of production, this satisfies criterion 4 if and only if the 'essence/appearance' relationship specified by Marx is a genuine causal relation, and not an instance of the speculative philosophical use of the contrast.[4] The *German Ideology*, on the other hand, says nothing about the historical-causal conditions for a science of history, though there are occasional references to the causal conditions of the natural sciences. The introduction to the *Grundrisse*, whilst having little to say on this question, does indicate that the production of certain scientific categories is limited to certain historical periods.[5]

It seems, then, that Marx and Engels, implicitly at least, recognised the four criteria for a materialist theory of knowledge which I have advanced. There are, though, several areas of internal difficulty in the way their theory of knowledge, as I have so far presented it, meets or fails to meet these criteria. These areas of difficulty can be distinguished as follows.

1 The essence/phenomena distinction. Does this, in Marx and Engels, mark a causal relationship between specifiable structures and processes, or is it merely the importation of a survival from speculative philosophy?

2 However problem (1) is solved, it must provide also an explanation of how it is that 'phenomenal forms', considered as realities, having certain causal relations with other realities, should also be the forms in which a given mode of production 'presents itself' to the experience of the 'agents' of that mode of production.

3 Whatever explanation is given in (2) must be capable of correcting the implication of this theory of ideology in Marx's work that these 'phenomenal forms' found only one ideology (the dominant ideology = the ideology of the mode of production concerned).

4 If it is conceded that the structures and practices of a single mode of production can generate distinct and antagonistic forms of 'social consciousness' (including what I have called theoretical and practical ideologies), then the mechanism by which one of these is sustained and reproduced as the dominant ideology requires to be specified.

5 If scientific knowledge is to be recognised as a reality, distinct from ideological forms of knowledge, then we need a theory of the mechanism of its production.[6] If, in turn, the empiricist thesis of Durkheim that this consists in a return to 'reality' itself through the medium of sense-experience is rejected as offering no solution, then the theory of the mechanism by which scientific knowledge is produced must involve some theory of the transformation of ideology into science. This latter transformation is the object of Marx's sketchy remarks about 'analysis' and 'synthesis' in the introduction to the *Grundrisse*, but what he says there, of course, in no sense constitutes an adequate theorisation of the problem.

6 If science and ideology are to be theorised as distinct historical

realities, then theoretical criteria need to be established for distinguishing them. Again, there is no satisfactory solution to this in Marx and Engels themselves. The most popular of the several solutions they hint at – the criterion of 'practice' – can be shown, by extension of the arguments I brought against Popper's paradoxically similar position in *The Poverty of Historicism*, to imply the abolition of any science/ideology distinction.[7]

Althusser and ideology

I shall use a critical discussion of the work of Louis Althusser to indicate in a very preliminary way how these problem areas might be tackled. I shall deal with problem areas 1–4, mainly concerned with the theory of ideology, first of all. Problem area 4, the mechanisms which sustain the dominance of the dominant ideology, is indicated in Marx and Engels by their references to control, by the ruling class, of the means of production and distribution of ideas.[8] These indicators are taken up and developed by Althusser in his theory of the ideological state apparatuses (ISAs, for short).[9] Althusser identifies two defects in classical Marxist theories of the state. First, the base/superstructure distinction upon which these theories depend is metaphorical, and there are only the merest beginnings of a theory of the causal relations between the two structures. Secondly, these theories of the state are incomplete in that they conceive it solely as a 'machine' of repressive class-domination through the legal apparatus (courts, police, etc.), armed forces and coercive administrative apparatus. Althusser terms these, collectively, the 'repressive state apparatuses', and argues that their function is, in part, to secure the political conditions (moderation of class-conflict within certain limits) under which another collection of apparatuses – the ideological state apparatuses – can operate. These 'apparatuses' include the educational system, the media of mass communications, the family, the trade unions, political parties and others. These function predominantly 'by ideology' rather than 'by repression', behind the 'shield' provided by the RSAs. Althusser further argues that the theory of the distinction and relationships between base and superstructure in Marxist theory can be developed through an analysis of the role of the superstructures in 'reproduction'. This is a technical term in Marxist theory which refers, primarily, to the necessity, if economic production is to be a continuous process through time, for the raw materials of production, the instruments of production, labour-power itself and, finally, the relations in which production takes place to be replaced or replenished as they are used up, or worn out, or when social agents themselves die. In the capitalist mode of production raw materials, instruments of production and, to some extent, labour-power and the relations of production are reproduced at the level of production itself. But certain aspects of the reproduction of labour-power and of the relationships of production, together with the reproduction of non-economic relations (e.g. the relations constituting the educational system, the political parties, etc. themselves), cannot be achieved solely within the economic system. According to Althusser, the principal non-economic systems – the RSAs and the ISAs – have the function of carrying out these aspects of 'reproduction'. The use of the term 'function' here does not imply that the existence of a 'requirement' which this function fulfils in any sense explains the existence or persistence of the state apparatuses, nor is there any implication that there is any necessity about the fulfilment of this function. Also, in capitalist societies, which are class societies, this 'function' of the reproduction of the relations of production is simultaneously and *ipso facto* the reproduction of the dominance of the dominant class in the mode of production constituted by those relations (i.e. the capitalist class). In this sense the 'function' of the state apparatuses is not to be conceived, as in some functionalist sociologies, as supplying the necessary conditions for 'society' as such, but as supplying the necessary conditions for the persistence of a specific form of *class-domination.*

With respect to the ISAs in particular, Althusser argues that the part they play in the reproduction of labour-power and of social relations in general can be summed up as the 'constitution' of individuals as subjects and their 'interpellation' into positions in the system of social relations. Through participation in 'material practices governed by material rituals which are themselves defined by the material ideological apparatus'[10] each individual becomes constituted as a 'subject' with certain practical attitudes, dispositions, customary habits and, in short, beliefs and ideas about himself, or herself, and his or her relationship to the social system. This ideological formation of individual subjects will involve different apparatuses, rituals and practices, therefore, for individuals destined for different places ('tasks', 'functions') in the system of social relations (cf. segregated educational systems, 'streaming' in schools, the various mechanisms which reproduce the sexual division of labour in the family, schools, political parties, etc.). The ISAs also play a key role in actually distributing social agents to these places (admissions, promotions, qualification, certification and so on).

This, put very schematically and abstractly, is Althusser's development of problem area 4, identified above. It also constitutes part of a theory of ideology which satisfies criterion 3 above as a materialist theory of ideology: ideology is held to have a real 'material' existence in the everyday practices and rituals of each ISA, into which individual social actions are 'inserted'. In short, Althusser utilises the concept of 'practical ideology', which I described in my critique of the Weberian theory of action, to solve one of the central problems in the theory of ideology which I identified, also in chapter 7, as insoluble within either a methodological individualist or, more generally, humanist perspective. Not only is there no special reason to believe that the subjects constituted and distributed by these mechanisms should be constituted so as to 'understand' the mechanisms by which they are constituted but, on the contrary, it is a condition of operation of many of the mechanisms that they are not understood by the subjects they 'constitute'.[11]

However, this theory has a number of obvious weaknesses, and it is seriously incomplete. Althusser's work has not surprisingly, then, been subject to criticism from a variety of sources, including his own 1970 'postscript' to his main article.[12] I shall summarise what seem to me the most pertinent criticisms, and add some of my own. First, and most important, there still is nothing in the basic theoretical structure (apart from certain verbal 'asides') capable of explaining the simultaneous co-existence, within capitalist societies in particular, of a multiplicity of ideological 'universes'. The 'imaginary relation to real conditions of existence' which, in Althusser's view, is represented in the consciousness of every subject who has been constituted by the ISAs will vary in its specific contents according to the destination of that subject. But always, in so far as the ISAs reproduce the relations of production, those variations will be variations under the 'domination' of the basic categories of the ruling ideology. In the learning of certain necessary skills, for instance, individuals are taught the technical operations involved under relations of authority and with disciplines which relate to the ultimate exercise of those skills under specifically capitalist social relations (the learning of medical skills is a currently topical example). But if all this 'reproduction' is reproduction of agents who think and act in terms of the basic categories of the ruling ideology, then how can it come about that there exists in societies of this type a multiplicity of ideologies? In short, Althusser has failed to give any help in problem area 3.

We can begin to see how work in this area might be developed by a second look at Althusser's 'list' of ISAs. There is some dispute as to the legitimacy of including even such 'apparatuses' as the media of communication, educational system and so on in the state, but the theoretical justification for this in the cases of the family, the trade unions and (especially) the working-class political parties[13] is even less clear. In the case of the family, its considerable autonomy, in the capitalist social formation, from centralised control renders its capacity to function as a means of ideological reproduction very insecure and vulnerable.[14] In the cases of the trade union and working-class party 'ISAs', they certainly may be said to contribute to the reproduction of capitalist social relations (and hence the domination of the dominant class) in so far as they formulate the demands of workers in relatively narrow economic terms and are integrated, particularly at the highest levels, with civil service and government; or in so far as they recognise, in theory and practice, the legitimacy of the established forms of political practice (parliamentary elections, cabinet government, limitation of political objectives to 'government' rather than state apparatus as a whole, and so on). But they also exist as instruments of practical struggle on the part of organised workers at the economic and political levels. Not only this, but in most capitalist societies they are looked to by a large proportion of their working-class base not simply as a means of promoting their interests in the existing social order, but also as a means of transition to a new social order. In so far as the trade unions and political parties of the working class embody social practices and rituals (forms of struggle – strikes, occupations, work-ins, machine-breaking etc.; forms of organisation – direct elections, decisions by mass meetings and so on; and even forms of language, forms of address, and so on) which are distinctive, then they can be treated as the material forms of existence of the ideology of the working class.[15] That these practices co-exist in tension with practices which are not distinctive of the working class, and tend towards the reproduction of the ruling ideology in the working class merely demonstrates the existence of class-antagonism within these apparatuses – it is no grounds for reducing them to the status of instruments of the class-domination of the ruling class (to do so would be to neglect the fundamental differences between capitalist societies with a liberal-democratic type of state and those with various forms of authoritarian rule – 'fascist', military dictatorships and so on). Equally, class-struggle can be recognised in those apparatuses – the mass media, the educational system, and so on – which do function predominantly to reproduce the prevailing social relations.

Now, whilst these considerations may have taken us some small way towards a solution of certain problems in problem area 3, they do not begin to help with 1 and 2. Here, it needs to be recognised that ideologies exist not only in the 'practices and rituals' of the churches, schools, colleges, parties and so on, but also in those of the courts, armed services, administrative institutions of the state, and industrial firms and corporations. Ideologies, in their practical forms, are present in all social practices, including economic ones. There is a recognition of this point implicit in Althusser's concluding remark of his postscript to 'Ideology and Ideological State Apparatuses':

> For if it is true that the I.S.A.s represent the *form* in which the ideology of the ruling class must *necessarily* be realised, and

> the form in which the ideology of the ruled class must *necessarily* be measured and confronted, ideologies are not 'born' in the I.S.A.s but from the social classes at grips in the class struggle: from their conditions of existence, their practices, their experience of the struggle, etc.[16]

The different class ideologies, then, have their material existence in the different practices and experiences of the opposed classes. The source of ideologies is therefore to be sought in the conditions of existence of the classes and their practices themselves.[17] That is to say, 'in the last instance', in the economic structure. In short, we are back with problem areas 1 and 2, with the problem of the 'essence/phenomenal forms' distinction, and with the problem of how 'phenomenal forms' can form the basis of more than one ideology. First, in the quotations from *Capital* which I used as sources in reconstructing this 'essence/phenomenal forms' conception of ideology, 'phenomenal forms' figure not as 'mere appearances' but as realities, though realities of a causally secondary kind, relative to the real, or 'essential' relations disguised by them: real social relations are not merely misleading in appearance, but wear a false beard and moustache. In the example of the wage form and that of the commodity form it is an exchange relation which is referred to by the expression 'phenomenal form', and a production relation which is referred to by the expression 'real relation'. Essence and phenomena, then, turn out to be two causally related aspects of the economic structure of the capitalist mode of production. Moreover, this is a causal relation which Marx has already grappled with in his introduction to the *Grundrisse*, distinguishing his conception of the relations between production, distribution, exchange and consumption as distinct, asymmetrically, related 'moments' of 'production' in a wider sense, both from the Hegelian conception of totality and the empiricist separation of these 'processes' in the work of the political economists.[18]

The relationship between real relations and phenomenal forms is, then, a relationship of a causal kind between two aspects of a single structure, one of which has causal (and therefore *explanatory*) primacy over the other. It follows that concepts of the capitalist social order formed on the basis of exchange relations, though they may well have a degree of adequacy in the negotiation of aspects of that reality, will be defective in so far as they fail to theorise the dependence of exchange relations on production relations. By contrast, conceptions of the capitalist social order 'based on' production relations will, since they theorise the relations which are causally primary, have greater explanatory power. It is here that the sense of the 'inversion' metaphor, so often found in Marx's writings on ideology, becomes a little clearer. In treating exchange relations as the fundamental realities, and in seeking to explain capitalist social relations generally in terms of such concepts as exchange between formally equal, and formally free individuals, contract, competition, and other categories derived directly, or by way of metaphor, from the market-place, such ideologies 'invert' the true explanatory priorities.

But in what sense are these conceptualisations 'based on' exchange and production relations, respectively, and why should either, rather than the other, be regarded as the 'phenomenal form' not just in the sense of a causally secondary aspect of reality, but also in the sense of 'that aspect of reality which presents itself to experience'? I am capable of giving only gestural answers to both these questions. As to the first question, the conflicting conceptualisations which I have represented as 'based on' exchange and production relations are, as 'conceptualisations', theoretical ideologies. As such they may be thought of as articulations, in theoretical form, of the practical ideologies of the different social classes, the totality of these together in each case constituting the 'form of social consciousness' peculiar to each class. Each theoretical ideology, then, is 'based on' a corresponding practical ideology, embodied in the practices, experiences, struggles, etc. of the corresponding class and its individual members. Here there is a fundamental asymmetry between the practices and experiences of productive workers, on the one hand, and capitalists and non-productive workers, on the other hand. Whereas the capitalist enters the market as a source of finance, of means of production, of labour-power, and of his own means of consumption, the worker enters the market also to purchase his or her means of consumption and for the sale of labour power. But the worker is also involved in productive practice, and has the daily experience of the antagonistic character of this form of production: working-class industrial and political organisation and struggle is both built out of and constitutes this experience. The market and production, then, both figure in the life-experience of workers. In so far as their experience of the market forms the basis of their theoretical understanding of their general social relations then what Marx says of them is true: 'this phenomenal form . . . forms the basis of all the juridical notions of both labourer and capitalist, of all the mystifications of the capitalist mode of production'.[19] But involvement in productive practices, and the struggles which develop from its antagonistic forms, constitute the elements of an alternative practical ideology which may, in turn, form the basis of an alternative theoretical understanding of the social formation.[20] This, like the theoretical articulations of the ruling ideology, will be structured in terms of the needs, interests, aspirations and values of the class in struggle: it will, in short, be a theoretical ideology in the sense I outlined in the course of my critique of the Weberian notion of value-relevance, and not a scientific theory.[21]

There is one (among the many) possible sources of misunderstanding in my argument which needs to be corrected. This is my talk of 'practice' and 'experience' as the source of theoretical ideologies. Is this not a resort to one, at least, of the doctrines of the empiricist theory of knowledge? The theory which I have been summarising does not involve any notion of 'theory-neutral', or 'pre-theorised' experience as the raw material of knowledge and so avoids this criticism. It does, though, involve the claim that certain ranges of life-experiences are more readily theorisable in terms of some theoretical ideologies than others and that, therefore, there is room for a degree of competition (!) between ideologies in the theorisation of any range of experience. It is the relative inadequacy of the ruling ideology as a means of theorising certain experiences of subordinate classes, strata, and social categories (for example certain groups of women, racial minorities,[22] and others) which provide the basis for the establishment of antagonistic ideologies, and for the necessity of the principal function of 'ideological reproduction' which Althusser attributes to the ISAs. When Marx implies that it is market relations themselves which ensure the subordination of workers to the dominant ideology he is wrong. The achievement of this subordination is the object of a sustained ideological and political struggle on the part of the ruling class and its allies.

Althusser and the theory of scientific knowledge

I have so far tried to show, in a very schematic way, how a materialist theory of ideology might be developed which solves at least some of the general problems listed above. No such theory of knowledge could make any serious claim to completeness of scope unless it also involved a theory of the nature of specifically scientific as distinct from ideological knowledge. This will involve some sort of investigation of both problem areas 5 and 6, outlined above: the problem of the 'mechanism' of the production of science, as a distinctive form of knowledge, and the question of criteria by which to distinguish science from ideology.

Again, I shall begin with a critical discussion of the Althusserian theory of science (basing my discussion, initially, on Althusser's writings prior to 1967 – principally the collections *For Marx* and *Reading Capital*). As I mentioned at the end of chapter 4,[23] Althusser's conception of theoretical knowledge involves a rejection of the notion, implicit in empiricist, and much anti-empiricist philosophy of science, of scientific knowledge as the creation of 'subjects', whether individual scientists, 'transcendental' subjects, or 'the scientific community'. For Althusser, the process of production of theoretical knowledge (including both science and theoretical ideologies) is a social practice. He calls such practices 'theoretical' practices, to distinguish them from the other practices constituting a society: economic, ideological and political practices. These practices co-exist in social formations, and are related to each other by the complex causal relationships described in chapter 8:[24] they are related by an order of 'dominance' between them, and are subjected to a 'determination-in-the-last-instance' by economic practice. Each practice is to be thought of as constituted by a structure which, in each case, is the structure of a production. The concepts by which Marx theorises the structure of economic production in general can, it is supposed, be generalised to ideological, political and theoretical practice. In each of these practices there will be elements and relationships to which the concepts 'raw materials', 'instruments of production', 'product', 'relations of production' and so on can be applied. In each case the 'practice' concerned will consist in the transformation of determinate 'raw materials' into 'products' by means of determinate instruments of production. In each case the role of individual human 'subjects' is not the role they may think they play, but the role assigned to them by the conditions (raw materials, instruments and relations) of production which are available to them.[25] The different practices, then, are analogous in that they share a common structure but, of course, are different in that different types of elements will count as, for example, 'raw materials', 'instruments of production', etc. in the different types of practice.

Althusser distinguishes within 'theoretical practice' both 'ideological' and 'scientific' theoretical practice, but has relatively little to say about the former (phlogiston theory in chemistry, astrology, classical political economy, most of what now passes for 'social science', theology, and most philosophy are all 'theoretical ideologies' and so presumably the results of a distinctive type of theoretical practice). In the case of scientific theoretical practice, the raw materials of the practice are 'concepts', 'notions', 'facts' generated by previous theoretical practice, or imported from other practices, but they are distinctive in being always 'general' in character. The raw materials of science are never 'raw' in the sense of being unconceptualised or untheorised 'pure data': Althusser here rejects the empiricist notion of theory-neutral experiences or perceptions as the basis of science. The contents of scientific knowledge are not to be thought of as 'imposed' on science by sense-experience, but as the results of a process of transformation of concepts into new concepts (in other words, Althusser contradicts Durkheim's strictures against what he called the 'ideological method'). The 'means of production' of a science are constituted by its theoretical system – its set of basic concepts – at each moment in time. The 'product' of scientific practice is also conceptual in character: it is a specific 'concrete-in-thought'.[26] The distinction between raw materials, means of production and product is a relative one in that the product of any specific labour of conceptual transformation may later serve as a means of production of new knowledge.

So far, then, it would seem that Althusser satisfies at least one of the criteria for a materialist theory of theoretical ideologies and sciences: this is that they be conceptualised as social realities in their own right. However, there is one symptom that this may not, after all, be so: although Althusser sometimes refers to relations of production in connection with theoretical practice, he never gives any indication of what these might be. I shall return to this.[27]

First, however, if Althusser's theory is to satisfy criterion 4 above, it must involve some theory not only of the nature of scientific practice itself, but also of the process of its generation and formation as a distinctive type of practice. That is to say, some solutions in problem area 5 are required. For Althusser, the 'pre-history' of any science is constituted by theoretical ideologies. It is through 'transformations', 'mutations' and 'fusions' of theoretical ideologies in a given 'ideological field' that a science is founded. These 'mutations', 'transformations' and so on are themselves not thought of as entirely self-generating, but as in part the effects of transformations in other practices, under the determination-in-the-last-instance of the economic. Marxist theory itself, for instance, was founded as a result of a fusion and transmutation of several theoretical ideologies (French socialist thought, classical political economy, and speculative philosophy, principally), which are in turn to be explained in part in terms of political class-struggle, the development of European capitalism, the underdevelopment of German capitalism, and so on.

Like Kuhn, Althusser conceptualises the history of each science as discontinuous, as marked by sharp qualitative breaks or 'ruptures'. The process of foundation of a new science out of a rupture with the ideologies of its pre-history is the most important of these discontinuities, from the point of view of the theory of knowledge, and in order to theorise it Althusser borrows the term 'epistemological break' from the French philosopher Gaston Bachelard.[28] This concept serves both to locate historically the emergence of the new type of theoretical practice (science) and to indicate the difference in epistemological status (status as knowledge) of the products of the new practice. This concept has been modified in Althusser's work, with the recognition that a new science does not spring fully formed from a sudden rupture with ideology, but rather the 'rupture' should be understood as opening up a new 'terrain' of problems and concepts within which a new scientific theoretical system may be produced. Also, and connected with this latter point, Althusser argues that theoretical ideologies do not disappear with the epistemological break, but persist as 'epistemological obstacles', combined with elements of the new scientific theory. This notion of epistemological break is crucial to Althusser's controversial anti-humanist interpretation of the later Marx: the claim is that 1845 marked a 'break', or discontinuity in Marx's theoretical position, which founded the scientific theory of history. A form of this thesis was involved in my argument in chapter 8.

Finally, Althusser's conception of scientific knowledge and its production, in order to theorise the 'epistemological break' separating theoretical ideologies from sciences, requires yet another concept. If the transition involved here is to be thought of as some sort of 'rupture' or 'transformation', it cannot simply be a question of the discovery of new evidence, or the invention of some new concepts. It must be a question of an upheaval in the whole system of concepts involved. Althusser, then, requires a concept which theorises the unity formed by the concepts of a theoretical system. This concept is the concept of 'problematic': each theoretical discourse presupposes, has as its foundation, or conceptual 'condition of possibility', a 'problematic'. Again, there is some inconsistency in Althusser as to the precise definition of this concept, but at the very least it involves the claim that the concepts constituting a theoretical system are systematically related in the sense that each concept may be identified or defined only in terms of the other concepts with which it is linked in the theory. To detach a concept from the theoretical corpus to which it belongs is necessarily to alter its meaning. The 'problematic' of a theory at any moment in its history constitutes the main element of the 'means of production' by which new knowledge is produced in that theoretical practice.

Already there are some fairly obvious internal difficulties in the theory of knowledge so far outlined. If theoretical ideologies continue to invade and co-exist with the scientific problematic after the 'epistemological break', what sense can we continue to make of the concept of 'problematic'? It seems that elements of different (ideological and scientific) problematic can co-exist in the same theoretical discourse, so what has happened to the internal coherence of the problematic? Related to this point, if any sense is to be made of the idea of production of knowledge as a process of transformation of concepts, it must be the case that there is a difference of epistemological status (and therefore a difference of problematic?) between those 'notions', 'concepts', etc. which form the raw material of a science and its problematic (means of production) at any point in the history of the science. It is necessary, therefore, to think of the 'unity' of a scientific theoretical system as a rather uneven, loose, and even contradictory one, in which there may be relatively autonomous clusters of concepts. Also, if any sense is to be attached to the idea of 'mutations' and transformations within theoretical ideologies, it must be conceded that the unity of their problematics, too, must have something of this unevenness and contradictoriness. These vague and metaphorical indicators require a much more precise and rigorous formulation which is nowhere to be found in Althusser. However, serious though this criticism is, it is not fundamental, in the sense that it leaves open the possibility of a revision in Althusser's system of ideas which may well be capable of answering it. There are other objections of this type, such as the claim that Althusser's theory of the social formation as a combination of practices, each having the structure of production, is entirely *a priori* and arbitrary, and that the application of terms such as 'raw materials', 'means of production' to knowledge is also a mechanical and *a priori* working-out of what is merely a metaphor in Marx.[29] These criticisms have their point, but are not decisive against Althusser's whole epistemological strategy.

There are, however, several rather more serious objections, some of which Althusser has conceded, and which involve the condemnation of his theories as 'idealist' and 'theoreticist'. The first of these objections is that Althusser at several points seems to be arguing that the epistemological break doesn't simply have the effect of founding a new social practice (science) but of projecting that practice quite out of the social formation. Science, alone of all the practices of a social formation, is exempt from determination-in-the-last-instance by economic practice. This notion of what amounts to the absolute autonomy of science seems to justify the claim that Althusser's theory of scientific knowledge is in certain respects idealist[30] (it fails to satisfy criterion 4 given above). Also related to this supposed autonomy of science is the failure in this earlier position of Althusser to pose the question of the relationship between scientific knowledge and politics in a rigorous way. This is clearly a serious omission, since Althusser's whole discussion of the nature of science is linked to a defence of the scientific status of the Marxist theory of history. I shall return to this point.[31]

But a further, and perhaps more fundamental respect in which Althusser is open to the charge of idealism concerns the way in which he attempts to reconcile the materialist thesis of the prior and independent existence of the reality which is 'grasped' in knowledge (criterion 1 above) with the conception of scientific knowledge as a product – as constructed. Althusser makes Marx's distinction (in the introduction to the *Grundrisse*) between the concrete real ('outside and independent of the intellect') and the concrete-in-thought, which is its conceptual representation, the basis of his own distinction between the so-called 'real object' and the 'object of knowledge'. In the process of production of knowledge a science constructs its own 'object of knowledge', which is distinct from the 'object' of the theoretical ideology which preceded it: 'phlogiston' is the object of a theoretical ideology, and is a distinct object from the 'oxygen' of the chemical theory of combustion. Similarly Marx, in producing the concept of 'surplus value', gives political economy a new object of knowledge.[32] But in each case these 'objects of knowledge' must be thought of as internal to knowledge, and not confused with the real object which remains throughout independent and 'outside' knowledge.

Althusser seems to regard this distinction between the 'real object' and the 'object of knowledge' as what saves his theory from empiricism, but there is a remarkable homology between Althusser's insistence on the 'constructed' character of the object of scientific knowledge and the Neo-Kantians' insistence on the same point, made all the more remarkable by the Althusserian criticism of Neo-Kantianism as a form of empiricism. But there are several other connected difficulties with Althusser's distinction. First, though it is effective in denoting the qualitative break involved in the shift from theoretical ideology to science (their problematics theorise different objects), it is perhaps too effective. This way of theorising the founding of a science (or, in general, the relationship between competing theoretical systems), like Thomas Kuhn's thesis of successive incommensurable 'paradigms', makes any conception of continuity through scientific revolutions unthinkable. It becomes, then, entirely problematic in what sense any theoretical ideology, or combination of them, can be regarded as the pre-history of any particular science. If phlogiston theory and the oxygen theory of combustion have different problematics, and have a different object, what sense is there in saying that one constituted the pre-history of the other, and what sense is there in the claim that problems produced in the one generated the formulation of the other? In what sense can it be said that such theoretical systems are in competition with one another, if they concern different objects? Further, what sense can be made of critical discourse between problematics, and progress in science as a result of the 'replacement' of an ideological by a scientific problematic, if this 'replacement' is a theory of a new object, rather than better knowledge of the same object? Significantly, Althusser's account of the 'epistemological break' in Marx does rely on a notion of continuity through the break, but as this cannot be a continuity of 'problematics' or of 'objects of knowledge', it is the continuity established by the 'subject', Marx, who was their creator! Back to 'humanism'![33]

Another, connected difficulty with the real object/object of knowledge distinction has to do with their relationship: how do we *know* that the production of the object of knowledge of a science is at the same time the production of knowledge of the real object, external to thought? In one text Althusser simply states, without explanation, that this relationship is 'non-problematic'.[34] Presumably we can just see that the 'object' of a theoretical ideology is not the knowledge of the real object, whereas that of a science is! But elsewhere, Althusser recognises the problem, and also its importance: '. . . the problem of the relation between these two objects (the object of knowledge and the real object), a relation which constitutes the very existence of knowledge'.[35] In this text, Althusser makes it clear that the search here is not, as in classical (empiricist and rationalist) epistemology, for some 'guarantee' of certainty in knowledge, for some timeless criterion by which to distinguish knowledge from mere belief. Rather, the search is for the 'mechanism of the knowledge effect'. Beyond making the search sound more scientific, it has to be recognised by Althusser that this is hardly a solution. However, what Althusser does not seem to recognise is that the problem as he has posed it cannot be answered. What kind of operation could compare the 'object of knowledge' (in thought) with the real world (outside thought) so as to declare whether or not the first was, indeed, the 'cognitive appropriation' of the second?

The 'real object' as an epistemological device has the same defect as the Kantian notion of a 'thing-in-itself' – it is a 'something' of which, by definition, nothing can be said, but of which something must be said if it is to have a place in a theoretical system. The distinction between the 'real object' and the 'object of knowledge' in Althusser's thought is, then, a second source for the charge of idealism: the theory satisfies neither criterion 1 nor criterion 2. The independence of the real world is asserted, but cannot be asserted consistently with the rest of the theory. Equally, there are places where Althusser recognises that the cognitive status of a theory is a function of its relationship to the reality of which it is the (putative) knowledge, but there is no way in which this relationship can be coherently theorised so long as the real object/object of knowledge distinction is retained.

Althusser's frequent explicit rejection of the classical epistemological search for universal criteria of certainty in knowledge co-exists uneasily with his equally frequent posing of the problem of knowledge in a way very little removed from that of the 'philosophy of guarantees'. This, too, is connected with the real object/object of knowledge distinction. If science and ideology are to be distinguished in terms of the different relationships between the 'real object' and their respective 'objects of knowledge', then this relationship must be thought of in a very abstract way. There is no room in such a theory of science for the relationship between science and the real world to be posed as a problem solved in different (though, perhaps, related) ways in each science. If, for instance, instead of posing the problem of the relationship between the 'object of knowledge' and the 'real object', we pose the problem of the relationships of the concepts 'dephlogisticated air' and 'oxygen' both to one another and to the substance they designate, the problem immediately appears less intractable. Certainly Lavoisier's new concept of oxygen, which avoided some of the theoretical difficulties which attended the notion of dephlogisticated air, involved a revolution in chemical theory, but a revolution with certain crucial continuities. Both the concepts 'dephlogisticated air' and 'oxygen' had a place in theories designed to explain combustion, and both concepts, despite their location in quite different 'networks' of concepts, could be recognised as designating one and the same substance. The possibility of this identity of reference of two quite different concepts, belonging to different 'problematics', is dependent upon the existence of procedures for producing the substance which may be taught, learned, copied, etc. without presupposing what is at issue between the two chemical theories. Lavoisier could copy the procedures adopted by Priestley to produce samples of dephlogisticated air whenever he wished to produce oxygen. That there are general connections between the realist conception of science which I began to outline in chapters 3 and 4, criteria 1 and 2[36] for a materialist theory of knowledge, and this notion of identity of reference as a major element of continuity through scientific revolutions should now be apparent. I shall try to develop these general connections a little further towards the end of the chapter. For the moment, suffice it to say that the search for such identities of reference of theoretical concepts across scientific revolutions is one method, at least, of avoiding the serious epistemological problems generated by Althusser's 'real object'/'object of knowledge' distinction.[37]

Finally, though, in this discussion of Althusser's theory of science, it is necessary to investigate Althusser's attempts at solving problem 6,[38] identified above: the problem of criteria for distinguishing science from ideology. I have already criticised one of Althusser's approaches to this problem: the 'mechanism of the knowledge effect' which produces an 'object of knowledge' which just is the 'cognitive appropriation' of the 'real object'. There are several other, sometimes mutually inconsistent, approaches scattered throughout Althusser's work. Sometimes the difference between science and ideology is represented as a matter of the relative importance of the 'practico-social' function of the theory.[39] Not only does this make the difference one of degree, but in the absence of any account of how 'practico-social functions' are to be measured and compared, the 'criterion' remains one which cannot be applied. Elsewhere, Althusser seems to suggest that it is in the mode of production of science that it differs from ideology, and alternatively, that it is a matter of the difference between their 'discourse-object unity'. But in neither case are the precise *differentia specifica* given.

Yet elsewhere, under the influence of his rejection of any philosophy of 'guarantees' of knowledge, Althusser seems to deny the very possibility of a general science/ideology distinction:

> Theoretical practice is indeed its own criterion and contains in itself definite protocols with which to *validate* the quality of its product, i.e., the criteria of the scientificity of the products of scientific practice. This is exactly what happens in the real practice of the sciences: once they are truly constituted and developed they have no need of verification from *external* practices to declare the knowledges they produce to be 'true', i.e. to be *knowledges*.[40]

Here Althusser either begs the question, or his position is relativist. When he says that 'truly constituted' sciences are not in need of any external criterion of validity, this presupposes that there is some prior way of telling whether or not a science is truly constituted. The alternative to this is that any theoretical discourse (theology, astrology, sociology . . .) which presents its internal criteria of validity and proclaims its status as a science is as justified in doing so as any other. This apparent concession to relativism, if it were accepted, would amount to a rejection not only of any general science/ideology distinction, but also of any critical role for the theory of knowledge in assessing knowledge-claims.

Finally, there is yet another approach to the science/ideology distinction in Althusser which does seem to offer more promise. This is the distinction between science and ideology in terms of the character of their internal unity. The problematic of a theoretical ideology is said to be 'closed' whereas that of a science is 'open'. The 'closure' of ideological problematics is, further, connected with the type of relationship they have with non-theoretical practices. The exigencies and demands of the other social practices present to theoretical ideology 'solutions' for which theoretical ideology must produce, in a theoretical form, the appropriate 'problem'. In other words, the concepts of a theoretical ideology will be structured around a problem, whose solution is already given in the form of a demand imposed by extra-theoretical practices. The 'problem-structure' of a theoretical ideology, then, is distinctive in that it is determined by extra-theoretical interests and demands and, connected with this, in that its 'solutions' are predetermined by this 'problem-structure'. An example of this would be the theoretical discourse of Durkheim's *Division of Labour*: the concepts constituting the theory are structured around the 'problem' of the maintenance of 'social order' under conditions of increasing division of social labour. The structure of concepts in terms of which this problem is theorised generate the 'solution', a normative and ultimately legal framework uniting differentiated functions. They also exclude the idea of a transition to a new social type as a conceivable solution. Durkheim's theory can, in this way, be understood as the theoretical expression and defence of problem-solutions required in a political practice extrinsic to theoretical practice.[41]

This notion of the 'closure' of ideological problematics, of course, requires much more theoretical elaboration. In particular, the 'tight' logical linkage between the concepts of a theoretical ideology which is implicit in the notion of 'closure' must not be such as to exclude the possibility of internal development in the field of theoretical ideology. If this possibility were to be excluded, then the theory of the founding of a science out of mutations in theoretical ideologies would become unintelligible. Also, and crucially, it is implicit in this way of conceptualising the relationships between theoretical ideologies and extra-theoretical social practices that there is a conceptual continuity or homogeneity between the 'meaning-structure' of theoretical ideologies and the practical ideologies at work in the practices which determine their problematics. Another way of stating the distinctive character of theoretical ideologies is in terms of this conceptual homogeneity with practical ideologies. However, the further elaboration of this point clearly requires the production of new categories in philosophical logic, which work in turn will require raw materials drawn from concrete work in the history of ideas.

So far, also, science has been defined only negatively by contrast with theoretical ideologies. By implication, the 'openness' of the problematic of a science consists in its 'solutions' not being predetermined by the structure of its theoretical problems and in its problems not being set by extra-theoretical requirements and interests: the 'objectivity' of science consists precisely in these differences between it and theoretical ideologies. Again, an implication of this notion of science will be a discontinuity and heterogeneity between its conceptual structures and those of both existing theoretical and practical ideologies. This notion of science enables, further, some notion of the autonomy of science which is not vulnerable to the charge of 'idealism' as was Althusser's. Scientific theories are 'autonomous' in that, and to the extent that, their conceptual structures, and the development of those conceptual structures, are not determined by extra-theoretical exigencies. Science may be held to have such a conceptual autonomy (and without such autonomy 'internalist'[42] accounts of the history of the sciences could not even have plausibility) without at all conceding that the social practice by which scientific knowledge is produced is autonomous, or is outside the social formation. Indeed, it may be argued that the production of scientific knowledge in the natural sciences has served, in the capitalist countries since the seventeenth century, very definite class interests. It has provided the theoretical basis for technological innovation in medicine, warfare and economic production, and has received political support for this reason. There is only a superficial air of paradox in the truth that this political support for scientific research has been based on a recognition that science could serve interests ('human' interests or 'class' interests) only if its conceptual autonomy and objectivity were conceded. The sixteenth- and seventeenth-century battle with the Catholic Church over intellectual freedom was not about freeing science from vested interests, but rather it was about which 'vested interests' should be served. The new social class whose economic power was to depend on the application of scientific knowledge clearly recognised that its interests could be served only by according conceptual autonomy to science, and institutionalising the conditions of this autonomy.

The late medieval cosmology, formed out of the combination of Catholic theology with Aristotelian physics and Ptolemaic astronomy, can be understood, on this basis, as a theoretical ideology. In its installation of hierarchy as the architectural principle of the universe, and its assignment of each element to a 'natural' place in this hierarchy, it legitimised the social hierarchies of the feudal order as 'natural' and as also divinely ordained. The structure of the universe also allowed the possibility of a physical location for the myths of Catholic theology. Heaven and hell had a literal physical location, so that the damnation or salvation consequent upon obedience or disobedience to divinely authoritative moral imperatives had a concrete meaning for social agents who lived their relationship to their physical and social world through the categories of this cosmology. In general outline, then, there is an intelligible homogeneity, or continuity between the categories of this theoretical cosmology, and the dominant practical ideologies at work in feudal social relationships. The theoretical revolution in astronomy and mechanics which spanned the 150 years or so from Copernicus to Newton's *Principia* had the effect of shattering the unity of the medieval cosmologies. The principle of hierarchy disappears from the world, the notion of an infinite universe abolishes the concept of the earth as the 'centre' of the universe, and opens the possibility of a plurality of worlds. There is no longer a clear physical location for heaven and hell, and the myths of religion, if taken literally, come to acquire a parochial and marginal significance in a morally indifferent universe.[43]

The new problematic of physics, then, establishes a clear conceptual break with the medieval cosmology and the practical ideologies with which it is homogeneous. Also, despite certain structural analogies between Newtonian physics and Enlightenment political philosophy (individualism/corpuscularianism; the laws of nature and the laws of the market), Newtonian physics never becomes integrated into a unified cosmology which will serve as a legitimisation of the bourgeois order as did the medieval cosmology with respect to the feudal order. The conceptual autonomy of physics with respect to social and political ideologies is retained. The politics is, so to speak, permanently taken out of physics.

Now this is a very provocative thing to say, and I shall be accused of restoring the 'theoreticism' of Althusser's theory of science: of constructing a theory of science which obscures its relationship to politics. My response to this is to argue that to take politics out of physics is not the same thing as to take physics out of politics. In other words, politics is taken out of physics in the sense that political requirements no longer determine the structure, content and development of physical theory, but physics is not taken out of politics in the sense that the theory so produced continues to have profound ideological and political effects, and is the stake in very bitter class-struggles. The reason why this is so is that in establishing a conceptual break with the prevailing ideological formations a scientific theory is necessarily subversive, and is a threat to the ideological dominance of the prevailing ruling class. The foundation of a new science is, in this respect, a process of great political importance. The response of the prevailing ruling classes may be a repressive one (as in the case of the Catholic Church's reponse to the new science of Copernicus and Galileo) or it may adopt a strategy of nullifying the subversive tendencies of the new science by re-articulating both the ruling ideological formation and the new science to re-establish some sort of ideological coherence. Where a revolutionary class also exists (the rising capitalist class in the example under discussion) there may well be a struggle between the contending classes for possession of the new science. An example here is the range of opposed political tendencies which contended for possession of Darwin's theory of the origin of species by natural selection. The theory was adduced to legitimate liberal capitalist competition, imperialism, the reformist socialism of A. R. Wallace, revolutionary socialism (by a 'struggle for survival' between social classes – Marx and Lenin), and many other diverse tendencies of thought.

In short, science may be objective, but it is never neutral in the struggles between classes. This point helps to focus on the fundamental political problems which have to be solved by any ruling class in the institutionalisation of science: the requirement that science be accorded conceptual autonomy in its development must be reconciled with its function in serving class interests: the subversive implications of fundamental theoretical innovation in the sciences must somehow be contained. It is in these aspects of the institutionalisation of scientific research that the concepts of relations of production, and relations of distributions of knowledge – which were, as we saw, absent from Althusser's conception of knowledge as production – have their role. The peculiar structural features of the western European universities, with their relative autonomy from the other state apparatuses, their hierarchical internal structure and restrictive criteria of entry, and the special features of academic 'communication', in small-circulation specialist journals, intelligible to only a narrow elite who have passed through the prescribed technical initiation, are explicable in terms of these political priorities. Knowledge is produced under relations which minimise direct ideological control over its content on the part of the ruling classes and strata, but which equally minimise the access to the knowledge so produced on the part of the subordinate classes.

What I have said above about the distinction between science and ideology is extremely conjectural and schematic. I have done no more than sketch, in a rather crude way, the outlines of a research programme. But a question arises here which also arises for Althusser's theory of science. Namely, is the theory of science outlined here a philosophical theory of knowledge, or is it merely a theoretical approach to the history of science as a social practice for the production of knowledge? Certainly there is only a limited continuity between the problems of the nature of scientific knowledge as I have posed them and the classical philosophical theories of knowledge (rationalism and empiricism). Any further attempt to develop and make more rigorous the general approach I have sketched would have to involve historical investigations of a very concrete kind in the history of ideas. On the other hand, the distinction between 'open' and 'closed' problematics, and the relationships of continuity/discontinuity between theoretical systems and social practices could not be developed without further work in fields at least recognisably related to what now goes under the title of philosophical logic and conceptual analysis.

The question of validity

Even if an adequate conception of the difference between science and ideology can be produced in the general terms of the theory I have outlined, this would still not necessarily answer the question which has been central to most philosophical theories of knowledge. The question of demarcation criteria between science and non-science has only been relevant to orthodox epistemologies in so far as it has been understood as a way of posing the question of criteria for distinguishing genuine from spurious knowledge-claims. Clearly, for those theories of knowledge which identify scientific knowledge as the only genuine knowledge, the two questions are identical. The theoretical approach I have adopted, however, recognises the cognitive character of both theoretical ideologies and sciences. To demonstrate the extra-theoretical interests at work in a theoretical ideology is not necessarily to demonstrate its cognitive inadequacy, though there will be close connections between the two processes.[44] The general distinction which I have begun to make, then, between science and theoretical ideology is not to be understood as a step towards a universal criterion for the recognition of genuine knowledge, which would replace the sense-experience and logical principles of the rationalists and empiricists. Within theoretical ideology it is possible to distinguish different types and degrees of cognitive defect, whilst even after the founding of a science revolutions continue to occur which involve the rejection of earlier scientific categories in favour of new ones. Any general criteria of validity of knowledge must, then, allow for some distinction between more and less adequate knowledge within science, as well as between science and theoretical ideology.

I shall approach this question of criteria for 'genuineness' or 'adequacy' of knowledge in two stages. I shall consider first the problem of criteria of validity, proof and demonstration internal to any theoretical system and secondly the more difficult question of general criteria of validity which transcend particular theoretical systems, and so allow of the possibility of comparing theoretical systems with respect to their relative cognitive adequacy – the possibility, in other words, of a concept of scientific progress. My approach to both problems should indicate the importance of a realist alternative to positivist and empiricist theories of knowledge.[45]

First, criteria of validity internal to a theoretical system. On the realist account of science, among the most fundamental concepts and propositions of a theory will be those which specify the range of entities, forces, structures, processes, etc. of which the theory purports to give knowledge. The most fundamental propositions of the theory will assert the existence and general characteristics of these entities, structures and so on. Also the theory will specify the general causal relationships between such items, with implications as to what types of event or process are possible or impossible. Implicit in the theory, then, will be conceptions of what is or is not to be considered a 'plausible mechanism', what may or may not count as an explanation, what standards of proof or demonstration are appropriate or inappropriate. Specific to each science, also, will be one or more conceptions of causality. Earlier in the book I have referred, all too summarily, to differences in conceptions of causality implicit in molecular physics, physiology, history and the theory of social action.

The specifically philosophical work of making explicit, for each science, the conceptions of explanation, causality, demonstration and proof appropriate to it, and implicit in its fundamental concepts and ontology, is important for the progress of science in a number of respects. First, it enables a more thorough and critical systematisation of what is already established in the science. Second, it provides rigorous guidelines for the production of new knowledge within the field defined by the basic concepts of the science. Although the establishment of the basic concepts and propositions of any science defines its scope, it does not at all follow that all areas within the scope of the science are equally thoroughly investigated and theorised. For instance, the scope of the research programme in molecular biology, established in the mid nineteenth century, is extremely broad and still includes within it areas – such as the molecular mechanisms involved in cell differentiation – which remain relatively underdeveloped. General criteria of what will count as an explanation in this field are provided by the overall structure of the theory and its basic concepts.

A third function of philosophical work in rendering explicit internal criteria of validity, concepts of causality and so on brings us closer to the key question of 'progress' in scientific knowledge through theoretical revolutions. Sometimes the rendering explicit of internal criteria of validity and concepts of causality exposes areas within the scope of the basic concepts of a science which are resistant to explanation in terms of the appropriate criteria of validity. This type of internal tension in a theory is both a cause of theoretical revolutions in science and a source of criteria of validity applicable outside the scope of a single theory. For example, the conception of mechanical explanation developed in the work of Galileo, and which formed the basis of Newtonian physics, involved a distinction between 'primary' and 'secondary' qualities of things. The primary qualities included shape, size, number and other quantifiable, measurable properties, whilst the secondary qualities included colours, tastes, scents and other supposedly more 'subjective' and relational properties. In general, a mechanical explanation was an explanation in terms of the primary qualities. Furthermore, this conception of explanation involved the restriction that changes in states of motion were to be explained in terms of forces impressed through direct contact, 'collision' being the paradigm. Paradoxically, Newton's fundamental law of universal gravitation was indispensable to his unification of celestial and terrestrial physics under a small number of universal laws, and yet entirely incompatible with the mechanical conception of explanation. Not only was gravitational attraction clearly not a primary quality, but the use of the concept of gravitational attraction to explain states of motion, and changes in states of motion seemed to involve the recognition of 'action at a distance' – a conceptual impossibility in the terms of the mechanical conception of explanation. Newton persisted, quite unsuccessfully, in attempting to postulate an underlying mechanism to explain gravitational attraction, and so render his theory consistent with the criteria of validity of explanation recognised in the physics of his period. Later physicists and philosophers, rather than abandon the hypothesis of universal gravitation, ceased to recognise the authority of the mechanical conception of explanation. For some, this led to a type of philosophical scepticism about scientific ontologies and mechanisms as such, and is one source of modern positivism: science is concerned with discovering laws governing phenomena (such as the law of gravitation) and has no business hypothesising about the basic constituents and structures of the world. Ultimately, however, the revolution in physics at the end of the nineteenth century involved a rejection of the ontology of the primary/secondary qualities distinction and of 'corpuscularianism' in favour of an ontology of forces and fields of force. In terms of this new ontology, and the conceptions of explanation and causality implicit in it, the adequacy of the Newtonian conception of gravitation is no longer suspect. Instead, the conception of mechanical explanation with which it was inconsistent has been 'demoted' as the paradigm for ultimate explanations in physics.[46]

In short, an incompatibility between forms of explanation established within the scope of a theory and the general criteria of validity established by that theory, on the basis of its fundamental concepts and ontology, may play a part in generating a theoretical revolution in the science. A consequence of that revolution may be to vindicate the 'suspect' forms of explanation against the general criteria of validity established within the overthrown theory. I am not committed to this scenario as a general theory of scientific revolution, but it does, I think, provide some sort of basis for reviewing some of the argumentative procedures I have employed in this book. At several points, and especially in my discussion of Max Weber's methodology, my arguments appealed to the reader's intuitive agreement that certain types of phenomena (for example, the coexistence of incompatible ideologies in a single social formation) call for explanation.[47] The argument then proceeded as a demonstration that the Weberian conception of sociological explanation either ruled out the possibility of such phenomena or rendered them insusceptible of sociological explanation. The obvious weakness in this type of argument is that it relies on the 'intuitive' agreement of the reader that such phenomena do, after all, exist and require explanation. The temptation, in the face of this problem, is to resort to the empiricist assertion of such phenomena as 'plain facts'. However, there is an alternative way of representing the force of these arguments. They seek to identify, in the corpus of Weber's substantive writings, a recognition and explanation of phenomena which are, in the terms of his general methodology, unrecognisable and inexplicable (for example, structural explanation of class consciousness, inexplicable on the methodological individualist paradigm of explanation). The argument of chapters 8 and 9 can be understood, in part, as the basis for an alternative, internally consistent, conception of explanation in defence of the 'suspect' parts of Weber's substantive work against his general methodology, and the fundamental concepts and ontology (actors, meanings, complexes of meaning) upon which it is based.

This begins, it seems to me, to approach the central question in epistemology: the problem of the validity of criteria of validity beyond the confines of a single theoretical system. If the certainties of sense-experience and logic as adequate universal criteria of validity for all knowledge-claims are abandoned, how can the descent into agnosticism and relativism be avoided? How can the claims of any theoretical system, with its internal criteria of validity, to provide genuine knowledge be critically assessed? The internal criteria of validity of any theoretical system have, as we have seen, a basis in the fundamental concepts and ontology of the theory, so long as theories are understood in a realist, non-positivist way. But what could form the basis of criteria of validity which have the function of critically assessing competing theories, and which must therefore be independent of either?

The problem is already reduced in scale once it is posed in this way. The classical epistemological question of universal criteria of knowledge is replaced by a search for criteria which do not 'beg the question' as between two, or possibly more, directly competing theories. The criteria of validity which I brought to bear on Weber (the indispensability of structural explanation, the necessity of a distinction between meaning systems and non-meaningful aspects of social reality, and others) are very clearly rooted in an alternative ontology and theoretical system – that of historical materialism. It may therefore be argued that they do beg the question against him and are not in the required way theory-neutral. This is of course true, but it is also true, as I have just argued, that there are aspects and parts of Weber's substantive theorising to which these criteria are appropriate and which they validate to some extent. Further, in exposing contradictions between the Weberian methodology and aspects of Weber's substantive theory, this form of argument involves an appeal to a still more generally applicable criterion of validity: the principle of non-contradiction.

A possible difficulty here is that the concept of contradiction, and concepts of logical proof in general are to some degree controversial, and have a history. That is to say, even logic does not provide absolute and universal criteria of validity. Considerations like this have seemed, to Kuhn and others who think like him, to justify the conclusion that there are no 'paradigm-neutral' standards to mediate in cases of fundamental conflict between theoretical systems. However, if the confrontation between theoretical systems is not a confrontation in logical theory, nor one which calls into question the prevailing logic, then there is no reason why logical principles should not be allowed to adjudicate between the theories. In general, theoretical revolutions in science do not call into question the whole of established scientific knowledge, including logic and mathematics. They are relatively localised affairs. This point is, in slightly more general terms, the thesis of the uneven development of scientific knowledge which, I argued above,[48] is a condition of science's being thought of as a form of theoretical production.

This thesis of uneven development in the history of the sciences opens up a general approach to the problem of the source of validity of 'paradigm-neutral' criteria of validity. The materialist thesis of the existence of a real world, prior to and independent of knowledge of it, together with the realist conception of science as knowledge of the nature, structure and constituent causal mechanisms of that reality, imply a conception of the unity of scientific knowledge such that the ontologies and basic concepts of each science and branch of science will, to the extent that they express genuine knowledge, be mutually consistent. Let us return, for instance, to the example of the transition from the 'phlogiston' to the 'oxygen' theory of combustion. One of the decisive arguments against the phlogiston theory was that substances were discovered to gain in weight as a result of combustion. Since the phlogiston theory explained combustion as expulsion of a substance, 'phlogiston', from the burning body, it had to be conceded either that phlogiston was a material substance with negative weight, or that the general law of conservation of matter was simply not applicable to combustion. Since weight was already generally established as a measure of 'quantity of matter', and the law of conservation of matter was widely accepted and presupposed in explanations of other physical and chemical processes, to continue to accept phlogiston theory would have been to accept a theory whose explanatory principles were in contradiction to some of the most fundamental propositions of the other sciences. The alternative, chemical theory did not involve any such basic incompatibilities.

In the above example, then, the wider scientific context within which a relatively limited paradigm-confrontation took place was capable of founding general criteria of validity to arbitrate between the competing paradigms. These criteria were not circular, in that they did not presuppose the truth of either theory in confrontation. Nor were these criteria produced by *a priori* philosophical speculation: they had their basis in a scientific knowledge broader in scope than either of the theoretical systems, or 'paradigms', between which they adjudicated. The general approach to the problem of paradigm-neutral criteria of validity, and hence to the problem of progress in science, which I am here suggesting, is contingent upon the assumption of the materialist and realist theses which I have just outlined, together with the theses of the unity and uneven development of science.

The materialist and realist theses are required to justify the mutual consistency of the basic concepts of the different sciences as itself a source of criteria of validity.[49] This normative conception of the unity of the sciences, in turn, can only exercise a critical function in the development of scientific knowledge if that development is itself uneven – that is, if the actual, historically produced, unity of the sciences at any point in time is complex and contradictory.

Of course, it is no part of my claim that the materialist and realist theses to which I refer can be, in any final way, proved. My claim is, rather, that their assumption offers an alternative to both relativism and the classical 'philosophy of guarantees' which gives some rational foundation for a conception of progress through scientific revolutions. If the core of my argument can be summed up, it is that the source of the objectivity of scientific knowledge is in the referential character of the theoretical concepts of a science: it is in the procedures for identifying, recognising and producing the entities, processes and structures to which the basic concepts of a theory refer that its objectivity is demonstrated. Even if two competing theories have no concepts in common, even if every phenomenon is conceptualised by them in mutually incompatible ways, so that all discourse between the theories is at cross-purposes (the extreme case, which Kuhn refers to with the concept 'incommensurability' of paradigms), still the possibility of a continuity between the two theories remains in the demonstrative element in the function of reference to particulars. P. F. Strawson's argument to the effect that all identifying reference to particulars involves an indispensably demonstrative element, that description in general terms is never sufficient to secure uniqueness of reference, allows for a solution to the problem of progress in science even in the extreme case of 'incommensurability' of paradigms.[50]

To return, in one final remark, to the question of objectivity and progress in the social sciences, the implication of my argument is that only through some notion of the unity of the sciences such as the one I have advocated (which is one fundamentally different from that of the positivists) which includes the social sciences, can there be any rational foundation for the notions of progress and objectivity in the social sciences. This in turn justifies the practice of looking to the natural sciences for analogues of the conceptions of causality and of explanation which are required in the social sciences, and also of demanding of social-science theories that they are consistent with the basic laws and propositions of the physical sciences.

In short, my argument can be understood as supporting the Marxian project of a 'natural science of history'.

Notes

1 Introduction

1 This chapter, pp. 7–9. The conception in question is that of Thomas Kuhn – a conception which could itself be described as revolutionary in its impact on a whole cluster of related disciplines which take the sciences as their object of study.

2 John Locke, *An Essay Concerning Human Understanding*, ed. A. D. Woozley (London, Collins, 1964), p. 58.

3 Ibid., p. 59.

4 This view is not, of course, confined to proponents of the under-labourer conception. One of the strongest antagonists of that conception, Peter Winch, also tends to speak as if scientists never faced conceptual issues. See, for instance, his *The Idea of a Social Science* (London, Routledge & Kegan Paul, 1958, 4th imp., 1965), p. 9. I shall refer to this book henceforth as *I.S.S.*

5 See, for example, Alan Ryan, *The Philosophy of the Social Sciences* (London, Macmillan, 1970), especially chapter 1; and C. G. Hempel, *Philosophy of Natural Science* (Englewood Cliffs, Prentice-Hall, 1966), pp. 1ff.

6 See, for example, Ryan, op. cit., pp. 4–5 and 24, and P. F. Strawson, *Introduction to Logical Theory* (London, Methuen, University Paperback edn, reprinted 1964), pp. 15ff.

7 See, for example, Ryan, op. cit., pp. 11–12. See also, a non-under-labourer, T. S. Kuhn, *The Structure of Scientific Revolutions* (University of Chicago Press, 1st edn, 1962), p. 87.

8 See Claude Bernard, *An Introduction to the Study of Experimental Medicine* (New York, Dover, 1957) esp. part 2, chapter 1.

9 For example, Peter Winch, *I.S.S.*, p. 4.

10 For two classic examples of this type of philosophising see Descartes, *Metaphysical Meditations* (various editions) and Leibniz, *Discourse on Metaphysics*, trans. Lucas and Grint (Manchester University Press, 1953).

11 See P. F. Strawson, *Individuals* (London, Methuen, University Paperbacks edn, 1959), especially the introduction.

12 See, for an introductory statement of Kant's arguments in this respect, the section on 'The Dialectic of Pure Reason' in Immanuel Kant, *Prolegomena to any Future Metaphysics* (Manchester University Press, 3rd imp., 1962), pp. 96–116.
13 K. Marx and F. Engels, *The German Ideology, Part I*, ed. C. J. Arthur (London, Lawrence & Wishart, 1970), p. 48.
14 K. Marx, preface to the *Contribution to the Critique of Political Economy* (1859) in most collections of the work of Marx and Engels.
15 P. Winch, *I.S.S.*, p. 3.
16 Ibid., p. 23.
17 See especially L. Wittgenstein, *Philosophical Investigations* (Oxford, Blackwell, 1963).
18 *I.S.S.*, p. 41.
19 *I.S.S.*, p. 43.
20 See especially chapter 5 of this book.
21 Marx and Engels, op. cit., p. 37.
22 In particular, in chapter 7.

2 Auguste Comte and positivist sociology

1 Descartes, *Discourse on Method*, trans. Wollaston (Harmondsworth, Penguin, 1964), p. 47.
2 Ibid., p. 36.
3 Ibid., p. 47.
4 W. V. Quine, 'Two Dogmas of Empiricism' in *From A Logical Point of View* (New York, Harper & Row, 1961), pp. 20–46.
5 In the writing of this section I have depended very heavily on Christopher Hill's *Intellectual Origins of the English Revolution* (London, Panther, 1972). L. Kolakowski's *Positivist Philosophy* (Harmondsworth, Penguin, 1972), is also a useful introductory work. George Novack's *Empiricism and its Evolution, a Marxist View* (New York, Pathfinder, 1971) is of some interest, but is far less reliable than the above works. The standard histories of philosophy by Russell and Copleston are also worth consulting, particularly the latter.
6 Hill, op. cit., p. 29.
7 A useful introduction to this debate can be gained from the earlier contributions in *Science and Religious Belief*, ed. C. A. Russell (Open University, 1973). See also Christopher Hill, *Puritanism and Revolution* (London, Panther, 1968).
8 See R. H. Popkin (ed.), *The Philosophy of the 16th and 17th Centuries* (London, Collier-Macmillan, 1968), p. 85.
9 The body of literature on the Enlightenment is enormous. Of the introductory material available, the collection *The Enlightenment*, edited by J. F. Lively (London, Longmans, 1966), provides a helpful diversity of brief extracts from primary sources, which can be followed up according to the student's interest. Ernst Cassirer's *The Philosophy of the Enlightenment* (Princeton University Press, 1951) is a classic secondary work, whilst Lucien Goldmann (*The Philosophy of the Enlightenment*, London, Routledge & Kegan Paul, 1973) and Eric

Hobsbawm (*The Age of Revolution, 1789–1848*, London and New York, Mentor, 1962) provides useful analyses of Enlightenment and post-Enlightenment thought in its social and historical importance. E. Barker's *Social Contract* (London, Oxford University Press, 1971) brings together three important texts of Enlightenment political philosophy.

10 See Maurice Dobb, *Studies in the Development of Capitalism* (London, Routledge & Kegan Paul, 1963), especially chapter 4.

11 P. L. Gardiner (ed.), *19th Century Philosophy* (New York, Free Press, 1969), p. 141. See also S. Andreski, *The Essential Comte*, trans. Margaret Clarke (London, Croom Helm, 1974), pp. 37–8.

12 'Invariable natural laws that will limit in each epoch, without the possibility of serious doubt, the extent and character of political action.' Andreski, op. cit., pp. 144–5.

13 Ibid., p. 20.

14 Ibid., p. 20.

15 Ibid., p. 24.

16 That knowledge has its source in experience is implicit in the first quotation given above. The doctrine of testability by experience is to be found in various places in the *Cours*. For example: 'Intellectual activity is sufficiently stimulated by the hope of discovering the laws of phenomena, the desire of confirming or refuting a theory' – Andreski, op. cit., p. 23. See also p. 139.

17 Ibid., p. 74.

18 Ibid., p. 100.

19 Ibid., p. 39.

20 Ibid., p. 56.

21 K. R. Popper, *The Poverty of Historicism* (London, Routledge & Kegan Paul, 1961), pp. 64ff.

22 Ibid., pp. 115ff.

23 Ibid., pp. 42–3.

24 See earlier in this chapter, p. 35.

25 Popper, op. cit., p. 128.

26 See, especially, chapter 4 of this book. For an authoritative, non-positivist treatment of the role of experimentation in the production of scientific knowledge, see the treatment of Gaston Bachelard's concept of 'phenomeno-technics' in D. Lecourt, *Marxism and Epistemology*, trans. Ben Brewster (London, New Left Books, 1975), pp. 76ff. and 137ff.

27 Popper, op. cit., p. 59.

28 Ibid., p. 62.

29 Ibid., p. 108.

30 Ibid., pp. 76ff.

31 See ibid., pp. 6–7 and 97–104.

32 K. Marx, *Capital*, vol. I (New York, International Publishers, 1967), pp. 644–5.

33 Andreski, op. cit., p. 167.

34 Herbert Marcuse, *Reason and Revolution* (London, Routledge & Kegan Paul, 1955), p. 342.

35 Ibid., p. 341.
36 The same point is made more fully in relation to the social theory of Durkheim, in chapter 5 of this book. A fuller exposition of the concept of ideology upon which this type of analysis is based is given in chapter 9.

3 The natural sciences I

1 See, for an important exception, the major contribution to contemporary debates in philosophy of the social sciences, R. Keat and J. Urry, *Social Theory as Science* (London, Routledge & Kegan Paul, 1975).
2 Winch, *I.S.S.*, chapter 3.
3 Especially in chapters 6 and 7.
4 They included Carnap, Neurath, Hahn, Waismann, Schlick and Reichenbach. A good account of the concerns and early development of the logical empiricist movement is given by Herbert Feigl in *The Legacy of Logical Positivism*, ed. Achinstein and Barker (Baltimore, Johns Hopkins University Press, 1969).
5 For a fuller account of logical atomism and of the differences between Russell's and Wittgenstein's versions of it see especially D. F. Pears, *Bertrand Russell and the British Tradition in Philosophy* (London, Fontana, 1967).
6 See P. F. Strawson, *Individuals* (London, Methuen, 1959), esp. chapter 4.
7 See, for instance, Wittgenstein's *Tractatus Logico-Philosophicus*, trans. Pears and McGuinness (London, Routledge & Kegan Paul, 1963), propositions 2.01231 and 2.0231.
8 For a fuller discussion of operationalism see R. Harré, *The Philosophies of Science* (London, Oxford University Press, 1972), especially pp. 76–8 and 161–3, and J. Losee, *A Historical Introduction to the Philosophy of Science* (London, Oxford University Press, 1972), especially pp. 181ff.
9 L. Wittgenstein, *Philosophical Investigations* (Oxford, Blackwell, 1963), esp. || 243–312 (pp. 88–103). See also the entertaining *Sense and Sensibilia* by J. L. Austin (London, Oxford University Press, 1962).
10 See, for instance, P. F. Strawson, op. cit., part 1.
11 See above, p. 501.
12 See above, p. 501.
13 For a discussion of this concept of explanation by one of its leading supporters, see C. G. Hempel, *The Philosophy of Natural Science* (Englewood Cliffs, Prentice-Hall, 1966), chapter 5. See also Losee op. cit., pp. 158–62.
14 M. Lessnoff (*The Structure of Social Science*, London, Allen & Unwin, 1974, pp. 19ff.) and Hempel (op. cit.) have useful introductory discussions of inductive generalisations.
15 Most of the apparatus of 'significance-testing' in orthodox social science research is aimed at providing a methodical way of estimating the strength of inductive support to generalisations provided by such results.

16 Lessnoff (op. cit., p. 71) seems to think that such laws must always be universal, but there seems to be no reason to suppose this.

17 See J. L. Mackie, 'Causes and Conditions', *American Philosophical Quarterly*, 2, 1965, pp. 245–64.

18 Lessnoff (op. cit., p. 65) uses this in an attempt to sidestep the supposed problem of individual free will in sociology.

19 See Hempel, op. cit., p. 67.

20 The by-now classic positivist treatment of functional explanation is C. G. Hempel's 'The Logic of Functional Analysis' in *Aspects of Scientific Explanation* (New York, Free Press, 1965). Accounts of functional explanation with more specific emphasis on their use in the social sciences are to be found in most of the standard textbooks. See, for example, Alan Ryan, *The Philosophy of the Social Sciences* (London, Macmillan, 1970), chapter 8; Lessnoff, op. cit., chapter 5; R. S. Rudner, *Philosophy of Social Science* (Englewood Cliffs, Prentice-Hall, 1966), chapter 5; and G. H. Von Wright, *Explanation and Understanding* (London, Routledge & Kegan Paul, 1971), chapter 3. See also R. P. Dore, 'Function and Cause', in *The Philosophy of Social Explanation*, ed. Alan Ryan (London, Oxford University Press, 1973).

21 See Hempel, *Aspects of Scientific Explanation*, pp. 314ff.

22 But see Mary B. Williams, 'Falsifiable Predictions of Evolutionary Theory', *Philosophy of Science*, 40, 1973, pp. 518–37.

23 R. Harré, op. cit., especially pp. 45–7. My whole discussion of the problems involved in the deductive-nomological model of explanation (and, indeed, my general approach to the philosophy of science) is greatly indebted to Harré's work.

24 See Harré, op. cit., pp. 116ff.

4 The natural sciences II

1 For a fuller, but still introductory exposition of the H-D account of scientific theories, see C. G. Hempel, *Philosophy of Natural Science* (Englewood Cliffs, Prentice-Hall), pp. 70ff.

2 See R. Harré, *The Philosophies of Science* (London, Oxford University Press, 1972), chapter 3, and R. Keat and J. Urry, *Social Theory as Science* (London, Routledge & Kegan Paul, 1975), esp. pp. 17–22, for introductory discussion on the status of theoretical entities. See also Hempel, op. cit., pp. 77ff.

3 On conventionalism, see J. Losee, *A Historical Introduction to the Philosophy of Science* (London, Oxford University Press, 1972), chapter 11 and Keat and Urry, op. cit., chapter 3.

4 Hempel, op. cit., pp. 81–2.

5 This work, chapter 3, pp. 61ff.

6 This work, chapter 3, pp. 61ff. See also Harré, op. cit., pp. 116ff.

7 See *The Science of Matter*, ed. M. P. Crosland (History of Science Readings, Harmondsworth, Penguin, 1971), p. 234.

8 The work of R. Carnap is the most well-known attempt to construct an 'inductive logic' on this basis.

9 Some of the work of Karl Popper adopts this approach, but beware of simplistic interpretations of Popper. I. Lakatos, 'Falsification and the Methodology of Scientific Research Programmes' (in I. Lakatos and A. Musgrave (eds), *Criticism and the Growth of Knowledge*, Cambridge University Press, 1970) gives a helpful classification of falsificationist and 'fallibilist' positions.

10 M. Lessnoff (*The Structure of Social Science*, London, Allen & Unwin, 1974), pp. 20–1 presents an argument which is supposed to support Popperian falsificationism on this point, but since the conclusion is that statistical laws are capable only of 'discorroboration' and not 'falsification' it is hard to recognise as such.

11 On the empiricist distinction between observation statements and theoretical statements see especially N. R. Hanson, *Patterns of Discovery* (Cambridge University Press, paperback edn, 1965), chapters 1, 2 and 4. See also T. S. Kuhn, *The Structure of Scientific Revolutions* (University of Chicago Press, 1962), chapter 6; and B. Hindess, *The Use of Official Statistics in Sociology* (London, Macmillan 1973), appendix. Hanson's discussion and the duck–rabbit figure are based on Wittgenstein, *Philosophical Investigations* (Oxford, Blackwell, 1963), II, xi, pp. 193ff.

12 See J. R. Partington, *A Short History of Chemistry* (London, Macmillan, 1965), pp. 200–11.

13 See, for example, Hempel, op. cit., pp. 73–4.

14 See, for examples, Kuhn, op. cit., chapter 13 and N. R. Hanson, *Observation and Explanation* (London, Allen & Unwin, 1971), p. 8.

15 See chapter 3 of this work, pp. 62ff.

16 See Hanson, *Patterns of Discovery*, chapter 4.

17 The work of Hanson, Kuhn, Lakatos (particularly his more recent work), Easlea and others is of this type. P. K. Feyerabend has oscillated between various forms of methodological relativism and the search for a broader and more 'humanitarian' conception of scientific rationality. Compare, for instance, pp. 217 and 228 in the same paper, 'Consolations for the Specialist', in Lakatos and Musgrave, op. cit.

18 Hanson, *Patterns of Discovery*, pp. 71–2 (final emphasis added).

19 See T. S. Kuhn, 'Logic of Discovery or Psychology of Research?' in Lakatos and Musgrave, op. cit.

20 'The new paradigm, or a sufficient hint to permit later articulation, emerges all at once, sometimes in the middle of the night, in the mind of a man deeply involved in crisis. What the nature of that final stage is . . . must here remain inscrutable and may be permanently so.' (Kuhn, *Structure of Scientific Revolutions*, 2nd edn, pp. 89–90.)

21 See this book, chapter 9.

22 Louis Althusser, 'From *Capital* to Marx's Philosophy', in L. Althusser and E. Balibar, *Reading Capital*, trans. Ben Brewster (London, New Left Books, 1970), pp. 41–2.

5 Positivism and ideology in the work of Emile Durkheim

1 See this book, chapter 2, p. 45.

2 In particular, my own account of Durkheim's methodology is very indebted to both the rather different accounts offered by P. Q. Hirst (*Durkheim, Bernard and Epistemology*, London, Routledge & Kegan Paul, 1975, and 'Morphology and Pathology', *Economy and Society*, vol. 2, no. 1, February, 1973) and Steven Lukes (*Émile Durkheim, his Life and Work*, Harmondsworth, Penguin, 1975).

3 Of the events of 1870 Durkheim said: 'The shock of those events was the stimulus which re-animated men's minds. The country found itself confronting the same question as at the beginning of the century. The system of organisation that constituted the imperial system . . . had just collapsed; it was a matter of rebuilding . . . a system with a real basis in the nature of things. For this purpose it was necessary to know what that nature of things was. In consequence, the urgency of establishing a science of societies did not delay in making itself felt.' (Quoted in Lukes, op. cit., p. 396.)

4 See Lukes, op. cit., pp. 66ff., and H. S. Hughes, *Consciousness and Society* (London, Macgibbon & Kee, 1967), especially chapter 2.

5 See P. Q. Hirst, 'Morphology and Pathology', pp. 3–6; and Lukes, op. cit., p. 73.

6 Comte, Espinas, Spencer, Tönnies, in particular.

7 See Lukes, op. cit., pp. 296–319.

8 See Durkheim, *The Rules of Sociological Method*, trans. from 8th edn by Solovay and Mueller, ed. G. E. G. Catlin (New York, Free Press paperback, 1964), p. lx.

9 Ibid., p. 145.

10 See 'Individual and Collective Representations', in E. Durkheim, *Sociology and Philosophy*, trans. D. F. Pocock (New York, Free Press, 1974), pp. 1–2.

11 This may justify the description of Durkheim as an 'objective' idealist in his ontological commitment – i.e. external (social) reality is conceded to exist, but argued to be essentially ideal, or spiritual in character. However, note that Durkheim sometimes, while asserting the homogeneity of social facts as a general type of fact (e.g. *Rules*, p. 13: 'No doubt, it may be of some advantage to reserve the term "morphological" for those social facts which concern the social substratum, but only on condition of not overlooking the fact they are of the same nature as the others'), nevertheless does distinguish within the field of social facts different 'degrees of crystallisation'. In the 1898 article, 'Individual and Collective Representations' (op. cit.), Durkheim actually implies that the 'collective substratum', social 'structure' or 'morphology' (here he seems to use the terms as equivalents, and gives as examples the merging of primitive clans, the organisation of the patriarchal family, etc.) is the foundation of the 'collective representations', which are nevertheless 'relatively autonomous'. This is to say, certain collective social facts are, whilst others are not, representational in character. Thus, in this text, at least, Durkheim's idealism is not in evidence (see especially *Sociology and Philosophy*, pp. 30–1).

12 See the *Rules*, p. xli.

13 Durkheim, *Sociology and Philosophy*, p. 19.

14 Durkheim, *The Division of Labour in Society* (New York, Free Press paperback, 1964), pp. 66–7.
15 For example, *Division of Labour*, pp. 68–9.
16 An example is Leibniz's metaphysics, in which 'monads', the ultimate constituents of the world, and analogues of human minds, carry in them 'marks' which 'represent' or 'express' the whole universe from the point of view of each monad.
17 For example, the distinction between primary and secondary qualities in seventeenth-century mechanics is sometimes expressed in this way, and there is, as I shall argue later, a comparable usage of the essence/appearance distinction in Marx's *Capital* (see chapters 8 and 9 of this book).
18 This book, chapter 2, pp. 28ff and 45.
19 *Rules*, p. xliii.
20 *Rules*, p. 30 ('external' is used in this passage in the sense of the first distinction, 'internal' in the sense of the second).
21 *Rules*, p. 7 (this seems to tell against Lukes's interpretation – cf. Lukes, op. cit., p. 11).
22 *Rules*, p. 8.
23 *Rules*, p. xliii.
24 *Rules*, p. xlv.
25 *Rules*, p. 6.
26 Lucien Goldmann, *The Human Sciences and Philosophy* (London, Jonathan Cape, 1969), pp. 36–42. For a critique from a broadly similar perspective, see I. M. Zeitlin, *Ideology and the Development of Sociological Theory* (Englewood Cliffs, Prentice-Hall, 1968), esp. pp. 234–80.
27 See, for example, P. L. Berger and T. Luckmann, *The Social Construction of Reality*, Harmondsworth, Penguin, 1967.
28 See, for the classic statement of this, Karl Marx, 'Economic and Philosophic Manuscripts of 1844', in Marx and Engels, *Collected Works* (London, Lawrence & Wishart, 1975, vol. 3, esp. pp. 270–82). See also chapter 8 of this book for a fuller treatment.
29 There may, of course, be more than one 'linguistic community' in this sense in any one society.
30 *Rules*, p. 14.
31 *Rules*, p. 15.
32 *Rules*, p. 15.
33 As we shall see, this is exactly the opposite of what Marx says in his important 1857 introduction to the *Grundrisse* (see chapter 8 of this book, pp. 167–8).
34 Chapters 8 and 9 of this book.
35 Compare this with: 'Scientific objectivity is possible only if one has broken with the immediate object, if one has refused to yield to the seduction of the initial choice, if one has checked and contradicted the thoughts which arise from one's first observation. Any objective examination, when duly verified, refutes the results of the first contact with the object. To start with, everything must be called into question: sensation, common sense, usage however constant, even etymology, for words, which are made for singing and enchanting, rarely make contact

with thought' (Gaston Bachelard, *Psychoanalysis of Fire* (Boston, Beacon Press, 1954, p. 1).

36 *Rules*, pp. 43–4.

37 *Rules*, p. xlv.

38 A point conceded implicitly by Durkheim with his mention of Copernicus's dissipation of the 'illusion of the senses' – see above, p. 95.

39 For example, *Rules*, p. 16. 'This encroachment of art on science, which prevents the development of the latter, is facilitated, moreover, by the very circumstances which determine the awakening of scientific reflection. For, since it comes into being only for the purpose of satisfying vital necessities, it finds itself quite naturally oriented toward the attainment of practical results. The needs which it is called to relieve are always urgent, and consequently hasten it on to a conclusion; they demand remedies, not explanations.'

40 *Rules*, p. 61.

41 *Rules*, p. 58

42 *Rules*, p. 60.

43 See 'Individual and Collective Representations' in *Sociology and Philosophy*, p. 1.

44 P. Q. Hirst, by a quite different argument, reaches a similar conclusion. See *Durkheim, Bernard and Epistemology*, pp. 115–35.

6 Kant and the Neo-Kantians

1 See this work, chapter 5, pp. 86–9.

2 See this work, chapter 1, p. 12.

3 I. Kant, *Critique of Pure Reason*, trans. N. Kemp Smith (London, Macmillan, 1964). There are several available introductory works on Kant's philosophy. Kant's own *Prolegomena to any Future Metaphysics*, trans. P. G. Lucas (Manchester University Press, 1953) is extremely useful. See also S. Körner, *Kant* (Harmondsworth, Penguin, 1955). More difficult and/or controversial texts on Kant include P. F. Strawson, *The Bounds of Sense* (London, Methuen, 1966); J. Bennett, *Kant's Analytic* and *Kant's Dialectic* (Cambridge University Press, 1966 and 1974, respectively); and Lucien Goldmann, *Immanuel Kant* (London, New Left Books, 1971).

4 Kant, *Critique of Pure Reason*, p. 218.

5 See H. Stuart Hughes, *Consciousness and Society* (London, Macgibbon & Kee, 1967), chapter 2.

6 Introductory works on the Neo-Kantian movement are somewhat sparse. W. Outhwaite, *Understanding Social Life* (London, Allen & Unwin, 1975) is of some use, as is Goldmann, op. cit. The following more general works contain useful discussions of the movement: G. H. Von Wright, *Explanation and Understanding* (London, Routledge & Kegan Paul, 1971, esp. chapter 1); T. Parsons, *The Structure of Social Action* (New York, Free Press, 1968), (esp. vol. 11, chapter XII); and H. Stuart Hughes, op. cit. (esp. chapters 2 and 6). Lukács's 'Reification and the Consciousness of the Proletariat' in *History and Class Consciousness* (London, Merlin Press, 1971) contains a critical

examination of 'classical' German philosophy from Kant by an author deeply involved in that development. Though most definitely not an 'introductory' text, it repays the effort required to read it. Also difficult, but worthwhile, is the short paper by Ben Brewster, 'Révai and Lukács', in the now defunct journal *Theoretical Practice*, no. 1, January 1971, pp. 14–21.

7 As we shall see in chapter 7, arguments closely related to this have been reintroduced into mid-twentieth-century British philosophy, especially in the later work of Ludwig Wittgenstein and Peter Winch. See also Marx and Engels, *The German Ideology*, *Part 1*, ed. C. J. Arthur (London, Lawrence & Wishart, 1970), p. 51.

8 W. Dilthey, *Gesammelte Schriften*, vol. VII, pp. 146ff., quoted in W. Outhwaite, op. cit., pp. 26–7. A selection of Dilthey's work is contained in H. P. Rickman, ed., *Meaning in History*, London, Allen & Unwin, 1961.

9 H. Rickert, *Science and History, a Critique of Positivist Epistemology*, trans. George Reisman, ed. A. Goddard (New York, Van Nostrand, 1962), p. 13.

10 Ibid., p. xvii.

11 Ibid., p. 32.

12 Ibid., p. 5.

13 Ibid., p. xv.

14 Ibid., pp. 28–9.

15 Ibid., p. 20.

16 See, for example, Ludwig Wittgenstein, *Philosophical Investigations* (Oxford, Blackwell, 1963), pp. 19ff.

17 For an interestingly similar position, see K. Marx, introduction to the *Grundrisse*, part 3 (in various selections of works by Marx and Engels). See also my treatment of this in chapter 8 of this book (pp. 167ff).

18 See P. F. Strawson, *Individuals* (London, Methuen, 1959), part 1.

19 Rickert, op. cit., p. 97.

7 The methodology of Max Weber, and Peter Winch's 'Corrections'

1 See, for instance, Lucien Goldmann, *Immanuel Kant* (London, New Left Books, 1971), esp. pp. 108–17. It does, however, seem to me that Goldmann's judgment is excessively harsh in this respect.

2 Max Weber, *The Theory of Social and Economic Organisations*, trans. T. Parsons and A. M. Henderson (New York, Free Press, 1964), p. 88.

3 Ibid., p. 101.

4 See, for a clarification of the very confused debate over the various types of individualism (methodological, ontological, logical, etc.), A. C. Danto, *Analytical Philosophy of History* (Cambridge University Press, 1968), pp. 257–84 (beware the slightly misleading terminology).

5 H. H. Gerth and C. Wright Mills, eds, *From Max Weber* (London, Routledge & Kegan Paul, 1970), p. 181.

6 Ibid., p. 184.

7 See this book, chapter 4, pp. 67ff.

8 Gerth and Mills, op. cit., p. 102.

9 See Steven Lukes, 'Methodological Individualism Reconsidered',

British Journal of Sociology, XIX (1968), pp. 119–29; reprinted in D. Emmet and A. MacIntyre (eds), *Sociological Theory and Philosophical Analysis* (London, Macmillan, 1970), and in A. Ryan (ed.), *The Philosophy of Social Explanation* (London, Oxford University Press, 1973).

10 See, for example, Weber's treatment of the vulgarisation of the Calvinist doctrine of predestination in *The Protestant Ethic and the Spirit of Capitalism* (trans. T. Parsons, London, Allen & Unwin University Books, 10th impression 1970), esp. p. 110; 'Quite naturally this attitude was impossible for his followers as early as Beza, and, above all, for the broad mass of ordinary men.' Calvinist doctrine runs up against what can only be understood as some sort of universal human need. This, in turn, brings about a change of doctrine.

11 Gerth and Mills, op. cit., pp. 182 and 184.

12 Weber, *Theory of Social and Economic Organisations*, p. 88.

13 Ibid., p. 93.

14 P. Winch, *I.S.S.*, pp. 49–50. See also the criticism of Winch's interpretation of Weber in W. G. Runciman, *A Critique of Max Weber's Philosophy of Social Science* (Cambridge University Press, 1972), p. 21.

15 See this book, chapter 6, pp. 108–9.

16 Weber, *Theory of Social and Economic Organisations*, p. 88.

17 Ibid., p. 112.

18 Winch, *I.S.S.*, pp. 116–20.

19 Positivist critics of the concepts of *verstehen* include T. F. Abel, 'The Operation called Verstehen', *American Journal of Sociology*, vol. 54, 1948, pp. 211–18, and R. S. Rudner, *Philosophy of Social Science* (Englewood Cliffs, Prentice-Hall, 1966), pp. 71–3. 'Rescuers' of the concept include D. Leat, 'Misunderstanding Verstehen', *Sociological Review*, vol. 20, 1972, pp. 29–38; P. Winch, *I.S.S.*, pp. 111–16; and R. Keat and J. Urry, *Social Theory as Science* (London, Routledge & Kegan Paul, 1975), esp. chapter 7.

20 Weber, *Theory of Social and Economic Organisations*, p. 90.

21 Keat and Urry, in their excellent critical discussion of these concepts, seem to follow Weber in this. See their *Social Theory as Science*, pp. 147–8 and 167–75.

22 Elsewhere, Weber demonstrates that he is well aware of this point. See, for example, his *Methodology of the Social Sciences*, trans. and ed. E. A. Shils and H. A. Finch (Chicago, Free Press, 1949), pp. 179–80.

23 Winch, *I.S.S.*, pp. 113–16.

24 Similar points have been made by A. MacIntyre, 'The Idea of a Social Science', *Aristotelian Society, Supplementary Proceedings*, 1967, pp. 95–114 and E. Gellner, 'Concepts and Society', in *Sociological Theory and Philosophical Analysis*, eds D. Emmett and A. MacIntyre (London, Macmillan, 1970), pp. 115–49 (both articles reprinted in B. Wilson (ed.), *Rationality* (Oxford, Blackwell, 1974)).

25 Winch, *I.S.S.*, p. 89.

26 Winch, 'Understanding a Primitive Society', *American Philosophical Quarterly*, vol. 1, 1964, pp. 307–24, reprinted in Wilson, op. cit., pp. 78–111.

27 See L. Wittgenstein, *Philosophical Investigations* (Oxford, Blackwell, 1963), 1, pp. 241–2.
28 Weber, *Methodology of the Social Sciences*, pp. 143–6.
29 Ibid., p. 143.
30 Ibid., p. 160.
31 For a helpful discussion of these and other, less distinctively Weberian, theses on value-judgments, see Keat and Urry, op. cit., pp. 196ff.
32 W. G. Runciman, op. cit., pp. 37ff.
33 This follows from Weber's methodological individualism and his thesis that historical concepts are constructed according to the criterion of value-relevance.
34 I use the term 'couple' here to refer to two theoretical positions apparently opposed to each other, yet which share, at a fundamental level, common presuppositions.
35 This distinction, and the terminology I employ, are not of course original. They derive, with some modification, from L. Althusser's 'reading' of Marx. This will be subjected to further critical discussion in chapters 8 and 9.
36 Weber, *Methodology of the Social Sciences*, p. 175.
37 Weber, *Theory of Social and Economic Organisations*, pp. 94–5.
38 Ibid., p. 95.
39 Ibid., pp. 98–9.
40 Ibid., p. 99.
41 Winch, *I.S.S.*, pp. 111–16 and 75–86.
42 *Explananda* (singular *explanandum*) are events, phenomena, etc. which require, or are the objects of, a (scientific) explanation.
43 Donald Davidson, 'Actions, Reasons and Causes', *Journal of Philosophy*, vol. 60 (1963), pp. 685–700, reprinted in A. R. White (ed.), *The Philosophy of Action* (London, Oxford University Press, 1968), pp. 79–94.
44 Winch, *I.S.S.*, pp. 83ff.
45 Ibid., pp. 91ff.
46 'Rationalisation' is used here in its common-sense usage, not in the misleading technical sense which Davidson gives to it in the above article.
47 Keat and Urry, op. cit., pp. 151–3.
48 Winch, *I.S.S.*, pp. 89ff.
49 This argument being an attempt to demonstrate the plausibility of thesis 5 above.
50 Weber, *The Protestant Ethic and the Spirit of Capitalism*, pp. 21ff.

8 Karl Marx and Frederick Engels: philosophy of history and theory of knowledge

1 See the more extended discussion of Althusser's work in chapter 9.
2 See V. I. Lenin, *Materialism and Empirio-Criticism* (Moscow, Progress Publishers, 1970).
3 The literature on the relationship between Marx and Hegel is very extensive indeed. The following is a small, but fairly representative

sample: G. V. Plekhanov, *Fundamental Problems of Marxism* (London, Lawrence & Wishart, 1969), esp. chapters I–V; G. Lukács, *History and Class Consciousness*, trans. R. Livingstone (London, Merlin Press, 1971), especially the essay 'Reification and the Consciousness of the Proletariat'; H. Marcuse, *Reason and Revolution* (London, Routledge & Kegan Paul, 1955), *passim*; L. Althusser, *For Marx* (London, Allen Lane, 1969), *passim*, but especially the essay 'Contradiction and Over-determination'; L. Althusser, *Politics and History* (London, New Left Books, 1972), esp. pp. 161–86; L. Colletti, *Marxism and Hegel* (London New Left Books, 1973), *passim*.

4 My understanding of the relationship between Kant and Hegel has been helped by the following: J. Plamenatz, *Man and Society* (London, Longmans, Green, 1963), vol. 2, chapters 3 and 4; S. Rosen, *G. W. F. Hegel* (New Haven, Yale University Press, 1974); L. Colletti, op. cit., chapters VII and VIII; H. Marcuse, op. cit., pp. 16–30; G. Lukács, 'Reification and the Consciousness of the Proletariat', in *History and Class Consciousness*, op. cit.

5 G. W. F. Hegel, *Science of Logic*, trans. Johnston and Struthers (London, Allen & Unwin, 1929), pp. 33–4.

6 Ibid., p. 168.

7 See, for an elementary but nonetheless useful exposition of Hegel on self-realisation, Plamenatz, op. cit., vol. II, p. 143.

8 In this, of course, the interpreters of Marx and Engels have been led by Marx and Engels themselves. See, for instance, *Capital*, vol. 1, afterword to the 2nd German edition (New York, International Publishers, 1967, p. 20); 'With him [Hegel] it [the dialectic] is standing on its head. It must be turned right side up again, if you would discover the rational kernel within the mystical shell.' See also F. Engels, *Anti-Dühring* (London, Lawrence & Wishart, 1969, p. 35): 'This way of thinking [Hegel's Idealism] turned everything upside down, and completely reversed the actual connection of things in the world.'

9 L. Feuerbach, *Sämtliche Werke*, vol. II, p. 363, quoted in E. Kamenka, *The Philosophy of Ludwig Feuerbach* (London, Routledge & Kegan Paul, 1970), p. 71.

10 In this respect, Feuerbach's argument amounts to a reinstatement of certain aspects of Kant's epistemology (though without commitment to 'things-in-themselves'). Compare Colletti's argument that Marx, too, in his critique of Hegel (in the Introduction to the *Grundrisse*) reinstates Kant (Colletti, op. cit., chapter VIII).

11 L. Feuerbach, *The Essence of Christianity*, trans. Marion Evans (New York, Harper & Row, 1957).

12 Marx and Engels, *Collected Works*, vol. 3 (London, Lawrence & Wishart, 1975), p. 274.

13 Ibid., pp. 276–7.

14 Ibid., pp. 296–7.

15 See Ibid.; '. . . positive criticism as a whole – and therefore also German positive criticism of political economy – owes its true foundation to the discoveries of Feuerbach . . .' (p. 232) and: 'Feuerbach's great achievement is . . . (t)he establishment of *true materialism* and

of *real science* . . .' (p. 328). For Plekhanov, too, the philosophical identity of Marx and Feuerbach's materialism was the foundation of that of Marx and Engels (see especially *Fundamental Problems of Marxism*, pp. 25–6).

16 K. Marx, *A Contribution to the Critique of Political Economy* (London, Lawrence & Wishart, 1971), p. 22.

17 Ibid., p. 20.

18 K. Marx, 'First Thesis on Feuerbach', in *The German Ideology, Part 1*, trans. Chris Arthur (London, Lawrence & Wishart, 1970), p. 121.

19 Marx, 'Fourth Thesis', ibid., p. 122.

20 Marx and Engels, *German Ideology, Part 1*, p. 94 (my emphasis added).

21 Marx, 'Fourth Thesis on Feuerbach', in *The German Ideology, Part 1*, p. 122 (my emphasis added).

22 Consider, especially, Marx's use of the essence/appearance distinction, which I discuss later in this chapter, and on pp. 172–3 and 178ff.

23 Marx himself suggests this reading when he refers, in the afterword to the second German edition of *Capital*, to his having 'coquetted with the modes of expression peculiar to [Hegel]'. (Marx, *Capital*, vol. 1, New York, International Publishers, 1967, p. 20.)

24 N. Poulantzas, *Political Power and Social Classes*, trans. O'Hagan (London, New Left Books; Sheed & Ward, 1973), introduction.

25 There exists no satisfactory introduction to the general theory of historical materialism. Perhaps still the best introduction is one of the smaller collections of the writings of Marx, *Karl Marx: Selected Writings in Sociology and Philosophy*, ed. Bottomore and Rubel (Harmondsworth, Penguin, 1963). However, one defect of this collection is that its organisation takes little account of the historical development of Marx's thought. A useful introductory secondary source is R. Keat and J. Urry, *Social Theory as Science* (London, Routledge & Kegan Paul, 1975), chapter 5. More advanced and controversial, but extremely rewarding discussions of general theoretical questions in Marxism are Balibar's essay 'The Basic Concepts of Historical Materialism', which is part III of L. Althusser and E. Balibar, *Reading Capital* (London, New Left Books, 1970); and B. Hindess and P. Q. Hirst, *Pre-Capitalist Modes of Production* (London, Routledge & Kegan Paul, 1975).

26 Considerable recent work of elaboration and critical discussion has been carried out. See especially Hindess and Hirst, op. cit.

27 Probably still the best introduction to Marxist economic theory is P. Sweezy, *The Theory of Capitalist Development* (New York, Monthly Review Press, 1942, reprinted 1964).

28 See, for instance, L. Althusser, *For Marx*, especially pp. 100–7 and 252–3.

29 See, for a further exposition and critical discussion of this, pp. 163–5 and 178ff. of this book.

30 See this book, chapter 4, pp. 65ff. Note also Marx's preface to the first German edition of *Capital:* 'The physicist either observes physical phenomena where they occur in their most typical form and most free from disturbing influence or, wherever possible, he makes experiments

under conditions that assure the occurrence of the phenomenon in its normality. In this work I have to examine the capitalist mode of production, and the conditions of production and exchange corresponding to that mode. Up to the present time, their classic ground is England. That is the reason why England is used as the chief illustration in the development of my theoretical ideas' (*Capital*, p. 8).

31 Such concepts differ from Weberian 'ideal types' in that abstraction is not a 'value-guided' selection from a manifold, but a process of theoretical production carried out under the constraint of gaining an objective knowledge of a causally effective actual structure.

32 My distinction here between abstract entities and real theoretical entities is related to the contrast drawn in a rather unsatisfactory way in terms of 'weak' and 'strong' senses of existence by Nicos Poulantzas: 'The mode of production constitutes an abstract-formal object which does not exist in the strong sense in reality. . . . The only thing which really exists is a historically determined social formation, i.e. a social whole, in the widest sense, at a given moment in its historical existence. . .' (Poulantzas, op. cit., p. 15). My position differs importantly from Poulantzas's, however, in that I do, whereas he does not, ascribe real existence to particular instances of general theoretical concepts such as capitalist mode of production, capitalist state, etc.

33 Cf. Marx's 1957 introduction to the *Grundrisse*: '. . . the so-called general conditions of all and any production, however, are nothing but abstract conceptions which do not define any of the actual stages of production'. (Published as an appendix to Marx, *Contribution to the Critique of Political Economy*, London, Lawrence & Wishart, p. 193).

34 See especially F. Engels, *Anti-Dühring* (op. cit.) and *Dialectics of Nature*, trans. C. Dutt (London, Lawrence & Wishart, 1940).

35 Engels, *Anti-Dühring*, p. 31.

36 This chapter, p. 143.

37 Colletti, op. cit., esp. chapters I and III.

38 See V. I. Lenin, 'On the Question of Dialectics', *Collected Works*, vol. 38 (London, Lawrence & Wishart, 1961), p. 359.

39 See Colletti, op. cit., pp. 41–2.

40 See, for instance, the essay 'On the Materialist Dialectic', where Althusser says, referring to Engels, 'The application of the "laws" of the dialectic to such and such a result of physics, for example, makes not one iota of difference to the structure or development of the theoretical practice of physics; worse, it may turn into an ideological fetter' (Althusser, *For Marx*, p. 170). But a little later we get: 'The knowledge of the process of this theoretical practice in its generality . . . itself a specified form of the general process of transformation, of the "development of things", constitutes a first theoretical elaboration of theory, that is, of the materialist dialectic' (ibid. p. 173). But see also the self-criticism in the foreword to the Italian edition of Althusser and Balibar, *Reading Capital*, pp. 7–8.

41 See *Selected Readings from the Works of Mao Tse-tung* (Peking, 1967), especially 'On Contradiction' and 'On the Correct Handling of Contradictions among the People'.

42 Compare the Marx of the 1844 *Manuscripts*, still in the grip of the (inverted) Hegelian dialectic: '. . . the emancipation of the workers contains universal human emancipation – and it contains this, because the whole of human servitude is involved in the relation of the worker to production, and all relations of servitude are but modifications and consequences of this relation' (Marx and Engels, *Collected Works*, vol. 3, p. 280).

43 The term 'overdetermination', as Althusser uses it, is drawn from psychoanalytic theory and is quite distinct from the empiricist use of the term according to which an event is said to be 'overdetermined' if there occurs a multiplicity of causally sufficient conditions for it.

44 See L. Althusser, *For Marx*, especially the essays 'Contradiction and Overdetermination' and 'On the Materialist Dialectic'.

45 Especially in Colletti, op. cit., pp. 88–9.

46 'Marxism and the Dialectic', *New Left Review*, vol. 93 (Sept./Oct. 1975), pp. 3–29.

47 Colletti, op. cit., p. 29.

48 Mao Tse-tung, 'On Contradiction', *Selected Readings*, p. 96.

49 See chapter 5 of this book, p. 81.

50 In particular, Marx's critiques of other political economists; an excellent short account of the epistemological significance of these critiques is given in Keat and Urry, op. cit., chapter 5.

51 Marx, unlike many of his 'followers', was never content to substitute an analysis of the source or function of an ideology for a rational critique of its cognitive status. That Marx did separate the questions of the epistemological status and the genesis of ideas is evidenced by his attempts to describe and justify the 'materialist method' (see especially the *German Ideology*, pp. 42ff.) without reference to its causal relationship to material life. Also, significantly, Marx asserts the causal dependency of the natural sciences on material life (see, for instance, the *German Ideology*, p. 63), without thereby casting doubt on their status as knowledge. Indeed, for Marx and Engels the natural sciences served as paradigms of genuine knowledge.

52 Marx and Engels, *German Ideology*, *Part 1*, p. 52.

53 Ibid., p. 64.

54 Lenin, in *What is to be Done?* (various editions), was a victim of this theory, concluding that the 'spontaneous' development of the working-class movement necessarily led it into domination by the ruling ideology. The task of producing a revolutionary ideology was to be performed by a radical intelligentsia. Lenin's position on these questions shifted significantly, however, after the 'revolution' of 1905.

55 See John Mepham, 'The Theory of Ideology in Capital', in *Radical Philosophy*, vol. 2 (Summer 1972), for an exceptionally clear statement of this.

56 Marx, *Capital*, vol. 1, pp. 71–83 and 535–42 respectively.

57 Ibid., p. 73 (emphasis added).

58 Ibid., p. 540 (emphasis added). See also p. 176 of the same volume.

59 See this book, chapter 5, pp. 94–7.

60 See Marx, *Capital*, vol. 1, p. 79. See also N. Geras, 'Essence and Appearance', *New Left Review*, 65, pp. 82 ff.
61 Various editions, including as an appendix to *A Contribution to the Critique of Political Economy*; a supplementary text in the *German Ideology*, part 1; and in Nicolaus (trans.), *Grundrisse* (Harmondsworth, Penguin, 1973). My page references are to the *Contribution to the Critique of Political Economy* version.
62 See, for example, L. Althusser, *Lenin and Philosophy and Other Essays* (London, New Left Books, 1971), p. 150.
63 Marx and Engels, *German Ideology*, p. 48.
64 Ibid., p. 48.
65 Ibid., p. 48.
66 Ibid., p. 42.
67 Ibid., pp. 42 and 47.
68 Ibid., p. 48.
69 Ibid., p. 48.
70 Marx and Engels, *Collected Works*, vol. 2, pp. 302 and 300 respectively.
71 This chapter, pp. 154–5.
72 See also Marx's letter intended (in 1877) for the editorial board of a Russian journal, *Otechestvenniye Zapiski*: 'By studying each of these forms of evolution separately and then comparing them one can easily find the clue to this phenomenon, but one will never arrive there by using as one's master key a general historico-philosophical theory, the supreme virtue of which consists in being super-historical.' (Marx and Engels, *Selected Correspondence*, Moscow, Progress Publishers, 2nd edn, 1965, p. 313.)
73 Marx, introduction to the *Grundrisse* (see above, note 61), p. 193.
74 Ibid., p. 190. Nicolaus (*Grundrisse*, p. 85) has the preferable 'rational' in place of 'sensible'.
75 Ibid., p. 190. My emphasis.
76 Ibid., p. 190. Compare Nicolaus, op. cit., p. 85; '. . . this common element, sifted out by comparison, is itself segmented many times over and splits into different determinations'.
77 Marx, op. cit., pp. 205–14.
78 Compare my earlier discussion of the various levels of abstraction in Marxist theory (this chapter, pp. 154–5).

9 Towards a materialist theory of knowledge

1 See chapters 3 and 4.
2 See chapter 5.
3 This criterion is intended to be quite general. Even where knowledge is itself an object of knowledge (as in the history of science, or epistemology), knowledge and its process of production is independent of explicit, theoretical knowledge of the history of science, the 'nature and scope' of knowledge and so on. The problems of epistemology do not require to be solved as a general condition of production of scientific knowledge.
4 See chapter 5, pp. 86–9.

5 Introduction to the *Grundrisse*, published as an appendix to Marx, *A Contribution to the Critique of Political Economy* (London, Lawrence & Wishart, 1971), p. 210.

6 This, I argued in chapter 7 (pp. 126–8), is the only way of avoiding the humanist commitment to relativism or a philosophical anthropology without simultaneously resorting to positivism.

7 See this book, chapter 2, pp. 40–1.

8 See this book, chapter 8, p. 163.

9 L. Althusser, *Lenin and Philosophy and Other Essays* (London, New Left Books, 1971), the essay 'Ideology and Ideological State Apparatuses'.

10 Ibid., p. 158.

11 See my essay 'Education and Politics' in D. Holly (ed.), *Education or Domination?* (London, Arrow, 1974), for a fuller presentation of a related point in connection with the educational 'ISA'. See also E. Gellner, 'Concepts and Society', in Bryan Wilson (ed.), *Rationality* (Oxford, Blackwell, 1974).

12 Althusser, op. cit., pp. 170–3. See also J. Rancière, 'On the Theory of Ideology', in *Radical Philosophy*, vol. 7, pp. 2–12.

13 I mean specifically, here, parties, (*a*) to which the principal economic organisations of the working class (trade unions, cooperatives, etc.) are affiliated or otherwise organisationally connected, (*b*) to which the mass of workers give electoral and other allegiance, and (*c*) which have their origins in the efforts of organised workers to pursue their perceived interests at the political level. That many of these may be said to have 'bourgeois' programmes is, for my purposes here, irrelevant.

14 There are also strong arguments, running counter to the whole Marxist tradition (apart from an occasional text by Engels), for regarding the family principally as an economic institution. I refer, in particular, to its role in the production and reproduction of agents of production. The significance of this for, e.g., the economic status of domestic labour is an issue which has been brought to the fore by the contemporary women's movement.

15 This is put admirably by Rancière: 'Proletarian ideology is neither the summary of the representations or positive values of the workers, nor the body of "proletarian" doctrines. It is a stopped assembly-line, an authority mocked, a system of divisions between particular jobs of work abolished, a mass fight-back against "scientific" innovations in exploitation . . .' (Rancière, op. cit., p. 12).

16 Althusser, op. cit., pp. 172–3.

17 Compare my discussion of Weber on class consciousness, chapter 7, p. 115–16.

18 Marx, op. cit., pp. 193–205, especially pp. 204–5.

19 Marx, *Capital*, vol. 1 (New York, International Publishers, 1967), p. 540.

20 The condensed form of my argument here renders it liable to be misread as implying that the sole source of working-class (and other subordinate class) ideologies is in economic practices and experience. It is my view that economic practices and experiences are crucial in

deciding the basic categories for economic ideologies, and that these economic ideologies play a fundamental role in structuring and providing metaphors in the other ideological regions (ideologies of the state, moral ideologies, etc.). However, struggles of a directly political (e.g. for legislative reforms), educational (e.g. for curriculum changes) or 'familial' (e.g. for the right to free abortion), etc. nature all contribute to the ideological formation of individuals, strata, and classes.

21 I am not arguing, of course, that such a working-class theoretical ideology usually, or even ever, exists in a 'pure form' in the consciousness of individual workers or even in the programme or literature of working-class parties or other organisations. Generally, it exists in a complex and contradictory unity with elements of the ideologies of other classes. For example, the British Labour Party's famous 'Clause 4' embodies a recognition of the necessity of social ownership of the means of production, distribution and exchange as an objective of the Labour movement, but this is combined in the programme with a social-democratic conception of the state as a neutral arbiter between competing interests and a corresponding conception of political practice.

22 Here, it will be the distinctive relationship of domestic labour to capitalist production in the narrow sense, the contradictions between ideologies of 'equality of opportunity' and patriarchal ideologies, the economic and ideological effects of imperialism and so on which will be decisive in the formation and inculcation of alternative ideologies to the ruling ideology in its various forms.

23 This book, pp. 79–80.

24 This book, chapter 8, p. 156.

25 See the quotation from *Reading Capital* which I gave at the end of chapter 4 (this book, pp. 79–80).

26 See my commentary on Marx's Introduction to the *Grundrisse* (this book, chapter 8, pp. 167–9).

27 This chapter, p. 192.

28 See D. Lecourt, *Marxism and Epistemology*, trans. Ben Brewster (London, New Left Books, 1975), esp. pp. 119–41. See also the introduction to the English edition (pp. 7–19) for a discussion of the relationship between Kuhn's and Bachelard's epistemologies.

29 See, for an example of such criticisms of Althusser's theory of knowledge, A. Glucksmann, 'A Ventriloquist Structuralism', *New Left Review*, 72 (March/April 1972), pp. 68–92.

30 N. Geras, for example, makes this claim, in his essay, 'Althusser's Marxism, an Account and Assessment', *New Left Review*, 71 (Jan/Feb. 1972), pp. 57–86, esp. pp. 82ff.

31 This chapter, pp. 191ff..

32 L. Althusser and E. Balibar, *Reading Capital*, trans. Ben Brewster (London, New Left Books, 1970), esp. chapter 6. See also Engels's preface to vol. II of *Capital* (London, Lawrence & Wishart, 1970), pp. 15ff.

33 See especially the essay 'On the Young Marx', in *For Marx* (London, Allen Lane, 1969, pp. 49–86). Althusser later criticises this earlier

essay (see *For Marx*, p. 187, footnote 23), but doesn't find an alternative.
34 Althusser, *For Marx*, p. 186.
35 Althusser and Balibar, op. cit., p. 52.
36 This chapter, p. 171.
37 As well as comparable difficulties in Kuhn's conception of a 'paradigm-shift'.
38 See this chapter, pp. 173–4.
39 See, for example, the glossary definition of 'ideology' in *For Marx*, p. 252.
40 Althusser and Balibar, op. cit., p. 59.
41 See my discussion of this aspect of Durkheim's work in chapter 5, pp. 97–9 of this book.
42 This term refers to the attempt to write the history of science without reference to any extrinsic economic, technical or social practices.
43 Still the best introductory account of the early development of modern science is, in my view, to be found in H. Butterfield, *The Origins oj Modern Science* (London, G. Bell, 1957). See also the various works by A. Koyré on Galileo and Newton.
44 To avoid misunderstandings, it is essential to stress that here, and throughout the present work, I treat the question of the cognitive status of a particular theoretical text – its status as knowledge – as a question to be answered independently of the question of the class, or other interests presupposed in its conceptual structure (i.e. its status as science or ideology). In general, a solution to the second question will presuppose a solution into the first. Conversely, a political critique of a text can never be a substitute for an epistemological one.
45 Here, as elsewhere in this book, I am greatly indebted to the works, in the philosophy of science, of R. Harré. Two other texts have recently appeared which also link this realist approach in the philosophy of science with Marxism. These are R. Keat and J. Urry, *Social Theory as Science* (London, Routledge & Kegan Paul, 1975), and R. Bhaskar, 'Feyerabend and Bachelard: Two Philosophies of Science', *New Left Review* (Nov/Dec. 1975), pp. 31–55. See also Bhaskar's *Realist Theory of Science* (Leeds, Alma Book Company, 1975); (unfortunately, the last mentioned texts appeared too late for me to take any account of them in this work).
46 See R. Harré's *The Philosophies of Science* (Oxford University Press, 1972), esp. chapter 4, for a fuller exposition of this general line of argument.
47 This book, chapter 7, pp. 123ff.
48 This chapter, pp. 183–4.
49 It is important to note that I am here arguing only that the requirement of consistency between basic concepts and ontologies of the various sciences may provide a basis for criteria of validity (and, in general, rational discourse) applicable across paradigm-boundaries. I am not arguing that the requirement of consistency with pre-established conceptual frameworks and ontologies will always actually be a criterion of validity within specific disciplinary specialisms. This was the effective criterion in my phlogiston-theory example, but in the notable

case of the Newtonian concept of gravitation the concept was retained despite its inconsistency with the prevailing ontology and conceptions of explanation. Any fully adequate account of a concept of 'scientific progress' along the lines I have suggested would have to demonstrate the considerations which dictate retention of a concept or type of explanation which runs counter to the prevailing scientific ontology, and this in turn would involve further work in the classification of the sciences. In particular, the cognitive authority of certain sciences vis-à-vis others is connected with the generality of the scope of their ontologies. Physics is, for instance, in this respect more 'fundamental' than biology or sociology. So far as I know, Comte is the only philosopher to have tackled these problems in a systematic way. How far his general solutions can be disentangled from the Comtian 'nature philosophy' and utilised for these purposes is a question which must remain, for the moment, unanswered.

50 P. F. Strawson, *Individuals* (London, Methuen, 1959), especially chapter 1.

Index

Routledge Social Science Series

Routledge & Kegan Paul London, Henley and Boston

39 Store Street,
London WC1E 7DD
Broadway House,
Newtown Road,
Henley-on-Thames,
Oxon RG9 1EN
9 Park Street,
Boston, Mass. 02108

Contents

Authors wishing to submit manuscripts for any series in this catalogue should send them to the Social Science Editor, Routledge & Kegan Paul Ltd, 39 Store Street, London WC1E 7DD.

● *Books so marked are available in paperback.*
○ *Books so marked are available in paperback only.*
All books are in metric Demy 8vo format (216 × 138mm approx.) unless otherwise stated.

International Library of Sociology
General Editor John Rex

GENERAL SOCIOLOGY

Barnsley, J. H. The Social Reality of Ethics. *464 pp.*
Brown, Robert. Explanation in Social Science. *208 pp.*
● Rules and Laws in Sociology. *192 pp.*
Bruford, W. H. Chekhov and His Russia. *A Sociological Study. 244 pp.*
Burton, F. and **Carlen, P.** Official Discourse. *On Discourse Analysis, Government Publications, Ideology. About 140 pp.*
Cain, Maureen E. Society and the Policeman's Role. *326 pp.*
● **Fletcher, Colin.** Beneath the Surface. *An Account of Three Styles of Sociological Research. 221 pp.*
Gibson, Quentin. The Logic of Social Enquiry. *240 pp.*
Glassner, B. Essential Interactionism. *208 pp.*
Glucksmann, M. Structuralist Analysis in Contemporary Social Thought. *212 pp.*
Gurvitch, Georges. Sociology of Law. *Foreword by Roscoe Pound. 264 pp.*
Hinkle, R. Founding Theory of American Sociology 1881–1913. *About 350 pp.*
Homans, George C. Sentiments and Activities. *336 pp.*
Johnson, Harry M. Sociology: *A Systematic Introduction. Foreword by Robert K. Merton. 710 pp.*
● **Keat, Russell** and **Urry, John.** Social Theory as Science. *278 pp.*
Mannheim, Karl. Essays on Sociology and Social Psychology. *Edited by Paul Keckskemeti. With Editorial Note by Adolph Lowe. 344 pp.*
Martindale, Don. The Nature and Types of Sociological Theory. *292 pp.*
● **Maus, Heinz.** A Short History of Sociology. *234 pp.*
Myrdal, Gunnar. Value in Social Theory: *A Collection of Essays on Methodology. Edited by Paul Streeten. 332 pp.*
Ogburn, William F. and **Nimkoff, Meyer F.** A Handbook of Sociology. *Preface by Karl Mannheim. 656 pp. 46 figures. 35 tables.*
Parsons, Talcott and **Smelser, Neil J.** Economy and Society: *A Study in the Integration of Economic and Social Theory. 362 pp.*
Payne, G., Dingwall, R., Payne, J. and **Carter, M.** Sociology and Social Research. *About 250 pp.*
Podgórecki, A. Practical Social Sciences. *About 200 pp.*
Podgórecki, A. and **Łos, M.** Multidimensional Sociology. *268 pp.*
Raffel, S. Matters of Fact. *A Sociological Inquiry. 152 pp.*
● **Rex, John.** Key Problems of Sociological Theory. *220 pp.*
Sociology and the Demystification of the Modern World. *282 pp.*
● **Rex, John.** (Ed.) Approaches to Sociology. *Contributions by Peter Abell, Frank Bechhofer, Basil Bernstein, Ronald Fletcher, David Frisby, Miriam Glucksmann, Peter Lassman, Herminio Martins, John Rex, Roland Robertson, John Westergaard and Jock Young. 302 pp.*
Rigby, A. Alternative Realities. *352 pp.*
Roche, M. Phenomenology, Language and the Social Sciences. *374 pp.*
Sahay, A. Sociological Analysis. *220 pp.*
Strasser, Hermann. The Normative Structure of Sociology. *Conservative and Emancipatory Themes in Social Thought. About 340 pp.*
Strong, P. Ceremonial Order of the Clinic. *267 pp.*
Urry, John. Reference Groups and the Theory of Revolution. *244 pp.*
Weinberg, E. Development of Sociology in the Soviet Union. *173 pp.*

FOREIGN CLASSICS OF SOCIOLOGY

● **Gerth, H. H.** and **Mills, C. Wright.** From Max Weber: *Essays in Sociology. 502 pp.*

● **Tönnies, Ferdinand.** Community and Association *(Gemeinschaft und Gesellschaft). Translated and Supplemented by Charles P. Loomis. Foreword by Pitirim A. Sorokin. 334 pp.*

SOCIAL STRUCTURE

Andreski, Stanislav. Military Organization and Society. *Foreword by Professor A. R. Radcliffe-Brown. 226 pp. 1 folder.*

Broom, L., Lancaster Jones, F., McDonnell, P. and **Williams, T.** The Inheritance of Inequality. *About 180 pp.*

Carlton, Eric. Ideology and Social Order. *Foreword by Professor Philip Abrahams. About 320 pp.*

Clegg, S. and **Dunkerley, D.** Organization, Class and Control. *614 pp.*

Coontz, Sydney H. Population Theories and the Economic Interpretation. *202 pp.*

Coser, Lewis. The Functions of Social Conflict. *204 pp.*

Crook, I. and **D.** The First Years of the Yangyi Commune. *304 pp., illustrated.*

Dickie-Clark, H. F. Marginal Situation: *A Sociological Study of a Coloured Group. 240 pp. 11 tables.*

Giner, S. and **Archer, M. S.** (Eds) Contemporary Europe: *Social Structures and Cultural Patterns, 336 pp.*

● **Glaser, Barney** and **Strauss, Anselm L.** Status Passage: *A Formal Theory. 212 pp.*

Glass, D. V. (Ed.) Social Mobility in Britain. *Contributions by J. Berent, T. Bottomore, R. C. Chambers, J. Floud, D. V. Glass, J. R. Hall, H. T. Himmelweit, R. K. Kelsall, F. M. Martin, C. A. Moser, R. Mukherjee and W. Ziegel. 420 pp.*

Kelsall, R. K. Higher Civil Servants in Britain: *From 1870 to the Present Day. 268 pp. 31 tables.*

● **Lawton, Denis.** Social Class, Language and Education. *192 pp.*

McLeish, John. The Theory of Social Change: *Four Views Considered. 128 pp.*

● **Marsh, David C.** The Changing Social Structure of England and Wales, 1871–1961. *Revised edition. 288 pp.*

Menzies, Ken. Talcott Parsons and the Social Image of Man. *About 208 pp.*

● **Mouzelis, Nicos.** Organization and Bureaucracy. *An Analysis of Modern Theories. 240 pp.*

● **Ossowski, Stanislaw.** Class Structure in the Social Consciousness. *210 pp.*

● **Podgórecki, Adam.** Law and Society. *302 pp.*

Renner, Karl. Institutions of Private Law and Their Social Functions. *Edited, with an Introduction and Notes, by O. Kahn-Freud. Translated by Agnes Schwarzschild. 316 pp.*

Rex, J. and **Tomlinson, S.** Colonial Immigrants in a British City. *A Class Analysis. 368 pp.*

Smooha, S. Israel: Pluralism and Conflict. *472 pp.*

Wesolowski, W. Class, Strata and Power. *Trans. and with Introduction by G. Kolankiewicz. 160 pp.*

Zureik, E. Palestinians in Israel. *A Study in Internal Colonialism. 264 pp.*

SOCIOLOGY AND POLITICS

Acton, T. A. Gypsy Politics and Social Change. *316 pp.*

Burton, F. Politics of Legitimacy. *Struggles in a Belfast Community. 250 pp.*

Crook, I. and **D.** Revolution in a Chinese Village. *Ten Mile Inn. 216 pp., illustrated.*

Etzioni-Halevy, E. Political Manipulation and Administrative Power. *A Comparative Study. About 200 pp.*

Fielding, N. The National Front. *About 250 pp.*

● **Hechter, Michael.** Internal Colonialism. *The Celtic Fringe in British National Development, 1536–1966. 380 pp.*

Kornhauser, William. The Politics of Mass Society. *272 pp. 20 tables.*

Korpi, W. The Working Class in Welfare Capitalism. *Work, Unions and Politics in Sweden. 472 pp.*

Kroes, R. Soldiers and Students. *A Study of Right- and Left-wing Students. 174 pp.*

Martin, Roderick. Sociology of Power. *About 272 pp.*

Merquior, J. G. Rousseau and Weber. *A Study in the Theory of Legitimacy. About 288 pp.*

Myrdal, Gunnar. The Political Element in the Development of Economic Theory. *Translated from the German by Paul Streeten. 282 pp.*

Varma, B. N. The Sociology and Politics of Development. *A Theoretical Study. 236 pp.*

Wong, S.-L. Sociology and Socialism in Contemporary China. *160 pp.*

Wootton, Graham. Workers, Unions and the State. *188 pp.*

CRIMINOLOGY

Ancel, Marc. Social Defence: *A Modern Approach to Criminal Problems. Foreword by Leon Radzinowicz. 240 pp.*

Athens, L. Violent Criminal Acts and Actors. *104 pp.*

Cain, Maureen E. Society and the Policeman's Role. *326 pp.*

Cloward, Richard A. and **Ohlin, Lloyd E.** Delinquency and Opportunity: *A Theory of Delinquent Gangs. 248 pp.*

Downes, David M. The Delinquent Solution. *A Study in Subcultural Theory. 296 pp.*

Friedlander, Kate. The Psycho-Analytical Approach to Juvenile Delinquency: *Theory, Case Studies, Treatment. 320 pp.*

Gleuck, Sheldon and **Eleanor.** Family Environment and Delinquency. *With the statistical assistance of Rose W. Kneznek. 340 pp.*

Lopez-Rey, Manuel. Crime. *An Analytical Appraisal. 288 pp.*

Mannheim, Hermann. Comparative Criminology: *A Text Book. Two volumes. 442 pp. and 380 pp.*

Morris, Terence. The Criminal Area: *A Study in Social Ecology. Foreword by Hermann Mannheim. 232 pp. 25 tables. 4 maps.*

Rock, Paul. Making People Pay. *338 pp.*

● **Taylor, Ian, Walton, Paul** and **Young, Jock.** The New Criminology. *For a Social Theory of Deviance. 325 pp.*

● **Taylor, Ian, Walton, Paul** and **Young, Jock.** (Eds) Critical Criminology. *268 pp.*

SOCIAL PSYCHOLOGY

Bagley, Christopher. The Social Psychology of the Epileptic Child. *320 pp.*

Brittan, Arthur. Meanings and Situations. *224 pp.*

Carroll, J. Break-Out from the Crystal Palace. *200 pp.*

● **Fleming, C. M.** Adolescence: Its Social Psychology. *With an Introduction to recent findings from the fields of Anthropology, Physiology, Medicine, Psychometrics and Sociometry. 288 pp.*

● The Social Psychology of Education: *An Introduction and Guide to Its Study. 136 pp.*

Linton, Ralph. The Cultural Background of Personality. *132 pp.*

● **Mayo, Elton.** The Social Problems of an Industrial Civilization. *With an Appendix on the Political Problem. 180 pp.*

Ottaway, A. K. C. Learning Through Group Experience. *176 pp.*

Plummer, Ken. Sexual Stigma. *An Interactionist Account. 254 pp.*

● **Rose, Arnold M.** (Ed.) Human Behaviour and Social Processes: *an Interactionist Approach. Contributions by Arnold M. Rose, Ralph H. Turner, Anselm Strauss, Everett C. Hughes, E. Franklin Frazier, Howard S. Becker et al. 696 pp.*

Smelser, Neil J. Theory of Collective Behaviour. *448 pp.*

Stephenson, Geoffrey M. The Development of Conscience. *128 pp.*

Young, Kimball. Handbook of Social Psychology. *658 pp. 16 figures. 10 tables.*

SOCIOLOGY OF THE FAMILY

Bell, Colin R. Middle Class Families: *Social and Geographical Mobility. 224 pp.*
Burton, Lindy. Vulnerable Children. *272 pp.*
Gavron, Hannah. The Captive Wife: *Conflicts of Household Mothers. 190 pp.*
George, Victor and **Wilding, Paul.** Motherless Families. *248 pp.*
Klein, Josephine. Samples from English Cultures.
1. Three Preliminary Studies and Aspects of Adult Life in England. *447 pp.*
2. Child-Rearing Practices and Index. *247 pp.*

Klein, Viola. The Feminine Character. *History of an Ideology. 244 pp.*
McWhinnie, Alexina M. Adopted Children. *How They Grow Up. 304 pp.*
● **Morgan, D. H. J.** Social Theory and the Family. *About 320 pp.*
● **Myrdal, Alva** and **Klein, Viola.** Women's Two Roles: *Home and Work. 238 pp. 27 tables.*
Parsons, Talcott and **Bales, Robert F.** Family: Socialization and Interaction Process. *In collaboration with James Olds, Morris Zelditch and Philip E. Slater. 456 pp. 50 figures and tables.*

SOCIAL SERVICES

Bastide, Roger. The Sociology of Mental Disorder. *Translated from the French by Jean McNeil. 260 pp.*
Carlebach, Julius. Caring For Children in Trouble. *266 pp.*
George, Victor. Foster Care. *Theory and Practice. 234 pp.*
Social Security: *Beveridge and After. 258 pp.*
George, V. and **Wilding, P.** Motherless Families. *248 pp.*
● **Goetschius, George W.** Working with Community Groups. *256 pp.*
Goetschius, George W. and **Tash, Joan.** Working with Unattached Youth. *416 pp.*
Heywood, Jean S. Children in Care. *The Development of the Service for the Deprived Child. Third revised edition. 284 pp.*
King, Roy D., Ranes, Norma V. and **Tizard, Jack.** Patterns of Residential Care. *356 pp.*
Leigh, John. Young People and Leisure. *256 pp.*
● **Mays, John.** (Ed.) Penelope Hall's Social Services of England and Wales. *368 pp.*
Morris, Mary. Voluntary Work and the Welfare State. *300 pp.*
Nokes, P. L. The Professional Task in Welfare Practice. *152 pp.*
Timms, Noel. Psychiatric Social Work in Great Britain (1939–1962). *280 pp.*
● Social Casework: *Principles and Practice. 256 pp.*

SOCIOLOGY OF EDUCATION

Banks, Olive. Parity and Prestige in English Secondary Education: a Study in Educational Sociology. *272 pp.*
● **Blyth, W. A. L.** English Primary Education. *A Sociological Description.*
2. Background. *168 pp.*

Collier, K. G. The Social Purposes of Education: *Personal and Social Values in Education. 268 pp.*
Evans, K. M. Sociometry and Education. *158 pp.*
● **Ford, Julienne.** Social Class and the Comprehensive School. *192 pp.*
Foster, P. J. Education and Social Change in Ghana. *336 pp. 3 maps.*
Fraser, W. R. Education and Society in Modern France. *150 pp.*
Grace, Gerald R. Role Conflict and the Teacher. *150 pp.*
Hans, Nicholas. New Trends in Education in the Eighteenth Century. *278 pp. 19 tables.*
● Comparative Education: *A Study of Educational Factors and Traditions. 360 pp.*
● **Hargreaves, David.** Interpersonal Relations and Education. *432 pp.*
● Social Relations in a Secondary School. *240 pp.*
School Organization and Pupil Involvement. *A Study of Secondary Schools.*

- **Mannheim, Karl** and **Stewart, W. A. C.** An Introduction to the Sociology of Education. *206 pp.*
- **Musgrove, F.** Youth and the Social Order. *176 pp.*
- **Ottaway, A. K. C.** Education and Society: An Introduction to the Sociology of Education. *With an Introduction by W. O. Lester Smith. 212 pp.*

Peers, Robert. Adult Education: *A Comparative Study. Revised edition. 398 pp.*

Stratta, Erica. The Education of Borstal Boys. *A Study of their Educational Experiences prior to, and during, Borstal Training. 256 pp.*

- **Taylor, P. H., Reid, W. A.** and **Holley, B. J.** The English Sixth Form. *A Case Study in Curriculum Research. 198 pp.*

SOCIOLOGY OF CULTURE

Eppel, E. M. and **M.** Adolescents and Morality: *A Study of some Moral Values and Dilemmas of Working Adolescents in the Context of a changing Climate of Opinion. Foreword by W. J. H. Sprott. 268 pp. 39 tables.*

- **Fromm, Erich.** The Fear of Freedom. *286 pp.*
- The Sane Society. *400 pp.*

Johnson, L. The Cultural Critics. *From Matthew Arnold to Raymond Williams. 233 pp.*

Mannheim, Karl. Essays on the Sociology of Culture. *Edited by Ernst Mannheim in co-operation with Paul Kecskemeti. Editorial Note by Adolph Lowe. 280 pp.*

Merquior, J. G. The Veil and the Mask. *Essays on Culture and Ideology. Foreword by Ernest Gellner. 140 pp.*

Zijderfeld, A. C. On Clichés. *The Supersedure of Meaning by Function in Modernity. 150 pp.*

SOCIOLOGY OF RELIGION

Argyle, Michael and **Beit-Hallahmi, Benjamin.** The Social Psychology of Religion. *256 pp.*

Glasner, Peter E. The Sociology of Secularisation. *A Critique of a Concept. 146 pp.*

Hall, J. R. The Ways Out. *Utopian Communal Groups in an Age of Babylon. 280 pp.*

Ranson, S., Hinings, B. and **Bryman, A.** Clergy, Ministers and Priests. *216 pp.*

Stark, Werner. The Sociology of Religion. *A Study of Christendom.*
Volume II. *Sectarian Religion. 368 pp.*
Volume III. *The Universal Church. 464 pp.*
Volume IV. *Types of Religious Man. 352 pp.*
Volume V. *Types of Religious Culture. 464 pp.*

Turner, B. S. Weber and Islam. *216 pp.*

Watt, W. Montgomery. Islam and the Integration of Society. *320 pp.*

SOCIOLOGY OF ART AND LITERATURE

Jarvie, Ian C. Towards a Sociology of the Cinema. *A Comparative Essay on the Structure and Functioning of a Major Entertainment Industry. 405 pp.*

Rust, Frances S. Dance in Society. *An Analysis of the Relationships between the Social Dance and Society in England from the Middle Ages to the Present Day. 256 pp. 8 pp. of plates.*

Schücking, L. L. The Sociology of Literary Taste. *112 pp.*

Wolff, Janet. Hermeneutic Philosophy and the Sociology of Art. *150 pp.*

SOCIOLOGY OF KNOWLEDGE

Diesing, P. Patterns of Discovery in the Social Sciences. *262 pp.*

- **Douglas, J. D.** (Ed.) Understanding Everyday Life. *370 pp.*
- **Hamilton, P.** Knowledge and Social Structure. *174 pp.*

Jarvie, I. C. Concepts and Society. *232 pp.*

Mannheim, Karl. Essays on the Sociology of Knowledge. *Edited by Paul Kecskemeti. Editorial Note by Adolph Lowe. 353 pp.*

Remmling, Gunter W. The Sociology of Karl Mannheim. *With a Bibliographical Guide to the Sociology of Knowledge, Ideological Analysis, and Social Planning. 255 pp.*

Remmling, Gunter W. (Ed.) Towards the Sociology of Knowledge. *Origin and Development of a Sociological Thought Style. 463 pp.*

Scheler, M. Problems of a Sociology of Knowledge. *Trans. by M. S. Frings. Edited and with an Introduction by K. Stikkers. 232 pp.*

URBAN SOCIOLOGY

Aldridge, M. The British New Towns. *A Programme Without a Policy. 232 pp.*

Ashworth, William. The Genesis of Modern British Town Planning: *A Study in Economic and Social History of the Nineteenth and Twentieth Centuries. 288 pp.*

Brittan, A. The Privatised World. *196 pp.*

Cullingworth, J. B. Housing Needs and Planning Policy: *A Restatement of the Problems of Housing Need and 'Overspill' in England and Wales. 232 pp. 44 tables. 8 maps.*

Dickinson, Robert E. City and Region: *A Geographical Interpretation. 608 pp. 125 figures.*

The West European City: *A Geographical Interpretation. 600 pp. 129 maps. 29 plates.*

Humphreys, Alexander J. New Dubliners: *Urbanization and the Irish Family. Foreword by George C. Homans. 304 pp.*

Jackson, Brian. Working Class Community: *Some General Notions raised by a Series of Studies in Northern England. 192 pp.*

- **Mann, P. H.** An Approach to Urban Sociology. *240 pp.*

Mellor, J. R. Urban Sociology in an Urbanized Society. *326 pp.*

Morris, R. N. and **Mogey, J.** The Sociology of Housing. *Studies at Berinsfield. 232 pp. 4 pp. plates.*

Mullan, R. Stevenage Ltd. *About 250 pp.*

Rex, J. and **Tomlinson, S.** Colonial Immigrants in a British City. *A Class Analysis. 368 pp.*

Rosser, C. and **Harris, C.** The Family and Social Change. *A Study of Family and Kinship in a South Wales Town. 352 pp. 8 maps.*

- **Stacey, Margaret, Batsone, Eric, Bell, Colin** and **Thurcott, Anne.** Power, Persistence and Change. *A Second Study of Banbury. 196 pp.*

RURAL SOCIOLOGY

Mayer, Adrian C. Peasants in the Pacific. *A Study of Fiji Indian Rural Society. 248 pp. 20 plates.*

Williams, W. M. The Sociology of an English Village: *Gosforth. 272 pp. 12 figures. 13 tables.*

SOCIOLOGY OF INDUSTRY AND DISTRIBUTION

Dunkerley, David. The Foreman. *Aspects of Task and Structure. 192 pp.*

Eldridge, J. E. T. Industrial Disputes. *Essays in the Sociology of Industrial Relations. 288 pp.*

Hollowell, Peter G. The Lorry Driver. *272 pp.*

- **Oxaal, I., Barnett, T.** and **Booth, D.** (Eds) Beyond the Sociology of Development.

Economy and Society in Latin America and Africa. 295 pp.

Smelser, Neil J. Social Change in the Industrial Revolution: *An Application of Theory to the Lancashire Cotton Industry, 1770–1840. 468 pp. 12 figures. 14 tables.*

Watson, T. J. The Personnel Managers. *A Study in the Sociology of Work and Employment, 262 pp.*

ANTHROPOLOGY

Brandel-Syrier, Mia. Reeftown Elite. *A Study of Social Mobility in a Modern African Community on the Reef. 376 pp.*

Dickie-Clark, H. F. The Marginal Situation. *A Sociological Study of a Coloured Group. 236 pp.*

Dube, S. C. Indian Village. *Foreword by Morris Edward Opler. 276 pp. 4 plates.*

India's Changing Villages: *Human Factors in Community Development. 260 pp. 8 plates. 1 map.*

Fei, H.-T. Peasant Life in China. *A Field Study of Country Life in the Yangtze Valley. With a foreword by Bronislaw Malinowski. 328 pp. 16 pp. plates.*

Firth, Raymond. Malay Fishermen. *Their Peasant Economy. 420 pp. 17 pp. plates.*

Gulliver, P. H. Social Control in an African Society: a Study of the Arusha, Agricultural Masai of Northern Tanganyika. *320 pp. 8 plates. 10 figures.*

Family Herds. *288 pp.*

Jarvie, Ian C. The Revolution in Anthropology. *268 pp.*

Little, Kenneth L. Mende of Sierra Leone. *308 pp. and folder.*

Negroes in Britain. *With a New Introduction and Contemporary Study by Leonard Bloom. 320 pp.*

Tambs-Lyche, H. London Patidars. *About 180 pp.*

Madan, G. R. Western Sociologists on Indian Society. *Marx, Spencer, Weber, Durkheim, Pareto. 384 pp.*

Mayer, A. C. Peasants in the Pacific. *A Study of Fiji Indian Rural Society. 248 pp.*

Meer, Fatima. Race and Suicide in South Africa. *325 pp.*

Smith, Raymond T. The Negro Family in British Guiana: *Family Structure and Social Status in the Villages. With a Foreword by Meyer Fortes. 314 pp. 8 plates. 1 figure. 4 maps.*

SOCIOLOGY AND PHILOSOPHY

Adriaansens, H. Talcott Parsons and the Conceptual Dilemma. *About 224 pp.*

Barnsley, John H. The Social Reality of Ethics. *A Comparative Analysis of Moral Codes. 448 pp.*

Diesing, Paul. Patterns of Discovery in the Social Sciences. *362 pp.*

● **Douglas, Jack D.** (Ed.) Understanding Everyday Life. *Toward the Reconstruction of Sociological Knowledge. Contributions by Alan F. Blum, Aaron W. Cicourel, Norman K. Denzin, Jack D. Douglas, John Heeren, Peter McHugh, Peter K. Manning, Melvin Power, Matthew Speier, Roy Turner, D. Lawrence Wieder, Thomas P. Wilson and Don H. Zimmerman. 370 pp.*

Gorman, Robert A. The Dual Vision. *Alfred Schutz and the Myth of Phenomenological Social Science. 240 pp.*

Jarvie, Ian C. Concepts and Society. *216 pp.*

Kilminster, R. Praxis and Method. *A Sociological Dialogue with Lukács, Gramsci and the Early Frankfurt School. 334 pp.*

● **Pelz, Werner.** The Scope of Understanding in Sociology. *Towards a More Radical Reorientation in the Social Humanistic Sciences. 283 pp.*

Roche, Maurice. Phenomenology, Language and the Social Sciences. *371 pp.*

Sahay, Arun. Sociological Analysis. *212 pp.*

● **Slater, P.** Origin and Significance of the Frankfurt School. *A Marxist Perspective. 185 pp.*

Spurling, L. Phenomenology and the Social World. *The Philosophy of Merleau-Ponty and its Relation to the Social Sciences. 222 pp.*

Wilson, H. T. The American Ideology. *Science, Technology and Organization as Modes of Rationality. 368 pp.*

International Library of Anthropology
General Editor Adam Kuper

● **Ahmed, A. S.** Millennium and Charisma Among Pathans. *A Critical Essay in Social Anthropology. 192 pp.*

Pukhtun Economy and Society. *Traditional Structure and Economic Development. About 360 pp.*

Barth, F. Selected Essays. *Volume I. About 250 pp.* Selected Essays. *Volume II. About 250 pp.*

Brown, Paula. The Chimbu. *A Study of Change in the New Guinea Highlands. 151 pp.*

Foner, N. Jamaica Farewell. *200 pp.*

Gudeman, Stephen. Relationships, Residence and the Individual. *A Rural Panamanian Community. 288 pp. 11 plates, 5 figures, 2 maps, 10 tables.*

The Demise of a Rural Economy. *From Subsistence to Capitalism in a Latin American Village. 160 pp.*

Hamnett, Ian. Chieftainship and Legitimacy. *An Anthropological Study of Executive Law in Lesotho. 163 pp.*

Hanson, F. Allan. Meaning in Culture. *127 pp.*

Hazan, H. The Limbo People. *A Study of the Constitution of the Time Universe Among the Aged. About 192 pp.*

Humphreys, S. C. Anthropology and the Greeks. *288 pp.*

Karp, I. Fields of Change Among the Iteso of Kenya. *140 pp.*

Lloyd, P. C. Power and Independence. *Urban Africans' Perception of Social Inequality. 264 pp.*

Parry, J. P. Caste and Kinship in Kangra. *352 pp. Illustrated.*

Pettigrew, Joyce. Robber Noblemen. *A Study of the Political System of the Sikh Jats. 284 pp.*

Street, Brian V. The Savage in Literature. *Representations of 'Primitive' Society in English Fiction, 1858–1920. 207 pp.*

Van Den Berghe, Pierre L. Power and Privilege at an African University. *278 pp.*

International Library of Phenomenology and Moral Sciences
General Editor John O'Neill

Apel, K.-O. Towards a Transformation of Philosophy. *308 pp.*

Bologh, R. W. Dialectical Phenomenology. *Marx's Method. 287 pp.*

Fekete, J. The Critical Twilight. *Explorations in the Ideology of Anglo-American Literary Theory from Eliot to McLuhan. 300 pp.*

Medina, A. Reflection, Time and the Novel. *Towards a Communicative Theory of Literature. 143 pp.*

International Library of Social Policy
General Editor Kathleen Jones

Bayley, M. Mental Handicap and Community Care. *426 pp.*

Bottoms, A. E. and **McClean, J. D.** Defendants in the Criminal Process. *284 pp.*

Bradshaw, J. The Family Fund. *An Initiative in Social Policy. About 224 pp.*

Butler, J. R. Family Doctors and Public Policy. *208 pp.*
Davies, Martin. Prisoners of Society. *Attitudes and Aftercare. 204 pp.*
Gittus, Elizabeth. Flats, Families and the Under-Fives. *285 pp.*
Holman, Robert. Trading in Children. *A Study of Private Fostering. 355 pp.*
Jeffs, A. Young People and the Youth Service. *160 pp.*
Jones, Howard and Cornes, Paul. Open Prisons. *288 pp.*
Jones, Kathleen. History of the Mental Health Service. *428 pp.*
Jones, Kathleen with **Brown, John, Cunningham, W. J., Roberts, Julian** and **Williams, Peter.** Opening the Door. *A Study of New Policies for the Mentally Handicapped. 278 pp.*
Karn, Valerie. Retiring to the Seaside. *400 pp. 2 maps. Numerous tables.*
King, R. D. and **Elliot, K. W.** Albany: Birth of a Prison—End of an Era. *394 pp.*
Thomas, J. E. The English Prison Officer since 1850: *A Study in Conflict. 258 pp.*
Walton, R. G. Women in Social Work. *303 pp.*
● **Woodward, J.** To Do the Sick No Harm. *A Study of the British Voluntary Hospital System to 1875. 234 pp.*

International Library of Welfare and Philosophy
General Editors Noel Timms and David Watson

● **McDermott, F. E.** (Ed.) Self-Determination in Social Work. *A Collection of Essays on Self-determination and Related Concepts by Philosophers and Social Work Theorists. Contributors: F. P. Biestek, S. Bernstein, A. Keith-Lucas, D. Sayer, H. H. Perelman, C. Whittington, R. F. Stalley, F. E. McDermott, I. Berlin, H. J. McCloskey, H. L. A. Hart, J. Wilson, A. I. Melden, S. I. Benn. 254 pp.*
● **Plant, Raymond.** Community and Ideology. *104 pp.*
Ragg, Nicholas M. People Not Cases. *A Philosophical Approach to Social Work. 168 pp.*
● **Timms, Noel** and **Watson, David.** (Eds) Talking About Welfare. *Readings in Philosophy and Social Policy. Contributors: T. H. Marshall, R. B. Brandt, G. H. von Wright, K. Nielsen, M. Cranston, R. M. Titmuss, R. S. Downie, E. Telfer, D. Donnison, J. Benson, P. Leonard, A. Keith-Lucas, D. Walsh, I. T. Ramsey. 320 pp.*
● Philosophy in Social Work. *250 pp.*
● **Weale, A.** Equality and Social Policy. *164 pp.*

Library of Social Work
General Editor Noel Timms

● **Baldock, Peter.** Community Work and Social Work. *140 pp.*
○ **Beedell, Christopher.** Residential Life with Children. *210 pp. Crown 8vo.*
● **Berry, Juliet.** Daily Experience in Residential Life. *A Study of Children and their Care-givers. 202 pp.*
○ Social Work with Children. *190 pp. Crown 8vo.*
● **Brearley, C. Paul.** Residential Work with the Elderly. *116 pp.*
● Social Work, Ageing and Society. *126 pp.*
● **Cheetham, Juliet.** Social Work with Immigrants. *240 pp. Crown 8vo.*
● **Cross, Crispin P.** (Ed.) Interviewing and Communication in Social Work. *Contributions by C. P. Cross, D. Laurenson, B. Strutt, S. Raven. 192 pp. Crown 8vo.*

● **Curnock, Kathleen** and **Hardiker, Pauline.** Towards Practice Theory. *Skills and Methods in Social Assessments. 208 pp.*

● **Davies, Bernard.** The Use of Groups in Social Work Practice. *158 pp.*

● **Davies, Martin.** Support Systems in Social Work. *144 pp.*

Ellis, June. (Ed.) West African Families in Britain. *A Meeting of Two Cultures. Contributions by Pat Stapleton, Vivien Biggs. 150 pp. 1 Map.*

● **Hart, John.** Social Work and Sexual Conduct. *230 pp.*

● **Hutten, Joan M.** Short-Term Contracts in Social Work. *Contributions by Stella M. Hall, Elsie Osborne, Mannie Sher, Eva Sternberg, Elizabeth Tuters. 134 pp.*

Jackson, Michael P. and **Valencia, B. Michael.** Financial Aid Through Social Work. *140 pp.*

● **Jones, Howard.** The Residential Community. *A Setting for Social Work. 150 pp.*

● (Ed.) Towards a New Social Work. *Contributions by Howard Jones, D. A. Fowler, J. R. Cypher, R. G. Walton, Geoffrey Mungham, Philip Priestley, Ian Shaw, M. Bartley, R. Deacon, Irwin Epstein, Geoffrey Pearson. 184 pp.*

Jones, Ray and **Pritchard, Colin.** (Eds) Social Work With Adolescents. *Contributions by Ray Jones, Colin Pritchard, Jack Dunham, Florence Rossetti, Andrew Kerslake, John Burns, William Gregory, Graham Templeman, Kenneth E. Reid, Audrey Taylor. About 170 pp.*

○ **Jordon, William.** The Social Worker in Family Situations. *160 pp. Crown 8vo.*

● **Laycock, A. L.** Adolescents and Social Work. *128 pp. Crown 8vo.*

● **Lees, Ray.** Politics and Social Work. *128 pp. Crown 8vo.*

● Research Strategies for Social Welfare. *112 pp. Tables.*

○ **McCullough, M. K.** and **Ely, Peter J.** Social Work with Groups. *127 pp. Crown 8vo.*

● **Moffett, Jonathan.** Concepts in Casework Treatment. *128 pp. Crown 8vo.*

Parsloe, Phyllida. Juvenile Justice in Britain and the United States. *The Balance of Needs and Rights. 336 pp.*

● **Plant, Raymond.** Social and Moral Theory in Casework. *112 pp. Crown 8vo.*

Priestley, Philip, Fears, Denise and **Fuller, Roger.** Justice for Juveniles. *The 1969 Children and Young Persons Act: A Case for Reform? 128 pp.*

● **Pritchard, Colin** and **Taylor, Richard.** Social Work: Reform or Revolution? *170 pp.*

○ **Pugh, Elisabeth.** Social Work in Child Care. *128 pp. Crown 8vo.*

● **Robinson, Margaret.** Schools and Social Work. *282 pp.*

○ **Ruddock, Ralph.** Roles and Relationships. *128 pp. Crown 8vo.*

● **Sainsbury, Eric.** Social Diagnosis in Casework. *118 pp. Crown 8vo.*

● Social Work with Families. *Perceptions of Social Casework among Clients of a Family Service. 188 pp.*

Seed, Philip. The Expansion of Social Work in Britain. *128 pp. Crown 8vo.*

● **Shaw, John.** The Self in Social Work. *124 pp.*

Smale, Gerald G. Prophecy, Behaviour and Change. *An Examination of Self-fulfilling Prophecies in Helping Relationships. 116 pp. Crown 8vo.*

Smith, Gilbert. Social Need. *Policy, Practice and Research. 155 pp.*

● Social Work and the Sociology of Organisations. *124 pp. Revised edition.*

● **Sutton, Carole.** Psychology for Social Workers and Counsellors. *An Introduction. 248 pp.*

● **Timms, Noel.** Language of Social Casework. *122 pp. Crown 8vo.*

● Recording in Social Work. *124 pp. Crown 8vo.*

● **Todd, F. Joan.** Social Work with the Mentally Subnormal. *96 pp. Crown 8vo.*

● **Walrond-Skinner, Sue.** Family Therapy. *The Treatment of Natural Systems. 172 pp.*

● **Warham, Joyce.** An Introduction to Administration for Social Workers. *Revised edition. 112 pp.*

● An Open Case. *The Organisational Context of Social Work. 172 pp.*

○ **Wittenberg, Isca Salzberger.** Psycho-Analytic Insight and Relationships. *A Kleinian Approach. 196 pp. Crown 8vo.*

Primary Socialization, Language and Education

General Editor Basil Bernstein

Adlam, Diana S., *with the assistance of Geoffrey Turner and Lesley Lineker.* Code in *Context. 272 pp.*

Bernstein, Basil. Class, Codes and Control. *3 volumes.*

● 1. *Theoretical Studies Towards a Sociology of Language. 254 pp.*

2. *Applied Studies Towards a Sociology of Language. 377 pp.*

● 3. *Towards a Theory of Educational Transmission. 167 pp.*

Brandis, W. and **Bernstein, B.** Selection and Control. *176 pp.*

Brandis, Walter and **Henderson, Dorothy.** Social Class, Language and Communication. *288 pp.*

Cook-Gumperz, Jenny. Social Control and Socialization. *A Study of Class Differences in the Language of Maternal Control. 290 pp.*

● **Gahagan, D. M.** and **G. A.** Talk Reform. *Exploration in Language for Infant School Children. 160 pp.*

Hawkins, P. R. Social Class, the Nominal Group and Verbal Strategies. *About 220 pp.*

Robinson, W. P. and **Rackstraw, Susan D. A.** A Question of Answers. *2 volumes. 192 pp. and 180 pp.*

Turner, Geoffrey J. and **Mohan, Bernard A.** A Linguistic Description and Computer Programme for Children's Speech. *208 pp.*

Reports of the Institute of Community Studies

Baker, J. The Neighbourhood Advice Centre. A Community Project in Camden. *320 pp.*

● **Cartwright, Ann.** Patients and their Doctors. *A Study of General Practice. 304 pp.*

Dench, Geoff. Maltese in London. *A Case-study in the Erosion of Ethnic Consciousness. 302 pp.*

Jackson, Brian and **Marsden, Dennis.** Education and the Working Class: *Some General Themes Raised by a Study of 88 Working-class Children in a Northern Industrial City. 268 pp. 2 folders.*

Marris, Peter. The Experience of Higher Education. *232 pp. 27 tables.*

● Loss and Change. *192 pp.*

Marris, Peter and **Rein, Martin.** Dilemmas of Social Reform. *Poverty and Community Action in the United States. 256 pp.*

Marris, Peter and **Somerset, Anthony.** African Businessmen. *A Study of Entrepreneurship and Development in Kenya. 256 pp.*

Mills, Richard. Young Outsiders: *a Study in Alternative Communities. 216 pp.*

Runciman, W. G. Relative Deprivation and Social Justice. *A Study of Attitudes to Social Inequality in Twentieth-Century England. 352 pp.*

Willmott, Peter. Adolescent Boys in East London. *230 pp.*

Willmott, Peter and **Young, Michael.** Family and Class in a London Suburb. *202 pp. 47 tables.*

Young, Michael and **McGeeney, Patrick.** Learning Begins at Home. *A Study of a Junior School and its Parents. 128 pp.*

Young, Michael and **Willmott, Peter.** Family and Kinship in East London. *Foreword by Richard M. Titmuss. 252 pp. 39 tables.*

The Symmetrical Family. *410 pp.*

Reports of the Institute for Social Studies in Medical Care

Cartwright, Ann, Hockey, Lisbeth and **Anderson, John J.** Life Before Death. *310 pp.*
Dunnell, Karen and **Cartwright, Ann.** Medicine Takers, Prescribers and Hoarders. *190 pp.*
Farrell, C. My Mother Said. . . *A Study of the Way Young People Learned About Sex and Birth Control. 288 pp.*

Medicine, Illness and Society
General Editor W. M. Williams

Hall, David J. Social Relations & Innovation. *Changing the State of Play in Hospitals. 232 pp.*
Hall, David J. and **Stacey, M.** (Eds) Beyond Separation. *234 pp.*
Robinson, David. The Process of Becoming Ill. *142 pp.*
Stacey, Margaret *et al.* Hospitals, Children and Their Families. *The Report of a Pilot Study. 202 pp.*
Stimson, G. V. and **Webb, B.** Going to See the Doctor. *The Consultation Process in General Practice. 155 pp.*

Monographs in Social Theory
General Editor Arthur Brittan

● **Barnes, B.** Scientific Knowledge and Sociological Theory. *192 pp.*
Bauman, Zygmunt. Culture as Praxis. *204 pp.*
● **Dixon, Keith.** Sociological Theory. *Pretence and Possibility. 142 pp.*
The Sociology of Belief. *Fallacy and Foundation. About 160 pp.*
Goff, T. W. Marx and Mead. *Contributions to a Sociology of Knowledge. 176 pp.*
Meltzer, B. N., Petras, J. W. and **Reynolds, L. T.** Symbolic Interactionism. *Genesis, Varieties and Criticisms. 144 pp.*
● **Smith, Anthony D.** The Concept of Social Change. *A Critique of the Functionalist Theory of Social Change. 208 pp.*

Routledge Social Science Journals

The British Journal of Sociology. *Editor – Angus Stewart; Associate Editor – Leslie Sklair. Vol. 1, No. 1 – March 1950 and Quarterly. Roy. 8vo. All back issues available. An international journal publishing original papers in the field of sociology and related areas.*
Community Work. *Edited by David Jones and Marjorie Mayo. 1973. Published annually.*
Economy and Society. *Vol. 1, No. 1. February 1972 and Quarterly. Metric Roy. 8vo. A journal for all social scientists covering sociology, philosophy, anthropology, economics and history. All back numbers available.*

Ethnic and Racial Studies. *Editor – John Stone. Vol. 1 – 1978. Published quarterly.*
Religion. Journal of Religion and Religions. *Chairman of Editorial Board, Ninian Smart. Vol. 1, No. 1, Spring 1971. A journal with an inter-disciplinary approach to the study of the phenomena of religion. All back numbers available.*
Sociology of Health and Illness. *A Journal of Medical Sociology. Editor – Alan Davies; Associate Editor – Ray Jobling. Vol. 1, Spring 1979. Published 3 times per annum.*
Year Book of Social Policy in Britain. *Edited by Kathleen Jones. 1971. Published annually.*

Social and Psychological Aspects of Medical Practice
Editor Trevor Silverstone

Lader, Malcolm. Psychophysiology of Mental Illness. *280 pp.*
● **Silverstone, Trevor** and **Turner, Paul.** Drug Treatment in Psychiatry. *Revised edition. 256 pp.*
Whiteley, J. S. and **Gordon, J.** Group Approaches in Psychiatry. *240 pp.*

Printed and bound in Great Britain by
Redwood Burn Limited, Trowbridge & Esher

1279